ENTREPRENEURSHIP IN INDIA

PERSPECTIVE AND PRACTICE

Entrepreneurship in India

Perspective and Practice

S.S. Khanka

AKANSHA PUBLISHING HOUSE
NEW DELHI - 110002 (INDIA)

AKANSHA PUBLISHING HOUSE
4649-B,Ansari Road,
Daryaganj, New Dellii-11 0002
Phones: 23268193, 09435116718
Email: ektabooks@yahoo.com
visit us: www.akanshapublishinghouse.com

Entrepreneurship in India: Perspective and Practice

First Published 2009

ISBN 978-81-8370-193-8

PRINTED IN INDIA

Published by Akansha Publishing House, New Delhi-110002 and Printed at Capital Offset Press, Delhi.

In the profound memory of
my eldest brother
Shri Kalyan Singh Khanka
who left for his heavenly abode on 25th
November 2008,
This work is humbly dedicated.

Contents

Preface

The terms 'entrepreneur' and 'entrepreneurship' which were not in economic use a century ago, have by now become buzzwords in the economic terminology. The reason is the *primum mobile* role these play in industrial and economic development of a country. The kingpin role of entrepreneurship in economic development of a country is appreciated as "an economy is the effect for which entrepreneurship is the cause." Hence, ever increasing importance has been given to entrepreneurship development everywhere in the world including India. India operates the oldest and largest entrepreneurship development programmes (EDPs) in any developing country and by now EDP has emerged as a nation-wide movement in our country. It's a cliche to mention that in spite of EDPs being emerged as a national movement, there has not been perceptible development and improvement in the entrepreneurial front of the country, in general and in some regions, in particular. But unfortunately that is the case.

Then, the million dollar question is how to develop entrepreneurship in the country? Attempts have been made by researchers and policy makers from time to time to study, understand, analyze, and answer this question. As such, the literature on entrepreneurship by now is replete with prodigious volume of research giving various models and / or theories of entrepreneurship development. The hitherto literature on entrepreneurship research reveals that most of the researches have so far been done either from general perspective or particular perspectives. Such research orientation may be good in understanding the phenomenon of entrepreneurship from one particular perspective, but may be inappropriate and / or inadequate to understand the phenomenon as a whole. Unlike previous studies, therefore, a modest attempt has been made in the present study to try to understand the phenomenon of entrepreneurship by integrating both general and particular perspectives of entrepreneurship in India. Integrating the particular perspective with general is imbued with some genuine academic justifications. Like other developments, entrepreneurship development is also context-specific. The significance of practical experience gained in a particular perspective or context to the existing knowledge and new learning can be, by no account, contested on mainly two counts. *One,* proceeding from the general to the particular is, more often than not, perilous because authenticating the particular from the general that too based on secondary sources may not fit in a context. *Two,* secondary sources often offer contestable interpretations and alternative views. This is because the problems and prospects of development are, to a great extent, context-specific. Therefore, the context or perspective specific actual experiences assume relevance and significance in search of new learning of the phenomenon of entrepreneurship. The North Eastern Region (NER) of India presents an altogether different perspective in many respects including entrepreneurship development. Hence, the present study entitled "*Entrepreneurship in India—Perspective and Practice*" presents the entrepreneurial scenario in an integrated manner to better understand the phenomenon of entrepreneurship. The entire study is presented in seventeen chapters under two parts: Part I: The Perspective and Part II: The Practice. Part I, running into ten chapters, presents the overall perspective of entrepreneurship development in India. Part II, consisting of seven chapters, delineates the hitherto entrepreneurial scenario in the North-East India.

The present study is an enlarged and modified version of my research project entitled "*Entrepreneurship Development in North-East India (With Special Reference to Assam)*" financially supported by the All India Council for Technical Education (AICTE), New Delhi. Though the original work was done at Tezpur University (A Central University), Tezpur, Assam; much of the additions and modifications were carried out at the National Institute of Financial Management (Ministry of Finance,

Government of India), Faridabad, Haryana. I am indebted to these two institutions for the support they provided for this work.

Honestly speaking, no book of this nature can be conceived and developed without having been inspired from other books and authors and direct and indirect support received from different people and institutions. Mentioning all of their names is not possible here. Nonetheless, I am thankful to each of them for their help and support received for the preparation of this book. First of all, I express my sincere thanks to the AICTE for granting me the financial help and, thus, providing me the opportunity to undertake the study. The 243 'unknown warriors' in the pages of entrepreneurial history deserve the most sincere thanks for their cooperation in providing the required information for the study. The study would not have been possible at all but only for their ungrudging cooperation. Mr. Anjan Bhuyan worked as Investigator in the study and was responsible for data collection, compilation, and tabulation of the study. My appreciative thanks go to Bhuyan for the painstaking assistance provided in undertaking the study. The secretarial help in typing and retyping of several drafts of the book extended by my office steno Ms Anju Rani is acknowledged with great encomiums. I also owe my gratefulness from the deep core of my heart to Professor M. K. Chaudhury, the Vice Chancellor, Tezpur University for his inspiration and encouragement to my academic endeavours. Professor Chaudhury is a perfect epitome of a scientist of repute, an able administrator of recognition, and above all, a good human being of respect and regard to one and all I have ever come across during my over 30 years' teaching career.

As for my immediate family, I should thank Geetu (my loving wife) and Abhineet and Abhinav (my dear sons), for deferring or foregoing some of their demands on my personal time.

Finally, I thank the publishers of this book, Akansha Publishing House, who are the publishers of professional and developmental topics of North-East India, for bringing out the book in such an excellent shape and get-up that too within a very short period of about two months.

While I thank everyone who has contributed directly or indirectly to the development of this book, I take the responsibility for its limitations and inadequacies. The trekking that I did on the trail of these trail-blazing 243 entrepreneurs has been certainly long, but very-very academically enriching and enjoyable. I do hope that the readers too would get a similar experience from this book and, like other authors, that will be my intrinsic academic reward from this book.

—S.S. Khanka

List of Tables

Abbreviations

AWAKE	:	Association of Women Entrepreneurs of Karnataka
BRAC	:	Bangladesh Rural Advancement Committee
CCI	:	Confederation of Indian Industry
CED	:	Centre for Entrepreneurship Development
CEO	:	Chief Executive Officer
CIS	:	Comprehensive Insurance Scheme
CNPPA	:	Commission on National Parks and Protected Areas
DIC	:	District Industry Centre
EDII	:	Entrepreneurship Development Institute of India
EDP	:	Entrepreneurship Development Programmes
EMTC	:	Entrepreneurial Motivation Training Centre
FICCI	:	Federation of Indian Chamber of Commerce and Industry
GB	:	Grameen Bank
GDP	:	Gross Domestic Production
ICICI	:	Industrial Credit and Investment Corporation of India
IDBI	:	Industrial Development Bank of India
UIED	:	Institute of Entrepreneurship Development
IFCI	:	Industrial and Financial Corporation of India
IIE	:	Indian Institute of Entrepreneurship

IIYW	:	Indian Institute of Youth Welfare
ILO	:	International Labour Organization
IRDP	:	Integrated Rural Development Programme
ITI	:	Industrial Training Institute
KVIC	:	Khadi and Village Industries Commission
NAYE	:	National Alliance of Young Entrepreneurs
NEC	:	North East Council
NEDFL	:	North Eastern Development Finance Corporation Ltd.
NEIIPP	:	North East Industrial and Investment Promotion Policy 2007
NEUTC	:	North Eastern Industrial and Technical Corporation
NER	:	North East Region
NHM	:	National Horticulture Mission
NIESBUD	:	National Institute for Entrepreneurship and Small Business Development
NISIET	:	National Institute of Small Industry Extension and Training
NKC	:	National Knowledge Commission
OSC	:	Over Sight Committee
PNRY	:	Prime Minister Rojgar Yojana
NSIC	:	National Small Industry Corporation
RUDSETI	:	Rural Development and Self-Employment Training Institute
SBI	:	State Bank of India
SEWA	:	Self-Employed Women's Association
SIDBI	:	Small Industry Development Bank of India
SIDO	:	Small Industry Development Organization

SIETI	:	Small Industries Extension Training Institute
SISI	:	Small Industry Service Institute
SSI	:	Small Scale Industry
TCO	:	Technical Consultancy Organization
TRYSE	:	Training for Rural Youth for Self-Employment
UBUDC	:	United Nations Industrial Development Corporation
UNWTO	:	United Nations World Tourism Organization
WASME	:	World Assembly of Small and Medium Entrepreneurs
WIEGO	:	Women in Informal Employment Globalizing and Organizing
WTO	:	World Tourism Organization
WTO	:	World Trade Organization
WTTC	:	World Travel and Tourism Council
XISS	:	Xavier Institute of Social Studies

PART I

THE PERSPECTIVE

1

Entrepreneurship: A Conceptual Framework

Introduction

The term 'entrepreneur' is of a relatively recent origin and an evolving one also. It is basically associated with economic and industrial development of an economy. As such, the changes in the meaning of the term 'entrepreneur' have parallel the economic and industrial development taken place over the period. The term 'entrepreneur' has been defined differently by different people from time to time. In fact, it is often used in omnibus fashion. As a result, even today it is not crystal clear what does the term 'entrepreneur' exactly mean and who is an 'entrepreneur. Because of a plethora of definitions given to the term entrepreneur', Kilby (1971: 1-40) has likened the entrepreneur with an animal called 'Heffalump' hunted by many individuals, but all unable to capture him. All claim to have seen him and differently described him, nonetheless considerable disagreements still exist among them on his characteristics. The views differ widely on its meaning and significance. The variation of opinion is from complete rejection to marked emphasis upon entrepreneurship as the key agent of production and the *primum mobile* of economic development.

We believe that a clear understanding about the concept of entrepreneur and entrepreneurship is essential for better understanding and development of the subject. We, therefore, begin with a theoretical framework of entrepreneurship. For analytical convenience, the present chapter proceeds along two sections. While Section I traces out the evolution of the concept of entrepreneurship, section II examines the alternative approaches used to study and understand entrepreneurship.

Evolution of the Concept of Entrepreneurship

The word 'entrepreneur' has been taken from the French language *enterprendre* where it cradled literally means "between-taker" and "go-between" i.e. "to undertake" and meant to designate an organizer of musical or other entertainments. The Oxford English Dictionary (in 1897) also defined entrepreneur in a similar way as "the director or manager of a public musical institution, one who 'gets up' entertainment, especially musical performance". In the early 16th century, it was applied to those who were engaged in military expeditions. It was extended to cover civil engineering activities such as construction and fortification in the 17th century (Cochran, 1950: 304-307). It was only in the beginning of 18th century that the word was used to refer to economic aspects. In this way, the evolution of the concept of entrepreneurship is considered over more than three centuries. Since then, the term 'entrepreneur' is used in various ways and various senses. We briefly discuss below each of these views.

Entrepreneurship as Risk-Bearing

Richard Cantillon, an Irishman living in France, was the first who introduced the term 'entrepreneur' and his unique risk-bearing function in economics in the early 18th century (Gopakumar 1995: 1-17). He defined entrepreneur as an agent who buys factors of production at certain prices in order to combine them into a product with a view to selling it at uncertain prices in future (Cantillon, 1971: 2). He illustrated a farmer who pays out contractual incomes which are 'certain' to the landlords and labourers and sells at prices that are 'uncertain'. He further states that so do merchants also who make certain payments in expectation of uncertain receipts. Thus, they too are essentially 'risk-bearing' agents of production.

Knight (1965) also described entrepreneur to be a specialized group of persons who bear uncertainty. Uncertainty is defined as a risk which cannot be insured against and is incalculable. He, thus, draws a distinction between ordinary risk and uncertainty. A risk can be reduced through the insurance principle, where the distribution of the outcome in a group of instances is known. On the contrary, uncertainty is the risk which cannot be calculated. The entrepreneur, according to Knight, is the economic functionary who undertakes such responsibility of uncertainty which by its very nature cannot be insured, or capitalized or salaried.

Entrepreneurship as Coordination

Jean-Baptiste Say (1827: 285-286), the French political economist, with his unpleasant practical experiences developed the concept of entrepreneur a little further which survived for almost two centuries. His definition associates entrepreneur with the functions of coordination, organization and supervision. According to Say, an entrepreneur is one who combines the land of one, the labour of another and the capital of yet another, and thus, produces a product. By selling the produce in the market he pays interest on capital, rent on land, wages to labourers and what remains is his/her profit. Say, thus, views that the entrepreneur shifts economic resources out of an area of lower and into an area of higher productivity and greater yield (Cardullo 1999: 4). Thus, Say has made a clear distinction between the role of the capitalist as a financer and the entrepreneur as an organizer. To play such a role, according to Say, the entrepreneur must possess the art of superintendence and administration. He further elaborates that in the course of undertaking a number of complex operations like obstacles to be surmounted, anxieties to be repressed, and misfortunes to be repaired and expedients to be devised, three more implicit factors are deemed to be essential. These are:

(1) morale qualities for work – judgment, perseverance, and knowledge about the business world,

(2) command over sufficient capital, and

(3) uncertainty of profits.

Marshall (1936: 293) also advocated the significance of

organization among the services of a special class of business undertakers.

The line of argument, thus, pursued from Cantillon to Marshall was in the context of a stationary situation not related to the process of economic development. Also, nothing worthwhile was done on the supply side of entrepreneurship.

Entrepreneurship as Innovation

Joseph A. Schumpeter, for the first time in 1934, assigned a crucial role of 'innovation' to the entrepreneur in his *magnum opus* **'Theory of Economic Development'** (1934). Schumpeter considered economic development as a discrete dynamic change brought by entrepreneur by instituting new combinations of factors of production which he called 'innovation' (1939: 103). In other words, entrepreneur is, according to Schumpeter, a 'creative destructor' whos creates or causes a dynamic disequilibrium in the economy by taking innovation to commercialization by embedding it in an environment where it did not exist previously. The 'innovation', i.e. introduction of new combination of factors of production, according to him, may occur in any one of the following five forms:

(i) introduction of a new product;

(ii) introduction of a new method of production;

(iii) opening of a new market;

(iv) discovery of a new source of supply of raw materials; and

(v) carrying out of the new form of organization of any industry.

However, Schumpeter stressed the fact that these attributes unaccompanied by the ability to innovate would not be sufficient to account for entrepreneurship (Gopakumar 1995: 1-17). Schumpeter also made a distinction between an inventor and an innovator. An inventor is one who discovers new methods and new materials. And, an innovator utilizes inventions and discoveries in order to make new combinations. Schumpeter argued that the entrepreneur may or may not be the inventor, and similarly, the entrepreneur may or may not be the supplier of capital. The basic difference between the inventor and innovator is that the former produces idea, the latter gets that idea converted into reality. This difference is similar to the difference between 'discovery' and 'exploitation.' Discovery is fruition of insight and exploitation is the realization of the potential value of discovered idea or insight. In a sense, innovation is an invention that is replicated and commercially used at large-scale to sole a particular problem.

However, the applicability of the Schumpeterian 'innovative' concept of entrepreneur to underdeveloped economics is conditioned on certain grounds. For example, Schumpeter wrote his theory of economic development in the context of Industrial Revolution of presently advanced countries where some of the prerequisites of growth already existed. Inevitably, his theoretical explanation corresponds to the particular social and economic order that existed there during that specific period. Innovation was concentrated in a few fields in which big entrepreneurs rose as the spearheads of growth. Big innovations yielded a surplus for reinvestment and in this way; the entrepreneur could invade the various economic fields with spectacular success (Singh, 1966: 228). In the process, the forces of growth tended to penetrate into the whole fabric of economy emanated from large scale changes introduced by a few big entrepreneurs. Moreover, from the point of view of its magnitude of operation, the Schumpeterian theory is modeled on big private entrepreneurship.

Although the Schumpeterian concept and perspective of entrepreneurship had been criticized on certain grounds, the modern entrepreneurial explorations are mainly founded on the Schumpeterian concept of entrepreneurship (Greshenkron 1968: 99). The post-Schumpeterian thinking on entrepreneurship has proceeded along two major but different themes: the Harvard Tradition and the neo-Australian School. The former is an extension of the Schumpeterian view, while the latter is represented as an alternative approach (Kanungo 1998: 21-22). According to the Harvard School approach, entrepreneurship comprises any purposeful activity that initiates, maintains or develops a profit-oriented business or with the economic, political and social circumstances surrounding the business (Cole 1949: 85-107). The another exposition of the Harvard tradition emphasizes on activities like searching and evaluating economic opportunities, mobilizing resources required for production, connecting markets and expanding the enterprise (Leibenstein 1968: 75). On the contrary, the neo-Australian School emphasized on disequilibrium as the necessary condition for the emergence and development of entrepreneurship. According to Kirzner (1979), an entrepreneur is the arbitrageur who discovers opportunity at low prices and sells the same items at high prices because of intertemporal and interspatial demands.

The most recent and authentic definition of entrepreneurship with special reference to India is given by the National Knowledge Commission (NKC) (2008:1) of India. The NKC has defined entrepreneurship as "the professional application of knowledge, skills and competencies and/or of monetizing a new idea, by an individual or a set of people by launching an enterprise *de novo* or diversifying from an existing one (distinct from seeking self-employment as in a profession or trade), thus to pursue growth while generating wealth, employment and social good."

Synthesis of the Concept

In sum and substance, the term entrepreneur or entrepreneurship have been defined in many ways and various senses. Nonetheless, the common element implied in all expositions from Cantillon to Kirzner to NKC is that entrepreneur performs various functional roles as risk taker, decision maker, organizer or coordinator, innovator, employer of factors of production, arbitrageur, etc. To sum up, an entrepreneur can be defined as a person who tries to create something new, organizes production and undertakes risk and handles economic uncertainty involved in enterprise.

Alternative Approaches

Entrepreneur is such a thing like 'Heffalump" as likened by Peter Kilby (1971: 1-40) seen by all and attempted by many to describe but hardly any one could grab it what exactly it is.

Many thinkers have made their best theoretical efforts to describe and analyze 'who is an entrepreneur?' For the convenience of understanding, the major contributions made on this vexing issue are broadly classified into two approaches:

1. Sociocultural Approaches.
2. Psychological Approaches.

These are discussed in turn.

Sociocultural Approaches

Some scholars have tried to identify entrepreneurs investigating into where they do come from. Giving historical evidences, they try to affirm that socio-cultural milieu matters in the emergence and development of entrepreneurs and, in turn, economic development (Cochran 1947; Cole 1949). Speaking alternatively, some special type of socio-cultural milieu induces entrepreneurial behaviour. Leaving the stereotype cases of 'rags to riches', they catalogue certain distinct characteristics of entrepreneurs different from the common individuals. Writers supporting this approach have referred to societies evincing different attitudes, interests, and likings have produced different kinds of entrepreneurs and different patterns of entrepreneurial behaviour. For example, Weber (1930) referring to the Protestant faith exemplifies that Calvinism characterized by attributes like duty to be diligent, prudent, and sober which, in turn, resulted in the increased well being of the individuals. So is the case mentioned by Tripathi (2004) about the Indian Gujarati and Marwari communities who are found quite skillful in business operation in India. Nonetheless, the critics comment that socio-cultural milieu still remains unable to answer the vexing question: Who is an entrepreneur? What constitutes an entrepreneurial behaviour?

As a result, some writers have used the psychological approach to answer the vexing question: 'who is an entrepreneur?'

Psychological Approach

In his attempt to identify who is an entrepreneur, McClelland (1961) initiated the shift in focus from the action to the actor.

Table 1.1: Evolution and Development of the Term Entrepreneur

Stems from the French word *'enterprendre'* means ***"between-taker "or "go-between".***

Middle Ages:	actor and person in-charge of large-scale production projects.
17th century:	person bearing risk of profit (loss) in a fixed-price contract with government.
1725:	Richard Cantillon—person bearing risks is different from one supplying capital.
1803:	Jean Baptiste Say—separated profits of entrepreneur from profits of capital.
1876:	Fransis Walker—distinguished between those who supplied funds and received interest and those who received profit from managerial capabilities.
1934:	Joseph Scumpeter opined entrepreneur as—one who is an innovator and develops untried technology.
1961:	David McClelland—entrepreneur is an energetic, moderate risk taker.
1964:	Peter Drucker-entrepreneur maximizes opportunities.
1975:	Albert Shapero—entrepreneur takes initiative, organizes some social and economic mechanisms, and accepts risks of failure.
1980:	Karl Vesper—entrepreneur seen differently by economists, psychologists, business persons, and politicians.
1983:	Gifford Pinchot—intrapreneur is an entrepreneur within an already established organization.
1985:	Robert Hisrich-entrepreneurship is the process of creating something different with value by devoting the necessary time and effort, assuming the accompanying financial, psychological, and social risks, and receiving the resulting rewards of monetary and personal satisfaction.

The supporters of McClelland's view argue that the individual characteristics are more important for the emergence of entrepreneurs than simply belonging to a particular socio-cultural milieu. McClelland rechristens these characteristics as '*need for achievement* (n-ach).' Higher the n-ach, according to McClelland, more will be the entrepreneurial supply and vice versa. The n-ach can be inculcated and developed through imparting education and training in self reliance, rewarding hard word and persistence in goal achievement. Legendry story telling by grand parents to their grand children in the past and narrating the life histories of great personalities in different walks of life by the teachers to the students during the Morning Prayer till yesteryears have been found quite effective in inculcating n-ach among the students. This approach, thus, stresses on traits possessed by an individual to make him/her an entrepreneur rather the socio-economic background he/she belongs to (Hagen 1962). More recently, while emphasizing the psychological approach to understand entrepreneur, Hisrich (1990: 209-222) has identified several psychological characteristics of entrepreneurs in terms of (a) conditions that make entrepreneurship desirable and possible, (b) the childhood family background, (c) the education level, personal values and motivation, and (d) role modeling effects and other support systems. There are other researchers also (Bird 1989).who have studied the entrepreneurial behaviour by focusing on work and family background, personal values, and motivation.

The evolution and development of the term 'entrepreneur' over the period is given in a chronological order in the Table 1.1.

Difference between Entrepreneurship, Managership and Leadership

Managership and leadership are considered as two cousins of entrepreneurship. In order to understand entrepreneurship more clearly, it would be, therefore, appropriate to distinguish between entrepreneurship, managership, and leadership. Such distinction among them seems very important because entrepreneurs resemble and perform roles that lie in the domain of these two terms. We have already defined and described entrepreneurship. Let us try to distinguish between the two terms managership and leadership. The distinction between the two can be made on two criteria: (i) the roles played by managers and leaders, and (ii) the nature of influence made by them.

As regards the *role played* by managers and leaders is concerned, the managers play the role of supervision, administration, and care taker to keep the organization on maintaining *status quo*. On the other hand, the leaders play the role of showing the direction to run the organization. In other words, leaders by thinking and directing the people change the organization from *status quo* to superior equilibrium. Leaders transform the organization and, hence, play the role of a change agent (Kanungo & Conger 1995: 155-170).

Looking at the second criterion of *influence made* by managers and leaders on organization, managers by playing their supervisory roles ensure the compliance of tasks assigned to workers. They may use rewards and sanctions to get the work done from workers. Thus, the influence of managers is as '*transactional*'. Leaders, on the contrary, by using their ideas, vision, and articulation changes the attitudes, values, motivation, and in turn, behaviour of the workers in the organization. Thus, the influence the leader creates in the organization is '*transformational*' (Burns 1978).

Warren Bennis and Burt Nanus (1985: 21) have differentiated managership from leadership by stating that "managers are people who do things right, and leaders are people who do the right things. Management's efficiency lies in climbing the ladder of success, leadership determines whether the leader is leaning against the right wall."

Some one has distinguished leadership from managership by quoting: "When Noah heard the weather forecast he ordered the building of the ark—that was leadership. Then he looked around and said, "Make sure the elephants don't see what the rabbits are up to—that was managership (Anonymous 2006: 19)."

Having gone through the distinctions between managers and leaders, it becomes quite apparent that entrepreneurs at times play both the roles of managership and leadership. How? Managership role is played by entrepreneurs when they act as supervisor and perform actions to procure and allocate resources among the various sections / divisions of organization. Entreprenurs also play leadership role when they are driven by their ideas and vision to bring in change in the organization.

Kanungo (1998:34-36) has distinguished the three constructs based on task demands and personal dispositions as depicted in the following Table 1.2.

Table 1.2: Contrasting Entrepreneurship, Managership and Leadership

Task Demands	*Entrepreneurship*	*Managership*	*Leadership*
Major Goal	Profit	Efficiency	Change
Time Frame	Short & Long-run	Short-run	Future
Arena	Enterprise & Markets	Enterprises	Social systems
Personal Dispositions			
Resourcefulness	High	High	Medium
Achievement-orientation	Medium	High	Medium
Visioning	Medium	Low	High
Opportunity-seeking	High	Medium	Low
Innovativeness	High	Low	Medium

Types of Entrepreneurs

Clarence Danhof (1949: 22-24), on the basis of his study of American agriculture, classified entrepreneurs in the manner that at the initial stage of economic development entrepreneurs have less initiative and drive and as economic development proceeds they become more innovating and enthusiastic. Based on this, he classified entrepreneurs into four categories:

1. **Innovating Entrepreneurs**. Innovating entrepreneurs are those who introduce new goods, inaugurate new method

of production, discover new market and reorganize the enterprise. It is important to note that such entrepreneurs can work only when a certain level of development is already achieved, and people look forward to change and improvement.

2. **Imitative Entrepreneurs.** These are characterized by readiness to adopt successful innovations inaugurated by successful innovating entrepreneurs. Imitative entrepreneurs do not innovate the changes themselves, they only imitate techniques and technology innovated by others. Such types of entrepreneurs are particularly suitable for the underdeveloped regions for bringing a mushroom drive of imitation of new combinations of factors of production already available in developed regions.
3. **Fabian Entrepreneurs.** Fabian entrepreneurs are characterized by very great caution and skepticism in introducing any change in their enterprise. They imitate only when it becomes perfectly clear that failure to do so would result in a loss of the relative position in the enterprise.
4. **Drone Entrepreneurs.** Drone entrepreneurs are characterized by a refusal to adopt opportunities to make changes in production formulae even at the cost of severely reduced returns relative to other likewise producers. Such entrepreneurs may even suffer losses but they are not ready to make changes in their existing production methods.

Concluding Remarks

Entrepreneurship is an evolving concept and is defined in many ways and various senses. The process of entrepreneurship is more a state of becoming than a steady state or event. Therefore, there is no typical entrepreneur as such. Entrepreneurs can be gregarious or taciturn, analytical or intuitive, cautious or daring. As such, it is not crystal clear what the term entrepreneur actually means. Researchers have made efforts to answer the vexing question who is an entrepreneur by looking either at their socio-economic background they belong to or the psychological characteristics they display. Nonetheless, the foregoing analysis can provide us a framework to be used to develop entrepreneurial capabilities among the people by imparting relevant education and training.

2

Research Paradigm on Entrepreneurship

Introduction

Entrepreneurship, though a relatively young subject in behavioural sciences, has emerged as a hyperactive area of organizational and behavioural research. Over the past half century, entrepreneurial research has resulted in a prodigious volume of publication. But, this research has been rife with controversy and multiple dimensions and paradigms. The reason for which is absence of unanimity among the researchers on what actually matters in entrepreneurship: whether the environment or the entrepreneur. There is no agreement on this issue among the researchers. While some researchers consider 'environment' more important, other consider the 'entrepreneur'. As such, entrepreneurship research has often been criticised for not having an agreement on research paradigm (Chell and Haworth 1988: 16-33). What is a paradigm? A paradigm, according to Manimala (1999: 87), is a shared set of assumptions held by researchers, including their conceptions of what is possible, the boundaries of acceptable enquiry, and the limiting factors, if any. Alternatively speaking, research paradigm is like the 'grand theory' under the framework of which researchers conduct their researches.

Research Paradigm

It is true that entrepreneurship researchers while conducting their investigation generally do not explicitly draw a paradigm under which they conduct their researches. However, one kind or other theoretical models on entrepreneurship are always implicit in their researches. All these models are classified into two types where one is alternative to other. The two models are: (a) Environment-Based Model, also rechristined as 'The Population Ecology Model' and (b) Entrepreneur-Based Model, also rechristined as 'The Strategic Choice Model.' This chapter is devoted to discuss these two models with empirical evidences. These are discussed now one by one.

Environment-Based Model

The proponents of 'the Environment-Based Model of Entrepreneurship' believe that enterprise is a sub-system within the large system called 'environment.' In other words, entrepreneurship / enterprise operates within an environment and, hence, gets affected by the environment. In general, environment means all what exists in the physical surroundings, conditions, circumstances, etc. under which someone (be human being) or something (be enterprise) exists. Accordingly, business environment means the sum total of all conditions, events and influences that surround and affect a business (Davis 1975: 43). Business history is replete with evidences that environment in one way or other affects the operation of business. A researcher (Anonymous 2000: 10-12) has recounted 25 events such as independence and partition (in 1947), establishment of Industrial and Financial Corporation of India (IFCI) (in 1948), establishment of industrial estates (1955), the Mundhra scandal (in 1957), licensing era (during 1965-73), telecom revolution (in 1986), and liberalization (from 1991 onwards) that shaped business in India. Thus, the proponents of the Population Ecology Model, or say, environmental determinants of business have their logic supported by empirical evidences to suggest that business organizations are affected and are outcome of their environment within which they operate. In other words, they view that entrepreneurship/enterprise is an effect for which environment is a cause. Hence, the need for and significance of understanding entrepreneurship/enterprise development in the context of given environment.

Let us make an excursion into the entrepreneurship research carried out in India that shows how entrepreneurship / enterprise development has been dependent on environment.

In his rigorous attempt to trace out the origins of the modern Indian business class, Gadgil (1959: 186) finds one remarkable feature about the business evolution in India was its slowness. The reasons for this slowness, Gadgil attributed, comprise village self-sufficiency, non-industrial character as the dominant trait of Indian towns, the persistent government policy of *laissez faire,* lack of technical training for workers, etc. Tripathi and Mehta (1990: 12), in their study on entrepreneurial response, report that the entrepreneurial response finds its expression in relation to the context of the constellation of forces facilitating the birth and expansion of a business enterprise. For example, they draw our attention to the factors stifling entrepreneurial response in the pre-British India, viz., lack of political unity, a network of customs barriers, the existence of innumerable systems of currency, development of regional markets and village self-sufficiency, monopolization of trade in profitable commodities by provincial satraps, heavy taxation coupled with low yield of Indian agriculture impairing the ability of the community to save and harvest, religious system of education reinforcing the occupational structure sanctified by the caste system, technological stagnation, and low esteem accorded to businessmen in the country.

In his study of 50 manufacturing firms in Madras (now, Chennai) city and Coimbatore in Tamil Nadu, Berna (1960) found that traditional occupation and caste had very little impact in determining entry into entrepreneurial endeavours than economic factors such as access to capital, possession of business experience and knowledge.

What follows from above illustrative empirical evidences is some kind of agreement on the issue of what constitutes a favourable, or say, conducive business environment and its presence promotes and absence deters entrepreneurship/ enterprise development. A favourable business environment is understood as one in which resources are easily available, competition is limited and restricted, political environment is benign with regard to infrastructure development, licensing, texation, grants and subsidies, availability of credit on soft terms and nursing and rehabilitation of sick business enterprises ((Panda 1984). Such views are held in developed countries also where attempts are made to develop entrepreneurship based on key environmental determinants (Gnyawali and Fogel 1994: 43-62). Here, the emphasis apparently is on the favourable or conducive environment which some rechristined as *task* environment, and obviously not on the *general* environment. Then, the question arises is what constitutes *task* environment. According to one researcher (Thompson 1967), the *task* environment consists of the factors that have a specific impact on business activities, such as: (a) customers, including both distributors and users; (b) suppliers of materials, labour, capital, and workspace; (c) competitors for markets and resources; and (d) regulatory groups including governmental agencies, unions and inter-firm associations. While reviewing environmental factors in entrepreneurship, Bruno and Tyebjee (1982: 287-316) listed the most frequently cited essential factors in respect of 17 studies as venture capital availability, presence of experienced entrepreneurs, technically skilled labour force, accessibility of suppliers, accessibility of customers or new markets, favourable government policies, proximities of universities, availability of land and facilities, accessibility to transportation, respective population, availability of supporting services, and attractive living conditions. As regards *general* environment, it, according to Khandwalla (1977), consists of economic, legal-political, socio-cultural, and educational aspects.

In a sense, the task and general environments of entrepreneurship are somewhat similar to the two factors of Herzberg's (two-factor) theory of motivation. The two factors are maintenance, also called, hygiene factors and motivational factors. According to Herzberg et al. (1959), the hygiene factors such as company policy and administration, supervision and salary when adequate in job only placate workers. So to say, workers will not be dissatisfied, neither will they be satisfied. The factors directly associated with the work such as promotional opportunities, opportunities for personal growth, achievement, recognition, reward, and responsibility, termed as motivational factors, satisfy and motivate workers at work. Thus, the hygiene and motivational factors represent the general and task environments of entrepreneurship respectively.

Let us produce some evidences on how environment affects entrepreneurship. There is ample evidence to show and believe that the favourable environment attracts people to the domain of entrepreneurship and, thus, promotes entrepreneurship (Saxena 2005: 140-142). It is with this realization that the Government of India has instituted a host of policy and institutional arrangements from time to time, since Independence, with an objective to create a favourable or conducive environment for entrepreneurship and industrial development in the country. The development of industrial estates or clusters, creation of special economic zones, export promotion zones, the announcement of industrial policies especially ***"Policy Measures for Promotion and Strengthening and Supplementing Small, Tiny and Village Enterprises 1991"***, and the announcement of special economic packages for some relatively less developed regions of the country in the recent past can be seen in this light. Promotion of industrial estates / industrial clusters, for example, is increasingly being recognized and recommended by many as an effective route to entrepreneurship and small enterprise development (Ministry of Industry 1997, Awasthi 1997, Gulati 1997). Very recently, the Government of India has announced its ***"North East Industrial and Investment Promotion Policy (NEIIPP), 2007"'*** with an objective to create the favourable environment for entrepreneurship, industrial and, in turn, economic development of North East India. The impact of favourable environment is reflected by the increasing number of small-scale enterprises, or say, entrepreneurs especially first-generation entrepreneurs in different regions of the country. An excursion into the industrial history of India also reflects a tendency of spatial concentration of enterprises at the places with the availability of transport facilities, raw materials, labour, and market (Tripathi 2004: 111-138, Shridharan and Manimala 1999: 165-193, Kristiansen 2001: 43-69), thus, confirming the importance of favourable environment in entrepreneurship and/ or enterprise development.

That the environment, entrepreneurship, industrial, and economic development are related in a lockstep manner is evident from cross-country and cross-region comparisons. Higher economic development, or call it favourable environment vis-à-vis more entrepreneurship development in the Punjab and Gujarat and less economic development in Bihar and Orissa lend support to the above statement that environment influences and determines entrepreneurship development. Industrial history is witness that a favourable or conducive environment and entrepreneurship sustain and support each other in a virtuous cycle. How? Favourable environment creates entrepreneurial opportunities and entrepreneurial initiatives create favourable environment and this virtuous cycle goes on and on. Thus, entrepreneurship begets entrepreneurship. This is because the favourable environment enables entrepreneurs to become more responsive to entrepreneurial opportunities available in the environment.

In order to verify whether or not environment affects entrepreneurship, the researchers have tried to test the hypothesis of environmental determinism. For example, Manimala (1999: 95-98) set the research hypotheses to test the environmental determinism like: if different kinds of environmental conditions can produce similar impacts on entrepreneurship, or if the same environment can produce differential responses from different individuals or entrepreneurs. The above hypothesis of environmental determinism will hold true if there is found a significant difference in the entrepreneurial responsiveness across the environments in terms of regions, time periods, and industries. It was found that environment did not have impact on entrepreneurship as none of the three Chi-squares was significant at 5 per cent or below. Thus, the research evidence does not offer any support to the theory of environmental determinism or the 'population ecology model' at least inasmuch as it concerns the favourable or task environment.

There are also some studies from historical perspectives

on refugees (Papanek 1962; Shapero 1975: 83-88), immigrants (Levenstein 1995: 106-122), marginal groups such as the Jews (Aris 1970), the Marwaris (Pavlov 1964), the Chettiars (Baldwin 1959), and the Parsis (Guha 1970: M107-M115); Sharma 1980), associating the entrepreneurial behaviour especially the innovativeness in those communities to certain unfavourable conditions they had endured and experienced, what Hagen (1962) terms, displacement and status withdrawal. The Marwaris in India, for example, could not establish themselves in their own birthplace because it was severely ravaged by feudal conflict and strife. This caused to their displacement to establish themselves at the emerging big business centers such as Calcutta (now Kolkata) and Bombay (now Mumbai). Similar is the story of Parsis as well who emerged and established themselves as the major business innovators in India during the British colonial rule providing unfavourable conditions by all means for the Indian businessmen. As reported by researchers (Sharma (1980), the same Parsi community seemed languishing in entrepreneurial pursuits during the post-Independence period which obviously provides a more favourable business environment. The available evidences also suggest that entrepreneurial behaviour especially innovative one takes places in unfavourable conditions as well. Manimala (1999: 93) takes global examples at industry level and reports that the oil boom in US brought about revolutionary innovations in the automobile industry, on the one hand, the like of which occurred again in opposite conditions, especially in Japan after the 1973 oil crisis. Thus, the entrepreneurial initiative, though of different nature and degree, may take place equally under conditions of abundance (say, favourableness) as well as scarcity (say, unfavourableness). This is duly illustrated by the national (entrepreneurial) performance of Japan and the USA. Japan with its scarcity of natural resources, could be as innovative as the United States with its abundance.

A more important reason for the neglect of environment in the entrepreneurial studies is the ambivalence of environmental influences on entrepreneurship. Let some facts be produced to substantiate this statement. Like many developing countries, India too has been adopting a policy of protecting its small-scale enterprises from competition with large organizations within the country and from foreign competition (Manimala 1999: 93-94). That is, the effort is to create a favourable environment for developing entrepreneurship and small-scale enterprises in the country. But it is found that in long-run, it has actually acted as a barrier to small-scale enterprises becoming innovative and competitive both at the national and international markets. Similarly, the Government's policy of reserving certain items for small and tiny-scale sectors was started with an objective to create favourable environment for developing entrepreneurship and small-scale enterprises in the country. But, it too actually created unfavourable environment for entrepreneurship development in the country. How? The reservations and restrictions were admissible to the industries with low economies of scale, using simple nature of technology, and utilization of traditional skills. The ultimate consequence of the reservations and restrictions was leading to jack up the cost of production and make the units non-competitive and non-viable in the long-run. This, Dasgupta (1969) points out, accounts for the large number of enterprise failure at small-scale sector culminating to high mortality rate in small sector. The reservation policy produced yet other implications for the development of small-scale enterprises. *One,* a small enterprise with low economies of scale may plan to change its nature of operation by introducing new technology. But, it becomes difficult for it because it needs to use simple technology to remain eligible for (availing of) reservation policy. *Two,* even the policy of reservation may prevent a small-scale enterprise to go for technological innovation, because that would change its size from small to large-scale. This will make the enterprise ineligible for the policy of reservation of items earmarked for small-scale enterprises.

Now that we have discussed and dissected the environment-based model or population ecology model and found it with ambivalence influences on entrepreneurship, we can proceed to examine the 'entrepreneur-based model' also called the 'strategic choice model' to see if it has impact on entrepreneurship, development.

Entrepreneur-Based Model

The entrepreneur-based model also called strategic choice model is based on the belief that the success or failure in business venture depends primarily on entrepreneur by making appropriate strategic decisions, rather than on the favourableness of the environment. The capable entrepreneur makes strategic decisions appropriate for his/her business even in an unfavourable business environment. The entrepreneur is capable enough to constantly adapt, even at times manipulate and control the environment through strategic choices (Hisrich 1975: 327-344). There are empirical evidences to believe that while ordinary entrepreneurs blame unfavourableness of environment for their failure or poor performance, the innovative ones are able to identify and exploit the limited opportunity even in so-called unfavourable environment and make big gains out of it. In a sense, the proponents of the strategic choice model vet the role of, what Rotter (1966) termed, the 'internal locus of control' in success in business venture. Then, this suggests that the perceptual differences among the entrepreneurs toward environment account for differences in their performances. The business world is replete with evidences to support above observations. For example, here is one such case of an innovative entrepreneur who identified an opportunity in a highly unfavourable business environment.

As reported by a researcher (Chandra 1985: 86-94), (Late) Dhirubhai Ambani started his textile company in India at the time when the textile industry in the country was facing absolutely unfavourable environment. The textile industry was suffering from the general recession in the country. The Government policy was in support of small powerloom units, on the one hand, and against the mill sector by imposing differential tax-structure, on the other. Expectedly, almost all small powerloom entrepreneurs were criticizing the discriminatory policy of the Government and demanding support from the Government to protect them in the market. The entrepreneur (Dhirubhai Ambani) with his uncanny knack identified an opportunity even in such unfavourable environment. He realized that the small powerloom units could produce goods with high quality, but were finding it difficult to market them. Therefore, he decided to get high quality goods produced by these small power loom units as per his specifications at a relatively low cost, got them duly processed and printed with exquisite designs, and then sold them under his widely accepted brand in the market. He earned huge margins of profits by doing so.

There is yet another instance of Ambani's strategic choice making. The Government of India imposed restrictions on the import of synthetic fibers by permitting imports only to the extent of foreign exchange earned through the export of textiles. As the Indian prices were higher than international prices, companies found it difficult to export textile and then import synthetic fibres. This caused short supply of synthetic yarn in the market. Dhirubhai Ambani again identified opportunity in such (unfavourable) environment. He decided to suffer losses on textile export, but was more than compensated for it through the resale of imported synthetic yarn, which was in short supply in the market. These are the excellent examples of entrepreneurial perceptions supporting the position that the entrepreneurial (innovative) behaviour depends primarily on individual's strategic choices, than on the environment.

The aforesaid cases lend support to the apparent neglect of the significance of environment in entrepreneurial studies. The cases well confirm that the impact of environment on entrepreneurship depends on the individual entrepreneur's perceptions of the environment, rather than on the objective reality. In case of entrepreneurial ventures, it is argued that the perceptual uncertainty rather than the actual uncertainty affects the choice and / or decision-making and strategy formulation of the entrepreneur (Boyle 1994: 63-69).

Now that we have discussed both the models of entrepreneurship research, the main features of the two models can easily be contrasted (Pennings 1982) in the following Table 2.1.

Table 2.1: Comparison between Population Ecology Model and Strategic Choice Model

Population Ecology Theory	*Strategic Choice Model*
1. The entrepreneur has little choice.	The entrepreneur has choice to choose.
2. The entrepreneur's actions are predicted, moulded and determined by the environment.	The entrepreneur makes strategic choice to secure the best transactions with the given environment.
3. The environment is a set of influences which selectively permit some ventures to survive.	The environment is a pool of resources which the entrepreneur selects and acquires to establish his ventures.
4. The entrepreneur is a creature of environment, and is used by the environment as its instrument.	The entrepreneur masters fate and makes strategic choices to minimize threats and exploit opportunities inherent in the environment.

We also think that a chronological overview of the evolution and development of entrepreneurship research will further help us better our understanding about the research paradigms in entrepreneurship studies. This is presented in Table 2.2.

A bird's eye view on the state-of-the-art review of entrepreneurship research (given in Table 2.2) reveals both types of research models, namely, population ecology model and strategic choice model in practice, yet the latter one is more explicit and in practice. The present study also operates under the theoretical framework of the strategic choice model. Based on Low and Macmillan (1988: 139-161) model, we have also made a modest attempt to position the present study in the context of future challenges and changes in entrepreneurship research (see Table 2.3).

Table 2.2: Research Paradigms in Entrepreneurship Studies: A Chronological Overview

Researcher(s)	*Year*	*Research Perspectives*
Cantillon	1755	Buys inputs at certain prices to market some thing at uncertain prices and, thus, becomes risk-taker.
Say	1803	Distinguished between investor and entrepreneur. The latter was seen as an organizer of business who buys land, labour and capital from respective owners and pays them rent, wages and interest respectively.
Weber	1930	Individual traits like hard work, thrift and desire for material advancement make one entrepreneur.
Schumpeter	1934	Innovation is the hallmark of entrepreneurship.
Baldwin	1959	Entrepreneurial behaviour varies between the communities.
Gadgil	1959	Economic opportunities rather than religion or communities are the cause of entrepreneurship.
McClleland	1961	Achievement motivation is the most critical element to become an entrepreneur.
Hagen	1962	Displacement or status withdrawal is the cause of becoming an entrepreneur.
Papanek	1962	Non-economic factors serve as cause for entrepreneurship.
Rotter	1966	Internal locus of control of an individual is a crucial construct to become an entrepreneur.
Guha	1970	Entrepreneurship is religious phenomenon like Parsi seths as entrepreneurs.
Cooper	1973	Entrepreneurship is a function of conducive environment.
Shapero	1975	Entrepreneurs come from among displaced persons who are characterized by a high degree of persistence.
McClelland and Burnham	1976	A high need for power, a low need for affiliation, and an ability to discipline oneself are the characteristic elements to become an entrepreneur.
Brockhaus	1980	One's ability to control the environment in his/her favour makes one entrepreneur.
Shapero and Sokol	1982	Entrepreneurship depends on situational and cultural factors.
Shepherd	1991	A constellation approach makes entrepreneurship happen.
Manimala	1992	The general and task environments affect entrepreneurship in different degrees and directions.
Clarke and Aram	1997	Behavioural ethics within the context of entrepreneurial dilemmas differ from country to country, though the fundamental values remain the same.
Knight, G.A.	1997	Entrepreneurial orientation of people/firms is determined by the cross-cultural reliability and validity of a scale known as ENTRESCALE).

Table 2.3: Entrepreneurship Research vis-à-vis The Present Study

Research Design	*Past Research*	*Model Research and Fugure Challenges*	*Features of the Present Study*
Purpose.	Lack of clarity and unity, more descriptive.	Clear description and explanation.	To promote economic development through entrepreneurship development
Theoretical Perspective.	Weak development of theory and implicit use of strategic choice model of research.	Theory-driven and variety of theoretical perspectives.	Strategic choice perspective.
Focus	Focus on personality traits and cultural determinants.	Focus on the entrepreneurial process in social context.	Focus on strategies of performing entrepreneurs
Analytical Level	Primarily single-level analysis.	Multiple-level analysis.	Enterprise—level analysis.
Time-frame	Narrow time-frame.	Wide time-frame	Longitudinal analysis covering the entire enterprise life cycle.
Methodology	Descriptive, case studies, and single method.	Explanatory, theory driven, *a priori* hypotheses, multiple method.	Case study method, explanatory, *a priori* hypotheses tested using statistical methods.

Concluding Remarks

The debate on what actually matters in entrepreneurship development, whether environment or entrepreneur, has so far been inconclusive. While some researchers consider environment more important in entrepreneurship development, others consider entrepreneur. As such, both the research models / perspectives have been in use attempting to explain the phenomenon of entrepreneurship. Nonetheless, as revealed from the review of research (see Table 2.2), the adoption of entrepreneur-based model has been more explicit, thus, implying its greater impact on entrepreneurship development. In a sense, there has been a paradigm shift in entrepreneurship research from focus on environment to entrepreneur and from 'who entrepreneurs are' to "what entrepreneurs do".

Accordingly, we have also positioned our study to examine the impact of both *i.e.,* environment and entrepreneur on entrepreneurship development, yet with more focus on entrepreneur.

3

Theorizing in Entrepreneurship

Introduction

The two entrepreneurial perspectives, namely, environment and entrepreneur perspectives, as discussed in the preceding chapter 2, are subject to certain criticism. These are: (i) each perspective is capable of covering only partial reflection of entrepreneurial behaviour; (ii) the assumptions made by each of the perspective are inappropriate to explain the entrepreneurial behaviour, (iii) each one of them focuses on some dimensions of entrepreneurial phenomenon and ignores others, and (iv) each one of them is suitable to explain especially bureaucratic large organizations rather than entrepreneurial organizations. That is why scholars have made attempts to theorize the phenomenon of entrepreneurship.

What is theory in general? Theory is a supposition of ideas explaining something. In other words, theory is the sphere of abstract knowledge or speculative thought. It is an explanation of something which has not been proved but which one believes is true. Thus, theory is speculation. Theory, in general, is needed:

- To be convinced about the knowledge or things happening
- To better understanding of the subject.
- To concrete and robust development of the knowledge in the subject.

In a sense, theory serves as a foundation for proper future expansion and development of an idea, a discipline, a subject and alike. The need for entrepreneurial theory is to better understand and develop knowledge in entrepreneurship. That is to say, to better know how entrepreneurship occurs or takes place. Efforts are made to speculate this from time to time by different thinkers and researchers. We produce some of these speculative explanations, of say, *'Theories of Entrepreneurship'* here.

Theories of Entrepreneurship

The major theories of entrepreneurship are discussed hereunder:

Innovation Theory

Joseph A. Schumpeter (1934) propounded the innovation theory of entrepreneurship. According to him, entrepreneurship is an outcome of innovation. Innovation, in his view, is the introduction of new combinations. He specifies five cases of new combinations that entrepreneurs introduce:

1. A new good or a new quality of a good.
2. A new method of production.
3. The opening of a new market.
4. The conquest of a new source of supply of raw materials.
5. The carrying out of the new organization of any industry.

In nutshell, the corner stone in the *'Innovation Theory'* is innovation, or say, new combination. Innovation is treated different from invention. In invention, inventor discovers new materials and methods. But, in innovations, new materials or methods discovered through inventions are used in order to make new combinations, i.e., in Schumpeterian sense, innovations. With the help of these new combinations, new goods are produced.

However, the innovation theory of entrepreneurship suffers from some limitations also. These are:

(i) It excludes those who operate established businesses.
(ii) Innovative entrepreneurs represent the most vigorous

type of enterprises which are rarely available in developing countries.

(iii) The entrepreneurial functions like risk bearing and organizing are ignored.

(iv) It does not provide any suitable answer to the question – why some regions / countries have more entrepreneurial talent than others.

(v) Like capitalists and workers, entrepreneurs are not a class in themselves.

(vi) Only carrying out new combinations makes an entrepreneur and ceases to be entrepreneur the moment he settles down to run an established business.

Need for Achievement Theory (n-achievement)

This theory developed by David C. McClelland (1961) is based on the assumption that internal factors i.e., human values and motives that lead man to exploit opportunities and to take advantage of favourable trade conditions, lead to entrepreneurship development in a society. These internal human values are known as "need for achievement." The n-achievement is to do / perform well not so much for the sake of social recognition and prestige, but for the sake of an inner feeling of personal accomplishment. The n-achievement and entrepreneurship are positively related. The higher the n-achievement, the higher is the level of entrepreneurship. Hence, the need for developing high 'n-ach' for higher levels of economic development.

Need for achievement theory of entrepreneurship is also not free from criticism. One of the criticisms labeled against need for achievement theory is that it is doubtful how many people with high n-ach can succeed in utilizing it in practice to become successful entrepreneurs especially in developing countries unless strengthened by other reinforcing circumstances. Yet another criticism attached to it is there is a need for creating a suitable climate to enable people to become individuals with high need for achievement. Besides, high need for achievement, it is possible to improve the performance of existing entrepreneurs through giving proper education and imparting required training.

Status Withdrawal Theory

The status withdrawn theory is propounded by E. Hagen (1962). The basic assumption in this theory is that when the members of some social groups feel that their values and status are not respected by the society, they turn to do something new, special (innovations) to get the respect of the society. Thus, according to this theory, entrepreneurship is a function of status withdrawal. The basic tenet of this theory is that a class or group which lost its previous prestige, (call it a minority group) tends to show aggressive entrepreneurial drive.

Hagen postulates that the occurrence of four types of events causes 'status withdrawal' by some members of the society:

(*i*) Displacement of one traditional group by another one by force.

(*ii*) Denigration of values and symbols through some change in the attitude of superior group.

(*iii*) Non-acceptance of expected status on migration to a new place.

(*iv*) Inconsistency of static symbol with a changing distribution of economic power.

Hagen believes status withdrawal propels creative personality. And, creative personality is a hallmark of entrepreneurship. There could be four responses that assess the type of personality the person possesses:

1. ***Retreatist***: One who continues to work in the society but remains indifferent to his work and position.
2. ***Ritualist***: One who adopts defensive ways and manners. He / she does not improve his position / status.
3. ***Reformist***: One who foments rebellion and attempts to establish a new society.
4. ***Innovator***: One who is creative and is likely to be an entrepreneur.

One of the shortcomings of this theory pointed out is it distinguishes between entrepreneurship and intra-preneurship. But, the evidence reveals that different factors and forces operating within the organization motivate executives to innovate some thing, not necessarily the withdrawal of status. Further, Hagen postulates that emergence of entrepreneurship as a result of status withdrawal usually takes three to five generations. Here again, the evidence is contrary. Examples of Sunil Mittal of Bharati Group and J. P. Gour of Jai Prakash Industries confirm that entrepreneurial emergence can take place with one generation itself, i.e., first-generation entrepreneurship.

Theory of Social Change

Max Weber's theory of social change is based on a stand that entrepreneurial growth is dependent upon ethical value system of the society. Protestant ethic (members of Western Christian churches that are separate from the Roman Catholic Churches) and the spirit of capitalism are the two central core elements in the 'Social Change Theory' of Weber (1930). This theory analyses religion and its impact on entrepreneurship. Weber believes that spirit of rapid industrial growth depends on rationalized technology, acquisition of money, and multiplication of money and these depend upon the specific value orientation of individuals i.e., their ethical value – base. In other words, according to Max Weber, the tendency of acquisition and rational attitude towards actions and endeavours are generated by specific kind of ethical value base.

Weber's this Theory of Social Change was based on the relationship he found between protestant ethic and the spirit of capitalism. Based on this, Weber concluded that the Protestants progressed fast in money acquisition and accumulation, which he considers 'capitalism', because of their ethical value system that provided them with rational attitude. He found his thesis holding true about other communities also, e.g. Hindu, Jain and Juda. On the contrary, as a corollary to his thesis, he held that 'Jews', for example, did not succeed in capitalism, i.e. industrial capitalism because of their distinct value-base, called 'Pariha' i.e. the social restrictions on having contact with other communities. Thus, the Weber's 'Theory of Social Change' shows that the religions or ethical beliefs supplied from outside generate driving forces for the emergence of entrepreneurial class. One core element in Weber's this ethically driven theory is that the entrepreneurial class (according to his Protestant Group) does hard work not only to meet their worldly desires met by acquisition of wealth, but also to have their spiritual needs satisfied.

According to critics, this theory is based on invalid assumptions. To quote, there is a single system of Hindu value. It remained immune to and insulated against external / exogenous changes and pulls and pressures. Hinduism is not averse to the spirit of capitalism and adventurous spirit. Business history is witness that the capitalism Hinduism has contributed a lot in entrepreneurship development in India.

Theory of Social Behaviour

John H. Kunkel (1970: 260-274) propounded a behavioural model of entrepreneurship. According to Kunkel, the supply of entrepreneurs is a function of economic, political, and social structure prevalent at a given time. His thesis is that out of various activities performed by the individuals, some are accepted by the society and others are not. The activities accepted are rewarded. The rewards act as reinforcing stimulus that increases the probability of repeating that activity / behaviour pattern. This pattern of social behaviour, he considers, is the entrepreneurial behaviour.

According to Kunkel, the supply of entrepreneurship depends upon four structures found in a society. These are:

1. *Limitation Structure*: Society limits specific activities and this affects all the members (including entrepreneurs) in the society.
2. *Demand Structure*: Material rewards influence the people to behave as entrepreneurs.
3. *Opportunity Structure*: Availability of capital, labour, technology, market, management, and information concerning

raw materials, production method also influence supply of entrepreneurs.

4. ***Labour Structure***: It is concerned with the availability and supply of competent and willing labour.

Like previous theories, this theory also suffers from the following limitations:

(i) It considers the ideal structure for the supply of entrepreneurs which is hardly found in the real world.

(ii) Entrepreneurs emerge through specific combinations of circumstances but these combinations are not available in the environment.

Theory of Leadership

B.F. Hoselitz (1960: 64-65) has propounded the entrepreneurial theory of leadership wherein he considers entrepreneurship as a function of managerial skills and leadership. He opines that the entrepreneur, no doubt, should have a drive to earn profit and amass wealth, but he/she also should have the ability to manage and lead his/her business venture. As regards leadership quality, Hoselitz classifies it into three types: (i) merchant money lenders, managers, and entrepreneurs. These are distinguished from each other in the sense that money lenders are market oriented, managers are authority oriented, and entrepreneurs are, in addition to these two, production oriented. Compared to the first two types of leaders, the entrepreneurs assume more risk in running their enterprises. As such, entrepreneurship can emerge and develop in the societies which are relatively less rigid. In other words, social conditions should be as such that ensure the development of enterprise-oriented personalities. McClelland (1961) considers the enterprising attitude as an essential ingredient for emergence of entrepreneurs. Drawing evidences from across the countries like Jews and Greeks in Medieval Europe and the Lebanese in West Africa, the Chinese in South Asia, and the Indians in West Africa, Hoselitz formulated the hypothesis that marginal men, because of their ambiguous position from a cultural or social stand point, tend to make creative adjustments with the environment and innovations in their behavioural adjustments. The creative and innovative attitude, in turn, breeds enterprising attitude.

Nonetheless, Hoselitz's above theory has been criticized on different counts. For example, it's true that the marginal groups do not have traditional bondage and, hence, are likely to be more prone to new and innovative behaviours. But, this is not the only reason for entrepreneurial emergence. The Indian evidence confirms that the political and economic conditions do also encourage people to establish enterprises. In the recent times, the Government of India has been encouraging people by offering various incentives and concessions to establish industries. In other words, the Government has been encouraging, what is popularly called, the first-generation entrepreneurs.

Theory of Systematic Innovation

Peter Drucker (1985) who is considered the 'management guru' of the present era, propounded the theory of systematic innovation. He describes his theory of systematic innovation consisting of purposeful and organized search for changes and in the systematic analysis of the opportunities such changes might offer for economic or social innovation. In developing his theory, Drucker has identified seven sources for innovative opportunity. He has further classified these seven sources into internal and external sources of opportunity as follows:

Internal Sources	*External Sources*
(i) The unexpected success, the unexpected failure, and the unexpected outside event.	(i) Demographic changes
(ii) The incongruity between the reality as it actually is and the reality as it is assumed to be or as it ought to be.	(ii) Changes taken place in perception, mood, emotion, and meaning.
(iii) Innovation on process need	(iii) New knowledge both in scientific and non-scientific areas.
(iv) Changes in industry structure or market structure that remains unknown to the enterprise.	

Drucker's theory is also not free from criticism. One of the criticisms labeled to this theory is the question of reliability and predictability of seven sources of innovative opportunity. For example, changes in scientific knowledge are both unreliable and unpredictable. As such, the formulation of entrepreneurial theory is subject to questions and doubts.

After having gone through the various theories of entrepreneurship, it becomes clear that there has not been a single factor causing the emergences of entrepreneurs. As a matter of fact, a host of factors led to entrepreneurial emergence. Yes, the combination and prominence of various factors may vary from entrepreneur to entrepreneur, from time to time, and from region to region. In nutshell, entrepreneurship has been a multi-disciplinary area influenced by different disciplines and factors.

Concluding Remarks

Entrepreneurship being an evolving concept has been understood differently by different people. This is a becoming and dynamic concept in its roles and dimensions. This has given emergence to different approaches or theories to explain and understand what makes entrepreneurship take place. As such, there has not been a single approach or theory of entrepreneurship, but host of it. Such diverse blending of entrepreneurial theories has helped understand the phenomenon of entrepreneurship more closely with its diverse dimensions.

4

Indian Entrepreneurship

The main objective of this chapter is to give a background note for understanding entrepreneurial history of India. The review of literature is being, therefore, presented in two sections. Section I gives a brief resume of the Indian entrepreneurship in its historical perspective. Section II highlights the main findings of some of the studies on Indian industrial entrepreneurship over time and clime.

Entrepreneurship in Historical Perspective

In fact, a proper understanding of the entrepreneurial history of any country must evolve itself within the context of the economic history of the particular country. The review of the history of the Indian entrepreneurship has, therefore, been divided into two sections, viz., Entrepreneurship during Pre-Independence and Post-Independence.

Entrepreneurship during the Pre-Independence

The evolution of the Indian industrial entrepreneurship can be traced back to even as early as *Rigveda,* when metal handicrafts existed in the society (Rao, 1969: 10). This would bring the point home that handicraft entrepreneurship in India was as old as the human civilization itself, and was nurtured by the craftsmen as a part of their duty towards the society. Before India came into contact with the West, people were organized in a particular type of economic and social system of the village community. Then, the village community featured the economic scene in India. The Indian towns were mostly religious and aloof from the general life of the country. The elaborated caste-base division of workers consisted of farmers, artisans and religious priests (the Brahmins). The majority of the artisans were treated as village servants. Such compact system of the Indian village community effectively protecting village artisans from the onslaughts of external competition was one of the important contributing factors to the absence of localization of industry in ancient India (Deshpande, 1984: 63).

Evidently, organized industrial activity was observable among the Indian artisans in a few recognizable products in the cities of Banaras, Allahabad, Gaya, Puri and Mirzapur which were established on the river basins. Very possibly, this was because the rivers served as a means of transportation facilities. These artisan industries flourished over the period because the Royal patronage was to them to support them, the workshops called 'Kharkhanas' came into existence. The craftsmen were brought into an association pronounced as 'guild system'. On the whole, perfection in art, durability beyond doubt and appeal to the eye of the individual were the distinguishing qualities inherent in the Indian craftsmanship that brought much everlasting laurels of name and fame to the illustrious India in the past. To quote, Bengal enjoyed world-wide celebrity for corahs, Lucknow for chintzes, Ahmedabad for dupattas and dhotis, Nagpur for silk-bordered cloths, Kashmir for shawls and Banaras for metal wares. Thus, from time immemorial till the earlier years of the eighteenth century, India enjoyed the prestigious status of the queen of the international trade with the help of its handicrafts.

Unfortunately, so much prestigious Indian handicraft industry, which was basically a cottage and small sector, declined at the end of the eighteenth century for various reasons (Gadgil, 1959: 36), like:

1. The disappearance of the Indian Royal Courts, who patronized the crafts earlier;
2. The lukewarm attitude of the British colonial Government towards the Indian crafts;

3. Imposition of heavy duties on the imports of the Indian goods in England;
4. Low-priced British-made goods produced on large scale which reduced the competing capacity of the products of the Indian handicrafts;
5. Development of transport in India facilitating the easy access of British products even to far-flung remote parts of the country;
6. Changes in the tastes and habits of the Indians, developing crazyness of foreign products; and
7. Unwillingness of the Indian craftsmen to adapt to the changing tastes and needs of the people.

Some scholars hold the view that manufacturing entrepreneurship in India emerged as the latent and manifest consequence of East India Company's advent in India (Chernovskaya 2005). The Company injected various changes in the Indian economy through export of raw materials and import of finished goods to India. Particularly, the Parsis established good rapport with the Company and were much influenced by the Company's commercial operations. The Company established its first ship building industry in Surat where from 1673 onwards the Parsis built vessels for the Company. The most important was shipwright Lowjee-Nushirvan, who migrated to Bombay around 1935. He belonged to a Wadia family which gave birth to many leading ship-builders of Bombay (Pavlov, 1964: 146-147). In 1677, Manjee Dhanjee was given a contract for building the first large gunpowder-mill in Bombay for the East India Company. Besides, a Parsi foreman of a gun factory belonging to the Company established a steel industry in Bombay in 1852. On the basis of these facts, it can be stated that the East India Company made some contribution towards entrepreneurial growth in India. But, whether the Company did it deliberately for the growth of entrepreneurship in India or it was just a coincidence that people came in contact with the Company and entered the manufacturing, nothing can be said with certitude.

The actual emergence of manufacturing entrepreneurship can be noticed in the second half of the nineteenth century. Prior to 1850, some stray failure attempts were, indeed, made by the Europeans to set up factories in India. In the beginning, the Parsis were the founder manufacturing entrepreneurs in India.

Ranchodlal Chotalal, a Nagar Brahman, was the first Indian to think of setting up the textile manufacturing on the modern factory lines in 1847, but failed. In his second attempt, he succeeded (Spodek, 1965: 483) in setting up a textile mill in 1861 at Ahmedabad. But before this, the first cotton textile manufacturing unit was already set up by a Parsi – Cowasjee Nanabhoy Davar – in Bombay in 1854 followed by Nawrosjee Wadia, who opened his textile mill in Bombay in 1880. The credit for the expansion of textile industries up to 1915 goes to the Parsis. Out of 96 textile mills existing in 1915, 43 per cent (41) were set up by Parsis, 24 per cent (23) by Hindus, 10 per cent (10) by Muslims and 23 per cent (22) by foreigners, ie., British citizens (Pavlok, 1964: 253). Later, the Parsis invaded other fields, mainly iron and steel industry, also. Jamshedjee Tata was the first Parsi entrepreneur who established the first steel industry in Jamshedpur in 1911.[1]

In the first wave of manufacturing entrepreneurship, except Parsis, all others hailed from non-commercial communities. Why the well-known commercial communities, namely, Jains and Vaishyas of Ahmedabad and Baroda, lagged behind in entrepreneurial initiative throughout the nineteenth century can be explained by two factors. *Firstly,* the improvement of business climate in the countryside during this period resulted in an increase in the quantum of trade which assured quick returns on investment. This proved the commercial activity more/lucrative during the period. *Secondly,* it can also be attributed to their conservative attitude to change from commercial entrepreneurship to industrial entrepreneurship (Tripathi, 1971).

The *Swadeshi* campaign. i.e., emphasis on indigenous goods, provided, indeed, a proper seedbed for inculcating and developing nationalism in the country. It was the influence of *Swadeshi* that

Jamshedji Tata even named his first mill 'Swadeshi Mill'. The spirit of indigenousness strengthened its roots so much in the country that the Krishna Mills in its advertisement of *Tribune* of April 13 made the following appeal: "Our concern is financed by native capital and is under native management throughout" (Joshi, 1975).

The second wave of entrepreneurial growth in India began after the First World War. For various reasons, the Indian Government agreed to 'discriminating' protection to certain industries, even requiring that companies receiving its benefits should be registered in India with rupee capital and have a proportion of their directors as Indians. The advantages of these measures were mostly enjoyed by the Indians. The Europeans failed to harness the protectionist policies to their interests (Bagchi, 1970:243). These measures helped in establishing and extending the factory manufacturing in India during the first four decades of the twentieth century. During these decades, the relative importance of the Parsis declined and Gujaratis and Marwari Vaishyas gained that pendulum in India's entrepreneurial scene.

The emergence of Managing Agency System which made its own contribution to the Indian entrepreneurship can be traced back to 1936 when Carr, Tagore & Co. assumed the management of Calcutta Steam Tug Association (King, 1966). The credit for this initiation goes to an Indian, Dwarkanath Tagore, who encouraged others to form joint-stock companies and invented a distinct method of management in which management remained in the hands of the 'firm' rather than an 'individual'. Historical evidences also do confirm that after the East India Company lost its monopoly in 1813, the European Managing Agency Houses entered business, trade and banking. And, these houses markedly influenced eastern India's industrial scene. It is stated that the Managing Agency Houses were the real entrepreneur for that period particularly in eastern India. Brimmer (1955: 555-560) holds the opinion that Agency Houses emerged to overcome the limitations imposed by a shortage of venture capital and entrepreneurial acumen though all may not agree squarely with this view.

Before we skip our review of entrepreneurial growth to the post-Independence era, it will be in the fitness of the context to shed some light on effects of partition on India's industrial economy so as to depict Independent India's industrial background. August 15, 1947 was the day on which India became independent with part of its land separated. Some major effects of partition on the Indian industrial economy seem worth mentioning.

Demographic Effects: Of the total land area of the undivided country, India got 77 per cent while 23 per cent went to Pakistan. As to the distribution of the population of the undivided country, 82 per cent came to India while only 18 per cent went to Pakistan.[2]

Industrial Activity: Of the total industrial establishments (12,675) in the country at the time of partition, 90 per cent (1,462) came to India with 93 per cent of total workers employed in the industrial establishments of the undivided country. As many as six industries with one lakh or more workers employed came to India and Pakistan was left with none of that magnitude. Industries like jute, iron and steel, paper, etc., came to the Indian land while industries like cotton textiles, sugar, cement, glass, and chemicals, which went to Pakistan, were not of high magnitude. Hence, it could be seen that India got a relatively diversified industrial activity as compared to Pakistan.

Mineral and Natural Resources: Out of the total value of mineral resources, India got 97 per cent and, thus, only 3 per cent went to Pakistan. Major deposits of coal, mica, manganese, iron ore, etc., were found in the areas which came to India. But with regard to some important minerals like gypsum, rock salt, etc., which are necessary for heavy chemical industries, India was at a loss as all the deposits of these minerals were existing in Pakistan area. Also, 81 per cent of the total raw jute and 40 per cent of total raw cotton growing areas, which went to Pakistan, severely affected the supply of raw materials for jute and cotton textiles in India.

Manpower and Managerial Skills: Many industries like cotton textiles, woolen, hosiery, glass, engineering, metal works, etc., suffered from the shortage of skilled workers in the industries who happened to be Muslims that migrated to Pakistan.

Foreign Trade: Undivided India enjoyed a favourable balance of trade prior to the war and even during the war period. By March 1946, India had accumulated sterling balances to the extent of nearly Rs. 17,330 million besides the repatriation of the pre-war sterling debt of Rs. 4,260 million. Particularly after partition, the era of surplus trade in favour of India was over. For example, the net disinvestment due to deficit in the balance of payments on current account amounted to Rs. 2,180 million in 1949 (Vakil and Rao, 1968).

Transport Facilities: Partition also affected adversely the transport facilities – both railways and ports. The railway system was very much dislocated. Though India got 83 per cent of the total route mileage in the undivided country (34,000 route miles) difficulties as to the staff arose. Many Muslims who opted to migrate to Pakistan were drivers, firemen, workshop technicians, etc., while the non-Muslims opting to remain in India were clerks, ticket collectors, guards, etc. As such, immediately after partition, there was surplus of non-technical personnel and shortage of technical personnel in India which resulted in the dislocation in the railway transport system in the country. With dislocation in the railways, many industries were hard hit since the movement of coal from the collieries became slow.

Major ports like Chittagoing in the eastern sector and Karachi in the western sector went to Pakistan. Exports from West Bengal and Assam used to be routed through the Chittagong port before partition. But after partition, these exports were diverted to Calcutta port. This necessitated the construction of a new rail link between Assam and West Bengal, making transport a costly one.

Entrepreneurship during the Post-Independence

After taking a long sigh of political relief in 1947, the Government of India tried to spell out the priorities to devise a scheme for achieving balanced growth. For this purpose, the Government came forward with the First Industrial Policy, 1948, which was revised from time to time.[3] The Government in her various industrial policy statements identified the responsibility of the state to promote, assist and develop industries in the national interest. It also explicitly recognized the vital role of the private sector in accelerating industrial development and, for this, enough fields were reserved for the private sector. The Government took three important measures in her industrial resolutions:

(i) To maintain a proper distribution of economic power between private and public sector:

(ii) To encourage the tempo of industrialization by spreading entrepreneurship from the existing centres to other cities, towns and villages; and

(iii) To disseminate the entrepreneurial acumen concentrated in a few/dominant communities to a large number of industrially potential people of varied social strata (Malenbaum, 1962)

To achieve the above adumbrated objectives, the Government accorded emphasis on the development of small-scale industries in the country. Particularly since the Third Five Year Plan, the Government started to provide various incentives and concessions in the form of capital, technical know-how, markets and land to the potential entrepreneurs to establish industries in the industrially potential areas to remove the regional imbalances in development. This was, indeed, a major step taken by the Government to initiate interested people of varied social strata to enter the small-scale manufacturing field. Several institutions like Directorate of Industries, Financial Corporation, Small Scale Industries Corporations, and Small Industries Service Institutes were also established by the Government to facilitate the new entrepreneurs in setting up their enterprises. Expectedly, the small-scale units emerged very rapidly in India witnessing a tremendous increase in their number from 121,619 in 1966 to 190,727 in 1970 registering an increase of 17,000 units per year during the period under reference (Government of India, 1971:2).

The recapitulation of the review of literature regarding entrepreneurial growth in India, thus, leads us to conclude that prior to 1850, the manufacturing entrepreneurship was negligible lying dormant in artisans. The artisan entrepreneurship could not develop mainly due to inadequate infrastructure and the lukewarm attitude of the colonial political structure to the entrepreneurial function. The East India Company, the Managing Agency Houses and various socio-political movements like *Swadeshi* Campaign provided one way or the other, proper seedbed for the emergence of the manufacturing entrepreneurship from 1850 onwards.

The wave of entrepreneurial growth gained sufficient momentum after the Second World War. Since then the entrepreneurs have increased rapidly in numbers in the country. Particularly since the Third Five Year Plan, small entrepreneurs have experienced tremendous increase in their numbers. But, they lacked entrepreneurial ability, however. The fact remains that even the small entrepreneurship continued to be dominated by business communities though at some place new groups of entrepreneurs too emerged. Also, there are examples that some entrepreneurs grew from small to medium scale and from medium to large scale manufacturing units during the period. The family entrepreneurship units like Tata, Birla, Mafatlal, Dalmia, Kirloskar and other grew beyond the normally expected and also established new frontiers in business in this period. Notwithstanding, all this happened without the diversification of the entrepreneurial base so far as its socio-economic ramification is concerned.

Some Studies on Indian Entrepreneurship

Many scholars interested in socio-economic change have studied the phenomenon of entrepreneurship in its various aspects in India. We review here some of the studies undertaken so far in this field in India. For the sake of the analysis, these studies can be classified into two categories, viz., Spatial Studies and Ethical Studies.

Spatial Studies

Madras City and Coimbatore: A study of fifty manufacturing units engaged in various kinds of light engineering products in and around Madras city and Coimbatore was undertaken by

James J. Berna (1960). Most of his sample firms were started on medium scale. With regard to the entrepreneurs' background and origins, Berna found that the initial entry to industry was embraced by the total spectrum of all social and economic strata in the region. Thus, his finding refutes the popular belief that caste and tradition play an important role in the emergence of entrepreneurs. That industries have grown from small scale to medium scale over the period is one of his important findings. Moreover, Berna feels that if certain package of help in techniques of production could be provided to the entrepreneurs, their performance could still be improved. He also pointed out that the medium scale entrepreneurs did not receive the adequate support and encouragement from the Government as the small-scale entrepreneurs do receive.

Tanuku Region (Andhra Pradesh): Gaikwad and Tripathi (1970) attempted to bring out the prerequisites of successful entrepreneurs in small sector in their study of Tanuku region of West Godavari district in Andhra Pradesh. The study observed entrepreneurs with initiative, drive and hard work, though most of them neither possessed any technical knowledge nor had strong economic and political backgrounds. Besides, very few had any idea of the business involved and any concrete idea about the Government policy in this regard. One important finding of their study is that even realizing the scope for industrial development in the region, the traders does not take up the industrial entrepreneurship because, in their opinion, it involves large capital, technical knowledge and high managerial skills which they lack. Due to the longer gestation period of industrial entrepreneurship, the traders are not prepared to wait for late returns. They also feel that industrialists enjoy better status in the business world than the traders. The policy point of view because the tradesmen are often looked upon prospective entrepreneurs in India.

Hyderabad and Secunderabad (Andhra Pradesh): The Small Industries Extension Training Institute (SIET) (1974), Hyderabad, also conducted a survey of 61 small entrepreneurs of Hyderabad and Secunderabad to investigate into why the entrepreneurs started their industrial units. The study brings forth that "economic gains" was the most important reason for starting the small industrial units followed by "ambition", "social prestige" and "social responsibility" in that order. "Capital shortages" and "government red-tape" were identified as the most inhibiting factors in the development of industry. The study hypothesized the following six stages in the process of adopting innovation in a small industry:

1) The awareness stage;
2) The interest stage;
3) The preparation stage;
4) The trial stage;
5) The evaluation stage; and
6) The adoption stage.

It was revealed that neither all the entrepreneurs passed all the six stages for adopting innovation nor were number and sequence constant in the case of all. The study affirms that younger age, formal education, urban background and experience in industry were some of the characteristics positively associated with the performance of entrepreneurship. At the same time, other factors like technical education, being first born or eldest among the male children, contacts with influential people and need for achievement were found not associated with the entrepreneurship, however.

Uttar Pradesh: Sharma (1975) studied the entrepreneurial performance in role perspective in Uttar Pradesh. His study revealed that entrepreneurs in Uttar Pradesh have higher entrepreneurial orientation than entrepreneurial commitment and achievement. In his view non-conducive socio-economic milieu, non-commitment of workers and officials and shortages of raw materials and capital were the main attributing factors to the entrepreneurs' low achievement in the state. A higher degree of entrepreneurial orientation and commitment to entrepreneurial functions in non-business communities than the traditional business communities is his another important finding. Why a lower degree of entrepreneurial orientation and commitment is displayed by business caste communities lies in inheriting a well established business base from their fathers.

In his study of 245 small entrepreneurs from Punjab and Uttar Pradesh, Sharma (1976) identified that inter-state variations in entrepreneurial performance was accounted for their differential industrial climates. He maintains that socio-economic background matters, to some extent, for one's entry into manufacturing. He also affirms the Government's role in expanding industrial units. In his model of entrepreneurship growth, Sharma envisaged four stages for entrepreneurship development:

(1) entry;

(2) expansion;

(3) perception of stability; and

(4) commitment to sustained growth.

Kanpur, Allahabad and Gorakhpur (Uttar Pradesh): Gupta (1987) studied entrepreneurial performance by surveying 60 small entrepreneurs, 20 each in Kanpur, Allahabad and Gorakhpur, in Uttar Pradesh. He found that out of 60 entrepreneurs, as many as 34 (56.67 per cent) hail from Vaishya community followed by 14 (23.33 per cent) from Khatris. This suggests that Vaishya caste still dominates the entrepreneurial scene in the State and the various incentives provided by the Government could not widen the base of entrepreneurship to embrace the total spectrum of all castes in the state. Again, two-thirds (40) of the total entrepreneurs belonging to the families of businessmen and industrialists affirm that family background of the entrepreneurs matters for one's entry into manufacturing. It is also revealed that the sons of industrialists and businessmen have displayed better in sales because of the extended contacts of entrepreneurs' fathers with customers as well as prior experience of the entrepreneurs themselves. A positive association was observed between the entrepreneurs levels of education and approach to innovation. Lastly, thin equity base of the units, dilatory and cumbersome procedure of debt, more emphasis on furnishing security in place of visualizing the viability of the projects, high rates of interest and delay in payments by parent units and other financing agencies were stated as the reported financial problems of the entrepreneurs discouraging them.

Ethical Studies

The analysis of Indian entrepreneurship from the ethical point of view seems more relevant to the Indian situation where entrepreneurial scene is dominated by the caste-system particularly during the pre-Independence era.

Parsi: The most important ethical group, which figured in the industrial scene in the latter half of the nineteenth century as discussed in the first section of the chapter, was Parsi. An intelligent attempt has been made by Robert Kennedy (1962) to analyse the commercial bent of the Parsi attitude. He maintains that the Parsi entrepreneurship is greatly influenced by Zoroastrianism.

Amalendu Guha (1970) reviews historic development of Parsi entrepreneurs for a century (1750-1850). He holds the view that religion of Puritanism cannot purely be accounted for the success of the Parsi entrepreneurs. Parsi' interest in European forms of business organization, exploration of new markets, acquisition of a working knowledge of the English language and quickness to adapt themselves to the changed political circumstances are, according to Guha, major contributory factors to the Parsis' commendable success in business and industry.

Marwari: The nature of entrepreneurship with respect to the Marwaris' success in business and their late entry into manufacturing is studied by Thomas Timberg (1978). In his study, he arrives to this conclusion that as entrepreneurs, the Marwaris displayed pivotal roles in northern India's industrial and commercial development.

On the whole, the above listed studies facilitate the researchers to have an idea about the various characteristics of the entrepreneurs with their varied spatial and ethnical origins.

NOTES AND REFERENCES

1. In fact, Tatas were not the first to have attempted the construction of a steel mill in India. There were two other attempts – one in 1830 and the other in 1875 – but both of them failed.

2. For effects of partition in more detail, reference can be made to: Vakil, C.N., 1950: *Economic Consequences of Divided India,* Vora & Company, Bombay.

3. For the details of industrial policies, Kuchhal, S.C., 1963: *The Industrial Economy of India,* Chaitanya Publishing House, Allahabad; *Industrial Development and Regulation Act,* 1951; *Karve Committee Report,* 1954; *Industrial Policy Resolution,* 1955; *The Industrial Licensing Policy,* 1970, and the *Industrial Policy Statement,* 1977; *Policy Measures for Promoting and Strengthening Small, Tiny and Village Industries, 1991; and North East Industrial and Investment Promotion Policy* (NEIIPP), 2007.

5

Women Entrepreneurship*

Women constitute around half of the total world population. So is in India also. They are, therefore, regarded as the better half of the society. In traditional societies, they were confined to the four walls of houses performing household activities. In modern societies, they have come out of the four walls to participate in all sorts of activities. The global evidences buttress that women have been performing exceedingly well in different spheres of activities like academics, politics, administration, social work and so on. Now, they have started plunging into industry also and running their enterprises successfully. Therefore, while discussing on entrepreneurial development, it seems in the fitness of the context to study about the development of women entrepreneurs also in the country. The present chapter, therefore, aims at discussing the growth and problems of women entrepreneurs in India.

Before we discuss development of women entrepreneurship in India, let us first make a case for women entrepreneurship. The review of developmental literature reveals that the focus on the contribution of women in direct productive work was first brought about in 1970 with Ester Boserup's book (1970), *'Women's Role in Economic Development'* which was an outcome of Boserup's research experience in India. If David C. McClelland's

---

* This chapter heavily draws from S.S. Khanka: "Women Entrepreneurship in India," *Journal of Assam University,* Volume III, Number I, January 1998, pp. 8-13.

experiment (1961) proved as seed for entrepreneurship development programmes (EDPs) in India, so was Boserup's research experience for women in development. It was during 1970s; more attention was given to the women's productive roles than the reproductive ones (like childbearing and rearing, housekeeping, and care of the elderly). In the 1980s, the gender and development approach took the women life into totality rejecting the public/private dichotomy which devalues women's role at home. The Planning Commission of the Government of India realized that economic development of country can take place only when women are brought in the mainstream of economic development. Development can not take place unless the people at the grassroots' level are not involved in the development programmes. This, among other things, underlined the need for entrepreneurship development programmes for women to enable them start small-scale industries. Accordingly, the focus on economic development made women the 'subjects' rather than 'objects' of development and 'change agents' rather than 'welfare recipients.' This also made women to move from margin to the centre (Hooks 1984) by empowering women to gain control over their lives. Considering the dual roles of women at home and work, developmental approaches tried to harmoniously combine women's home life with work life. For example, Bangladesh Rural Advancement Committee (BRAC) has developed flexible programmes which work around women's lives and within the context of broader policies and plans making women the subjects of development rather than welfare recipients (Ghosh, Gupta and Dhar 1998: 158-159).

Now that we have justified the case for women entrepreneurship, we can profitably discuss the important aspects of women entrepreneurship in India. Let us begin with understanding the concept of women entrepreneurs.

Concept of Women Entrepreneur

Based on the general concept of entrepreneur discussed earlier, women entrepreneur may be defined as a woman or group of women who initiate, organize, and run a business enterprise. In terms of Schumpeterian concept of innovative entrepreneurs, women who innovate, imitate or adopt a business activity are called "women entrepreneurs". The Government of India has defined women entrepreneurs based on women participation in equity and employment of a business enterprise. Accordingly, a women entrepreneur is defined as "an enterprise owned and controlled by a women having a minimum financial interest of 51 per cent of the capital and giving at least 51 per cent of the employment generated in the enterprise to women". However, this definition is subject to criticism mainly on the condition of employing more than 50 per cent women workers in the enterprises owned and run by the women.

In nutshell, women entrepreneurs are those women who think of a business enterprise, initiate it, organize and combine the factors of production, operate the enterprise and undertake risks and handle economic uncertainty involved in running a business enterprise.

Functions of Women Entrepreneurs

As an entrepreneur, a woman entrepreneur has also to perform all the functions involved in establishing an enterprise. These include idea generation and screening, determination of objectives, project preparation, product analysis, determination of forms of business organization, completion of promotional formalities, raising funds, procuring men, machine and materials, and operation of business.

Frederick Harbison (1956) has enumerated the following five functions of a woman entrepreneur:

1. Exploration of the prospects of starting a new business enterprise.
2. Undertaking of risks and the handling of economic uncertainties involved in business.
3. Introduction of innovations or imitation of innovations.
4. Coordination, administration and control.
5. Supervision and leadership.

The fact remains that, like the definition of the term 'entrepreneur', different scholars have identified different sets of functions performed by an entrepreneur whether man or women. All these entrepreneurial functions can be classified broadly into three categories:

- Risk-bearing
- Organisation
- Innovations

There functions are self-explanatory, hence not discussed in detail.

Growth of Women Entrepreneurship

Women in India constitute around half of the country's population. Hence, they are regarded as the "better half of the society". In the official proclamation, they are at par with men. But, in real life, the truth prevails otherwise. Our society is still male-dominated and women are not treated as equal partners both inside and outside four walls of the house. In fact, they are treated as *abla*, i.e., weak and dependent on men. As such, the Indian women enjoy a disadvantageous status in the society. Let some facts be given. The much low literacy rate (40%), low work participation rate (28%) and low urban population share (10%) of women as compared to 60%, 52% and 18% respectively of their male counterparts well confirm their disadvantageous position in the society. Our age-old socio-cultural traditions and taboos arresting the women within four walls of their houses also make their conditions more disadvantageous. These factors combinedly serve as non-conducive conditions for the emergence and development of women entrepreneurship in the country. Given these unfavourable conditions, the development of women entrepreneurship is expectedly low in the country. This is well indicated by a dismally low level of women (5.2%) in total self-employed persons in the country (Gupta and Khanka 1996:1.10). Further, women entrepreneurs in India accounted for 9.01% of the total 1.70 million entrepreneurs during 1988-89 (Desai 1992: 132).

A cross-country comparison reveals that emergence and development of entrepreneurship is largely caused by the availability of supporting conditions in a country. To quote, with improving supporting conditions, the share of women owned enterprises in the United States has risen from 7.1% in

1977 to 32% in 1990. It has reached to 50% by the turn of the 20th century.

In India, women entry into business is a new phenomenon. Women entry into business, or say, entrepreneurship is traced out as an extension of their kitchen activities mainly to 3 Ps, viz., Pickles, Power and Pappad. Women in India plugged into business for both pull and push factors. Pull factors imply the factors which encourage women to start an occupation or venture with an urge to do something independently. Push factors refer to those factors which compel women to take up their own business to tide over their economic difficulties and responsibilities. With growing awareness about business and spread of education among women over the period, women have started shifting from 3 PS to engross to 3 modern Es, viz., Engineering, Electronics, and Energy and other industries under Integrated Rural Development Programmes (IRDP) (David 1992). They have excelled in these activities. Women entrepreneurs manufacturing solar cookers in Gujarat, small foundries in Maharashtra and T.V. capacitors in Orissa have proved beyond doubt that given the opportunities, they can excel their male counterparts. Smt. Sumati Morarji (Shipping Corporation), Smt. Yamutai Kirloskar (Mahila Udyog Limited), Smt. Neena Malhotra (Exports), Kiran Majumdar Shaw (Bio-technology) Naina Lal Kidwai (Banking), Jaswantiben Jamnadas Popat (Food), and Smt. Shahnaz Hussain (Beauty Clinic) are some exemplary names of successful and accomplished women entrepreneurs in our country. Women have traditionally played an important role in the small business development as owners, managers, and workers. They dominate three important sub-sectors, constituting over 80 per cent of the employees in textile, clothing and leather production; 75 per cent in food, beverages and tobacco production; and over 60 per cent in wood and wood processing (quoted by Bhargava 2007: 28). Besides, they also act as micro-entrepreneurs and traders in agri-business.

In India, Kerala is a state with highest literacy (including women literacy) reflecting a congenial atmosphere for the emergence and development of women entrepreneurship in the State. According to a study of the Government of Kerala (1984), the number of women's industrial units in Kerala was

358 in 1981 which rose to 782 in March 1984. These 782 units included 592 proprietory concerns, 43 partnership firms, 42 charitable institutions, 03 joint stock companies and 102 co-operative societies covering a wide range of activities. On the whole, proper education of women in Kerala resulted in high motivation among them to enter into business. The financial, marketing and training assistance provided by the State Government also helped motivate women to assume entrepreneurial career. Women's desire to work at the place or residence, difficulty of getting jobs in the public and private sectors and the desire for social recognition also motivated women in Kerala for self-employment. Like Kerala, an increasing number of women is entering the business in the State of Maharashtra also.

Problems of Women Entrepreneurs

Women entrepreneurs encounter two sets of problems, viz., general problems of entrepreneurs and problems specific to women entrepreneurs. These are discussed as follows:

- **Problem of Finance**: Finance is regarded as "life-blood" for any enterprise, be it big or small. However, women entrepreneurs suffer from shortage of finance on two counts. *Firstly*, women do not generally have property on their names to use them as collateral for obtaining funds from external sources. Thus, their access to the external sources of funds is limited. *Secondly*, the banks also consider women less credit-worthy and discourage women borrowers on the belief that they can at any time leave their business. Given such situation, women entrepreneurs are bound to rely on their own savings, if any, and loans from friends and relatives who are expectedly meager and negligible. Thus, women enterprises fail due to the shortage of finance.
- **Scarcity of Raw Material**: Most of the women enterprises are plagued by the scarcity of raw material and necessary inputs. Added to this are the high prices of raw material, on the one hand, and getting raw material at the minimum of discount, on the other. The failure of many women

co-operatives in 1971 engaged in basket-making is an example how the scarcity of raw material sounds the death-knell of enterprises run by women (Gupta and Srinivasan 1992: 132).

- **Stiff Competition:** Women entrepreneurs do not have organizational set-up to pump in a lot of money for canvassing and advertisement. Thus, they have to face a stiff competition for marketing their products with both organized sector and their male counterparts. Such a competition ultimately results in the liquidation of women enterprises.
- **Limited Mobility**: Unlike men, women mobility in India is highly limited due to various reasons. A single women asking for room is still looked upon suspicion. Cumbersome exercise involved in starting an enterprise coupled with the officials humiliating attitude towards women compels them to give up idea of starting an enterprise.
- **Family Ties**: In India, it is mainly a woman's duty to look after the children and other members of the family. Man plays a secondary role only. In case of married women, she has to strike a fine balance between her business and family. Her total involvement in family leaves little or o energy and time to devote for business. Support and approval of husbands seem necessary condition for women's entry into business. Accordingly, the educational level and family background of husbands positively influence women's entry into business activities.
- **Lack of Education**: In India, around three-fifths (60%) of women are still illiterate. Illiteracy is the root cause of socio-economic problems. Due to the lack of education and that too qualitative education, women are not aware of business, technology and market knowledge. Also, lack of education causes low achievement motivation among women. Thus, lack of education creates problems for women in the setting up and running of business enterprises.

- **Male-Dominated Society**: Male chauvinism is still the order of the day in India. The Constitution of India speaks of equality between sexes. But, in practice, women are looked upon as abla, i.e. weak in all respects. Women suffer from male reservations about a women's role, ability and capacity and are treated accordingly. In nutshell, in the male-dominated Indian society, women are not treated equal to men. This, in turn, serves as a barrier to women entry into business.
- **Low Risk-Bearing Ability**: Women in India lead a protected life. They are less educated and economically not self-dependent. All these reduce their ability to take risk involved in running an enterprise. Risk-bearing is an essential requisite of a successful entrepreneur.

In addition to above problems, inadequate infrastructural facilities, shortage of power, high cost of production, social attitude, low need for achievement and socio-economic constraints also hold the women back from entering into business.

Developing Women Entrepreneurs

Days are gone when women in India remained confined to within four walls of their homes and their immense strength and potential remained unrecognized and unaccounted for. Now, they are increasingly participating in all spheres of activities. The fact remains that the citadels of excellence in academic, politics, administration, business and industry are no longer the prerogatives of men in India. The general consensus that is emerging in all discussions relating to the development of women is that promotion of women entrepreneurs should form an integral part of all development efforts. The experience of the United States where the share of women-owned enterprises is continuously on increase strengthens the view that the future of small-scale industries depends very much on the entry of women into industry. Several national and international organizations and agencies have appreciated the need for and importance of developing women entrepreneurs in recent years. A brief review of it is given here.

With a view to develop better half of the society, the

United Nations declared the decade 1975-85 as the *Decade for Women*. The UNIDO Preparatory Meeting on the *Role of Women in Industrialisation in Developing Countries* held at Vienna during 6-10 February, 1978 identified several constraints such as social, attitudinal and institutional barriers, inadequate employment opportunities, inappropriate and inadequate training, insufficient information and so on which held women back from participating in industrial activities. *The World Conference of the United Nations Decade for Women* held at Copenhagen in Denmark on 30th June, 1980 also adopted a programme aimed at promoting full and equal opportunities and treatment of women in employment and their access to non-traditional skilled trades (Prasad 1983: 147).

The First National Conference of Women Entrepreneurs held at New Delhi in November 1981 advocated the need for developing women entrepreneurs for the overall development of the country. It called for priority to women in allotment of land, sheds, sanction of power, licensing, etc. *The Second International Conference of Women Entrepreneurs* organized by the National Alliance of Young Entrepreneurs (NAYE) held in 1989 at New Delhi also adopted certain declarations involving women's participation in industry.

The Government of India has been assigning increasing importance to the development of women entrepreneurs in the country in recent years. The Sixth Five Year Plan, for example, proposed for promoting female employment in women-owned industries. The Government moved a step forward in the Seventh Five Year Plan by including a special chapter on *Integration of Women in Development*. The chapter suggested:

- To treat women as specific target groups in all development programmes.
- To devise and diversify vocational training facilities for women to suit their varied needs and skills.
- To promote appropriate technologies to improve their efficiency and productivity.
- To provide assistance for marketing their products.
- To involve women in decision-making process.

In her recent Industrial Policy 1991, the Government of India further stressed the need for conducting special entrepreneurship development programmes for women with a view to encourage women to their industry. Product and process-oriented courses enabling women to start small-scale industries are also recommended in the Policy Statement.

There are several institutional arrangements both at the centre and the state levels like nationalized banks, state financial corporations, state industrial corporations, district industry centres and voluntary agencies like FICCI's Ladies Organisation (FLO), National Alliance of Young Entrepreneurs (NAYE) which have been engaged in protecting and developing women entrepreneurs in the country. Added to these are national and international women associations set up with a purpose to create a congenial environment for developing women entrepreneurship in rural and urban areas.

Limits of Women Entrepreneurship

It is a cliché to mention that despite the various efforts of governmental and non-governmental organizations, the number of women entrepreneurs in India has so far been very small. But, unfortunately that is the case. Several factors/limitations explain this. The prodigious volume of entrepreneurial research on gender differences has highlighted several limitations of development of women entrepreneurship. The most important ones are discussed hereunder:

First, establishing and running enterprises always involve risk-taking. In case of women, the gender stereotyped perception like self, lake of confidence, and assertiveness pose limitations to risk-taking. Added to these are the fear of non-traditional and outside the home activities make women hesitant to involve in business.

Second, the Indian women are known as housewives bearing heavy domestic commitments and resistance of social structure to change the status from housewives to working wives also limits women's entry into entrepreneurship. Especially in a patriarchal social structure, women are dependent on the males – husband and father- in their lives. As such, family resistance is a major barrier to start an enterprise. In such social structures, male family members often make decisions for women.

Third, as indicated by much low literacy rate of women, lack of access to education and training for them serve yet other barriers for women to enter into entrepreneurship.

Fourth, as women generally lack in collateral, they find it difficult to obtain even small amounts from the banks. Banks have a perception about women as weak in repaying capacity.

Concluding Remarks

A women entrepreneur is one who owns and controls an enterprise having a share capital of not less than 51 per cent as partners / shareholders / directors of private limited company / members of co-operative society. The functions performed by a women entrepreneur are categorized as risk-bearing, organization and innovation. Women entry into business is a recent phenomenon. It is traced out as an extension of their kitchen activities to three Ps, i.e., pickle, power (masala) and pappad manufacturing. With growing awareness and spread of education over the years, women have started engrossing to modern activities like engineering, electronics and energy popularly known as 3Es. In certain businesses, women entrepreneurs are doing exceedingly well and excelling their male counterparts. Women entrepreneurs account for about 10 per cent of total entrepreneurs in the country.

Women entrepreneurs face two types of problems, *one,* general problems faced by all entrepreneurs and, *second,* problems specific to women. Male dominating society, family ties, lack of need achievement, education and risk-bearing abilities are the examples of problems specific to women entrepreneurs.

Women in India are no longer *abla* and remain confined to within four walls of house. They are participating and performing well in all spheres of activities such as academic, politics, administration, space, and industry. Efforts are on at the Government and voluntary agencies levels to tap the hitherto unrecognized and unaccounted for strength of women to integrate them in the process of industrial development, more especially small-scale industry development in the country.

6

Rural Entrepreneurship

As women forming about half of the India's population make a case for developing women entrepreneurship in the country, just discussed in Chapter 5, so is justified developing rural entrepreneurship by about three – fourth of the India's population living in its vast rural areas. The rural-urban dichotomy reveals wide disparities in various respects. The division of economic activities between rural and urban areas is one of them. Rural areas specialize more or less exclusively in agriculture while industries are exclusively located in urban areas. Given the weak rural-urban or agriculture-industry linkages, such a situation suffers from two serious shortcomings. *First,* as agriculture by itself has a tendency to develop at a slower pace than industry, the division of economic activities leads to uneven development. *Second,* since industry generally leads to higher level of output per worker than agriculture, the gap in income levels between those engaged in the two sectors tends to widen (Papola 1982:1). Further, the relationship between traditional agriculture and modern industry generally has a dependency structure which puts the rural sector at a greater disadvantage in appropriating the gains of development and, in turn, increases the disparities between rural and urban income levels (Sigurdson 1977: 233). As such, rural areas are ultimately marked by abject poverty and backwardness. In such situation, rural industrialization is viewed as an effective means of accelerating the process of rural development. Entrepreneurship precedes industrialization. Hence, the need for rural entrepreneurship.

This chapter is, therefore, devoted to deal with various aspects of rural entrepreneurship, such as, its meaning, need, present position, strategies for the future development of rural entrepreneurship in the country, and role of Non-Government Organisaitons (NGOs) in developing rural entrepreneurship.

Meaning of Rural Entrepreneurship

Like entrepreneurship, rural entrepreneurship also conjures different meanings to different people. Without going into semantics, rural entrepreneurship can simply be defined as entrepreneurship emerging in rural areas is rural entrepreneurship. In other words, establishing industrial units in the rural areas refers to rural entrepreneurship. Or say, rural entrepreneurship implies rural industries.

Let us know, for the sake of our knowledge, the meaning of rural industry.

Rural industries are generally associated with agriculture. According to the Khadi and Village Industries Commission (KVIC), "village industry or rural industry means any industry located in rural area, population of which does not exceed 10,000 or such other figure which produces any goods or renders any services with or without use of power and in which the fixed capital investment per head of an artisan or a worker does not exceed a thousand rupees (Soundarapandian 1999:1)."

The definition of village industry has been recently modified by the government so as to enlarge its scope. Accordingly, any industry located in rural area, village or town with a population of 20,000 and below and an investment of Rs. 3 crores in plant and machinery is classified as a village industry (Soundarapandian 1999:1). As a result of widening of the scope of village industries, 41 new village industries have been added making a total of 101 as against 70 industries earlier.

All the village industries have been grouped into seven major categories as follows:

(i) Mineral-based industry,

(ii) Forest-based industry,

(iii) Agro-based industry,

(iv) Polymer and chemical-based industry,

(v) Engineering and non-conventional industry,

(vi) Textile industry (including khadi), and

(vii) Service industry.

Having understood the meanings of rural entrepreneurship and rural industry, let us move on to appreciate the need for and significance of rural entrepreneurship in India.

Need for Rural Entrepreneurship

The need for rural entrepreneurship for developing industries in the rural areas is imbued with multiplicity of justifications (Matthai 1978) as listed below:

1. Rural industries being labour intensive have high potential in employment generation. Thus, they serve as an antedote to the widespread problems of disguised unemployment or under-employment stalking the rural territory.
2. By providing employment, these industries have also high potential for income generation in the rural areas. These, thus, help in reducing disparities in income between rural and urban areas.
3. These industries encourage dispersal of economic activities in the rural areas and, thus, promote balanced regional development.
4. Development of industries in the rural areas also helps build up village republics.
5. Rural industries also help protect and promote the art and creativity, i.e. the age-old rich heritage of the country.
6. Rural industrialisaton fosters economic development in rural areas. This curbs rural-urban migration, on the one hand, and also lessens the disproportionate growth in the cities, reduces growth of slums, social tensions, and atmospheric pollution, on the other.
7. Last but no means the least, rural industries being

environment friendly lead to development without destruction i.e., the most desideratum of the time.

Rural Industrialization in Retrospect

Prior to Independence, small industry occupied almost insignificant place in the national economy. Then the commonly used term was cottage industry / handicrafts, which were located in rural areas. The government sincerely took interest in the development of rural / village industries since Independence.

The important role which rural industries can play in ameliorating the socio-economic conditions of the rural areas has received emphasis in most of the major policy pronouncements on development in India (Behari 1976). The Industrial Policy Resolution of 1948 emphasized the "utilization of local resources and the achievement of local self sufficiency in respect of certain essential consumer goods" as the most suitable characteristics of cottage and small industries. This approach was followed in the First Five-Year Plan. But, the development of rural industries was conceived largely in isolation of the rest of the economy (Haan 1980:23). The First Five-Year Plan stressed the development of agriculture, industry, infrastructure, and social services, but all this in manner that maximum feasible additional employment opportunities were created to raise the standard of living of the people.

The Industrial Policy Resolution of 1956 while emphasizing the creation of employment, equitable distribution of incomes and an effective mobilization of capital and skills, pointed out that the characteristics of cottage, village and small-scale industries are favourable to the achievement of these objectives. Accordingly, the Second Five-Year Plan looked upon rural industries as an integral component of the national economy to some extent, forming the basis of a pyramidal industrial structure (Haan 1980:23). With the formulation of 26 Pilot Industrial Projects, which were intended to be an exercise in area development, a spatial dimension was added to the programme of rural and small industry. This approach was followed up in the Third Five-Year Plan (1961-62 – 1965-66).

Rural Industries Projects in 49 selected areas were taken up during the Third Plan. This plan envisaged the development of village and small industries sector to provide employment and to increase the consumer goods and some producer goods. The programme aimed at promoting village and small-scale industries, including ancillary units of large-scale units, in order to achieve a balanced regional development. This process of rural industrialization was continued during the Annual Plans (1966-69) and the Fourth Five-Year Plan (1969-70 to 1973-74), when a Backward Area Development Programme was adopted, which included industrial development as well. For this, agro-industries and dispersal of these industries in backward areas were accepted as instruments.

The Fifth Five-Year Plan emphasised the need to ensure industrial development in underdeveloped areas. The Industrial Policy Statement of 1980 promised to generate economic viability in the villages dependent on a strategy based on an industry cum-area development approach. This was aimed at injecting integration of the programme. The Direct Industries Centres (DICs) were set up during the period to provide the required services under one roof. Rural Industrialisation continued to receive the main focus of development efforts in the rural areas during the subsequent Sixth Five-Year Plan also. In order to strengthen the process of rural industrialization, the Sixth Plan redefined Small Scale Industry (SSI) so as to include those manufacturing and repairing units as having investment in plant and machinery up to Rs. 20 lakhs and in the case of the ancillary units Rs. 25 lakhs.

The Seventh and Eighth Plans accorded importance to the role of institution in marketing, credit, technology etc., in the promotion of rural industrialization in the country. With a view to step up rural industrialization, a number of projects covering a variety of rural industries, viz., food processing, pottery, leather items, ready made garments etc., have been taken up by the Khadi and Village Industries Commission (KVIC).

The Ninth Five Year Plan includes the following development strategies for the Village and Small-Scale Industries (VSI) sector (Planning Commission 1997-2002):

(i) The small-scale and village industries will be provided incentives and support to facilitate their growth and employment. It will be ensured that foreign investment does not displace such industries.

(ii) Credit facilities to small-scale industries will be increased. For this, the financial institutions will be motivated to offer factoring services to the SSIs in addition to the present system of discounting bills.

(iii) The investment limit for the SSI sector will be revised to Rs. 3 crore to take account of inflation and also to enable this sector the achievement of minimum economics of scale and upgradation of technology so as to withstand emerging competition.

(iv) Technology development and up gradation in the VSI sector, especially in the case of small-scale industries, handlooms, powerlooms, coir-handicrafts, wool, etc., will receive special attention.

(v) Special attention will be paid to sericulture to improve the quality of raw silk by introducing better silk worm breeding practices.

One way to look at the Government's concern for developing village and rural industries may be the financial provisions made in various Five-Year Plans for these industries. This is exhibited in Table 6.1.

That the government is assigning increasing importance to the development and role of rural industries sector in the Indian economy is well vindicated by its continuously increasing plan outlays from Rs. 97 crores in the First Five-Year Plan to Rs. 19,708 crores in the Seventh Plan. But, the percentage of plan outlay on the industry on the whole to the total public sector outlay has been declining from 24.08 per cent in the Second Plan to 10.95 per cent in the Seventh Plan. Though the expenditure on rural industries has been on increase from Rs. 42 crores in the First Plan to a staggering figure of Rs. 6,334 crore in the Eighth Plan, the percentage of allocation has been decreasing from 4 per cent in the Second Plan to 1.6 per cent

Table 6.1: Plan Outlays on Rural Industrialization

Plan Period	*Public Sector outlay (Rs.)*	*Plan provision for*		*% of Public Sector outlays on*	
		Industry (Rs.)	*Rural Industry (Rs.)*	*Industry as a whole (Rs.)*	*Rural Industries (Rs.)*
I Plan	1960	97	42	4.95	2.1
II Plan	4672	1125	187	24.08	4.0
III Plan	8577	1967	241	22.93	2.8
Annual Plan	6625	1636	126	24.69	1.9
IV Plan	15779	3107	293	19.69	1.9
V Plan	39426	9581	592	24.30	1.5
1979-80	12601	2639	289	20.94	2.3
VI Plan	97500	15018	1780	15.40	1.8
VII Plan	180000	19708	2753	10.95	1.5
VIII Plan	434100	NA	6334	NA	1.6

Source: Government of India, *Economic Survey: 1982-83 and Seventh Five-Year Plan*, Planning Commission, 1985-90, Vol.1.

in the Eighth Plan. What these trends imply that the increasing importance was given to the rural industries in the Five-Year Plans on the development of village and rural industries.

It seems pertinent to look at the actual performance of rural industries over the period against so enunciated plan emphasis on them. Table 6.2 bears data on performance of rural and village industries in terms of production, sales, earnings and employment.

It is clearly seen from the table that the production, sales, earnings and employment in village and rural industries are continuously on increase. This all means underlines the vibrant nature of the SSI sector in the economy.

Table 6.2: Performance of Village and Rural Industries

Year				
1971-72	93.69	81.24	16.30	8.38
1972-73	109.13	97.04	17.80	8.40
1973-74	122.40	115.64	22.16	9.25
1974-75	136.31	133.17	28.05	9.82
1975-76	148.48	151.58	35.21	11.20
1976-77	171.73	174.71	40.19	11.78
1977-78	192.54	190.29	50.10	14.91
1978-79	242.97	242.01	59.79	14.96
1979-80	347.98	358.97	78.84	16.18
1980-81	451.24	476.47	101.34	18.10
1989-90	170.53	1895.47	546.85	27.80
1990-91	1994.07	2228.97	647.31	29.21
1992-93	2523.45	2801.13	845.58	36.21
1996-97	3760.21	3926.20	1126.25	46.25
1997-98	3895.21	4319.38	1275.57	42.45

Source: *Annual Report of KVIC, 1971-72 to 1997-98*

Problems of Rural Entrepreneurship

Developing entrepreneurship especially rural entrepreneurship is as important is not so easy. It is constrained with several problems. The general bottle-necks in the development of village industries are financial constraints, lack of technical know how, lack of training and extension services, management problems, lack of quality control, high cost of production due to high input cost, lack of communication and market information, poor quality of raw materials, lack of storage and warehousing facilities, obsolete and primitive technology, and lack of promotional strategy (Soundarapandian 1999:6).

According to the Ninth Plan (Planning Commission 1997-2002), the major problems faced in developing entrepreneurship in rural areas are (i) inadequate flow of credit, (ii) use of obsolete technology, machinery, and equipment, (iii) poor quality standards, and (v) inadequate infrastructural facilities.

One of the major problems faced in developing entrepreneurship in rural areas is lack of awareness and knowledge about the importance of developing industries in rural areas. Added to this is disinterest shown by rural people towards assuming the career as an entrepreneur for one reason or other. Rural/Village people generally want to take up salaried employment because of assured income, lesser hours of work, lesser degree of responsibility etc. This is supported by the society's higher degree of status accorded to the salaried people than to self-employed ones, or say, entrepreneurs. Further, the rural people are generally not aware about the entrepreneurial opportunities available and also about support organizations and other information required to take the first step in their entrepreneurial career. Even those who are aware about the facilities and support system for starting entrepreneurial career find organizational climate to be not so helpful. Thus, the environment in the family, society and the support system is generally not conducive to encourage the rural people to consider self-employment and entrepreneurial career as an option to salaried employment (Sangita 1990).

How to Develop Rural Entrepreneurship?

Establishing an industry and, thereby developing entrepreneurship is not one-man activity. In fact, it involves multi-pronged activities. Though the answer to the question how to develop entrepreneurship lies in the solutions of the problems faced in this regard, yet the following measures are suggested for developing entrepreneurship in the rural areas in the country.

1. Raw material is a must for any industry. However, the non-availability of raw materials accompanied by their prohibitive cost has weakened the viability of these industries. Past experience bears evidence that rural industries with employment potential can not be sustained for long unless a strong raw material-base is created in rural areas itself. Therefore, an urgent policy is called

for to strengthen the raw material base in rural areas.

2. Finance is considered as lubricant for setting up and running an industry. Funds, therefore, need to be made available on time at soft terms and conditions to those who really need it.

3. In order to solve the problem of marketing for rural industries, common production-cum-marketing centers need to be set up and developed with modern infrastructural facilities, particularly, in the areas having good production and growth potential. This would help in promoting export business, on the one hand, and bringing the buyers and sellers is close interaction avoiding the middleman in between them, on the other. Legislative measures have to be taken to make the government purchases compulsory from rural industries.

4. One peculiarity of rural entrepreneurs is that most of them join their entrepreneurial career not by choice but by chance. Lack of aptitude and competency on the part of such entrepreneurs makes the units sick. Hence, there is a need to develop entrepreneurial attitude and competencies among the prospective entrepreneurs through the training interventions like Entrepreneurship Development Programmes (EDP), Women Entrepreneurship Development Programmes and TRYSEM.

5. One effective way to inculcate the entrepreneurial acumen and attitude may be imparting entrepreneurial education in the schools, colleges, and universities. That younger minds are more susceptive to be moulded is well evidenced by the popularly known *'Kakinada Experiments'* in Andhra Pradesh (McClelland 1966:22).

6. Sometimes the real problem in setting up industries is not the non-availability of facilities, but non-awareness of facilities whatever is available. The need is, therefore, to disseminate information about all what is available to provide to the entrepreneurs to facilitate them in setting up industries.

7. Proper provisions need to be made to impart the institutional training to orient the entrepreneurs in specific products and trades so that the local resources can be harnessed properly.

8. Our accumulated experience bears ample evidences to the fact that the non-governmental organizations, popularly known as NGOs, can prove instrumental in developing rural entrepreneurship in the country. The role of NGOs in developing entrepreneurship is, therefore, discussed separately.

NGOs and Rural Entrepreneurship

There is no denying of the fact that development of entrepreneurship has emerged as a national movement due to its strengths to solve the twin problems of unemployment and poverty. In fact, the need for development of 'spirit of enterprise' among the target population intensified more during the nineties with the failure of the 'trickle down theory' to percolate the development benefits to the masses at grass-root level. It is against this back-ground, several self-employment and anti-poverty programmes like PMRY, TRYSEM etc., involving some entrepreneurial qualities were introduced by the government as a tool of bottom up mode of development. However, these programmes executed by the Government agencies proved ineffective due to their weaknesses of one type or other. Such a situation necessitated the NGOs to come out of their traditional bounds like health, sanitation, education, family planning, environment protection etc., to join a noble mission to entrepreneurise the lesser known target groups (Singh 1992). The government agencies engaged in this activity strengthened the NGOs by co-opting and collaborating with them to reach the lower rungs of the society.

Today, we have several NGOs contributing to entrepreneurship development in the country. The major ones are National Alliance of Young Entrepreneurs (NAYE), World Assembly of Small and Medium Entrepreneurs (WASME), Xavier Institute for Social Studies (XISS), SEWA of Ahmedabad, 'Y' Self-Employment of Calcutta, AWAKE (Association of Women

Entrepreneurs of Karnataka), and Rural Development and Self-Employment Training Institute (RUDSETIs) based in Karnataka.

The NGOs involved in entrepreneurship development can be classified into three types:

1. *Primary Level NGOs:* The NGOs who mobilize their own resources, operate at international level and execute developmental activities themselves or through intermediate fall within this category. ACTIONAID, OXFAM, Christian Children Fund etc. are prominent examples of the primary level NGOs in India.
2. *Intermediate NGOs:* These NGOs procure funds from various agencies, impart training, and conduct workshops for target work force. SEWA and AWAKE are examples of intermediate NGOs.
3. *Grass Root Level NGOs:* These NGOs are those who conduct field activities by establishing direct contact with the grass root people (needy). Examples of such NGOs are RUDSETIs, ANARDE Foundation (Gujarat), Indian Institute of Youth Welfare (IIYW) of Maharashtra etc.

The training imparted to the needy by the NGOs can be classified into three broad types:

1. ***Stimulation***: Conducting EDPs and other training programmes for the target people with a view of stimulate enterprising attitude among them.
2. ***Counselling***: Providing counseling and consultancy services to the needy ones how to prepare a project, feasibility report, purchase of plant and machinery, and performing other procedural activities.
3. ***Assistance:*** Assisting the target group in marketing their products and securing finance from financial institutions.

Lastly, the role of NGOs in entrepreneurship development can better be understood in terms of their strengths and weaknesses in the context of entrepreneurship development. The NGOs have revealed the following *strengths* as an edge over others (Bhat 1999: 18):

- The lean overhead and operating costs to reach the poor and needy.
- Flexibility and responsiveness in operation to invent appropriate solution.
- Nearness to client groups made them to be sensitive to community need.
- Capacity for innovation and experimentation with new groups and untried development approach.
- Stimulating and mobilizing interest in the community.
- Dependence on customer satisfaction.
- Act as a test bed and sound board for government policies and programmes.

That' one can not imbue in others what one cannot possess oneself' applies to the NGOs also. The well-noted weaknesses the NGOs suffer from are listed as follows:

- Role conflict as to the traditional areas of operation and micro-entrepreneurship development.
- Doubtful leadership and succession.
- Anti-business philosophy, lack of programme integration due to lack of proper understanding of entrepreneurship approach.
- Inadequate opportunities to work as trainer/motivator.
- Absence of impact assessment because of self righteousness on the part of NGO leaders.
- Not all NGOs are ready and equipped to take up this activity.

In spite of these so-called weaknesses, the role of NGOs in entrepreneurship development cannot be undermined. Evidences are galore to mention that a few NGOs in India have succeeded largely in imparting entrepreneurial skills among the weaker sections of the society. This is duly confirmed by a case *YCB – Dedicated to Rural Development.*

Concluding Remarks

Entrepreneurship emerging in rural areas is called rural entrepreneurship. Rural entrepreneurship symbolizes rural industrialization. Rural industrialization provides the best solution to tackle with the twin problems of unemployment and poverty stalking the rural areas in the country. That is why the Government of India has been assigning increasing importance to the development of rural industrialization or entrepreneurship in her subsequent Five-Year Plan.

However, the development of rural industrialization is plagued by some major problems like inadequate flow of credit; use of obsolete technology, machinery and equipment, and inadequate infrastructural facilities. Solving these problems is necessary for developing rural industries / entrepreneurship. Of late, NGOs have proved as an effective agent in developing entrepreneurship in rural areas of the country.

7

Agri-Entrepreneurship

Entrepreneurship involves seeking and exploiting opportunities available for the benefit of the society. In this way, like other kinds of developments, entrepreneurship development is also contextual. Entrepreneurial context changes from region to region and even from time to time in the same region. Viewed from this angle, the changing agro-economic conditions for quite some time in our country have offered a prospective context for developing entrepreneurship in agri-business in the country. It is against this backdrop, the present chapter makes a modest attempt in unfolding the opportunities for developing entrepreneurship in agri-business and also identifying the challenges in doing so. For the convenience of discussion, the entire chapter has been subsumed in four parts. Part I gives the rationale for developing entrepreneurship in agri-business in India. While part II delineates the opportunities available for developing entrepreneurship in agri-business, the penultimate part III identifies the major challenges faced in this regard. The last part IV, based on preceding description, submits suggestions how to develop agri-entrepreneurship in more effective manner.

Why Entrepreneurship in Agri-business?

Agriculture forms the backbone of the Indian economy. Hence, India is nomenclatured as an agriculturally dominated country. That agriculture plays a pivotal role in the Indian economy is evidenced by the facts that it contributes 22 percent to the total gross domestic products, provides employment to around 65 percent of the total work force, and contributes 14.7 percent of total exports of the country. That is precisely the reason why the Tenth Five Year Plan considered, agricultural development as central to economic development of the country (Dutt and Sundharam 2005: 486). In view of this, the Government of India has been giving increasing importance to the development of agriculture in the country. That agriculture has developed over the years is reflected by various indicators such as increasing productivity, cropping intensity, high-yielding variety seeds, diversification, mechanization, and modernization of agriculture. The need for and signification of agricultural development in the country can be imbued with multiplicity of justifications as follows:

- Availability of land for agricultural purposes.
- Low requirement of funds for agricultural activities.
- Illiterate and/or less educated population.
- Lack of employment opportunities in formal sector.
- Prevalence of large-scale unemployment
- Both backward and forward inducements of agricultural development for industrial development.

An economy broadly consists of two sectors, namely, agriculture and industry. While agriculture refers to the rural economy; industry to that of the urban economy. Still, 72 percent of India's population resides in rural areas and the rural areas are characterized by widespread unemployment and abject poverty. Thus, economic development of India means and depends on the economic development of her vast agrarian or rural economy. As regards how to develop rural economy, it depends on development of all what prospects and possibilities exist therein. Of late, the new agro-economic conditions have offered a good scope for development of agri-business especially in rural areas of the country. Given its good promise for attracting huge investment including foreign investment, agri-business worldwide is considered to be a sun rise industry including India.

What is the meaning of agri-business? Agri-business is an old concept but relatively new term used in business literature. As referred by Hansra and Vijayaragavan (2003: 29), the term 'agri-business' was formally introduced by Professor Ray Goldberg of Harvard University during mid-fifties. It is a comprehensive word encompassing a wide variety of activities related to production, processing and marketing of crops, livestock, and forest products. According to Surya Kumar (1999), agri-business includes activities relating to production, propagation, and distribution of products and services relating to agriculture, floriculture, horticulture, sericulture, aquiculture, and animal husbandry. In other words, agri-business comprises of organizations and enterprises which in some way contribute for value and supply chain elements such as production, processing, marketing, packaging, transportation and whole sale and retail trade. The supply chain includes the entire spectrum from firm gate to plate (Moharana 2006: 112). In a sense, agri-business includes all operations involved in the manufacture and distribution of farm supplies. Some researchers have tried to differentiate agri-business in terms of on-farm and off-farm activities. They call on-farm activities as agriculture and off-farm activities as agri-business (Chandrakandan 2002: 2).

Having made a case for agri-business development, let us now justify the need for entrepreneurship development in agri-business also. This we shall do by looking at it from two angles: (i) Which comes first entrepreneurship or business, i.e., agri-business? Alternatively speaking, is entrepreneurship development necessary for agri-business development? (ii) How does agri-business development benefit the economy? Let us address to these one by one.

There has not been consensus among researchers on what actually develops business enterprises: whether entrepreneur or environment. While some consider entrepreneur as a precondition for business-enterprise development, others consider the environment as necessary condition for emergence and development of business enterprises. The proponents of the two views give arguments and evidences in support of their views. One way to resolve the debate on whether entrepreneurship comes first or business is to refer to the analogy of horse and jockey in a race to say that both are equally important. Nonetheless, it is important to mention that while the jockey is not the creator of his horse; the entrepreneur is, to a large extent, responsible for the creation of his / her enterprise. Thus, there is pre-eminence of the entrepreneur in the process of enterprise or venture creation.

Agri-business development benefits an economy in various forms and ways, viz., it generates immediate large-scale employment, utilizes the idle human and natural resources, promotes capital formation by mobilizing the idle savings of the public, reduces unemployment, promotes balanced regional development, reduces concentration of economic power, promotes equitable distribution of wealth, income and even political power, induces backward and forward linkages for industrial and economic development, and promotes country's exports.

Opportunities for Developing Entrepreneurship in Agri-business

Now that we have justified the need for developing entrepreneurship in agri-business, we can logically proceed to unfold the opportunities available for developing entrepreneurship in agri-business in India, in general, and in rural areas, in particular. The recent World Trade Organization (WTO) agreements have opened new vistas for agricultural development and diversification and, in turn, agri-business in the member countries including India. As such, increasing opportunities have emerged for developing entrepreneurship in agri-business sector especially agriculture, horticulture, floriculture, sericulture, animal husbandry and veterinary, fishery, etc. Following table 7.1 gives the summary view of the same:

Table 7.1: Entrepreneurial Opportunities in Agri-business

Sector	*Opportunities*
Agriculture	• Organic Farming
	• Agro-based Industry
	• Farm Mechanization
	• Pulse and Oilseeds Post Harvest and Processing
	• Quality Input Production and Supply Chain
Horticulture,	• Organic Farming
Fruits	• Commercial Production
Vegetables	• Marketing
Flowers	• Processing
Aromatic and Herbal	• Packaging
Plantation	• Off-Season Vegetables and Quality Flower Production
	• Commercial Flower Production
	• Aromatic and Herbal Plantation
Animal Husbandry	• Dairy Processing and Chilling
and Veterinary	• Meat Processing
	• Broiler and Egg Production and Marketing
	• Livestock Feed
	• Livestock Vaccine/ Drug Production
Fishery	• Scientific and Commercial Production
	• Integrated and Intensive Farming
	• Carp Hatchery
	• Ornamental Fish
	• Fish Feed
Sericulture	• Silkworm Rearing Technology
	• Silk Yarn Production
	• Handloom and Textile/ Garment Design

	• Exports
Others	• Mass Production of Bio Pesticides
	• Bio-Fertilizers Production and Marketing
	• Mushroom Marketing
	• Vermi Compost
	• Bee Keeping and Honey Marketing

Some highlight on some of these seems in logical sequence.

Agriculture

Agriculture has always been the backbone of the Indian economy and despite concerted industrialization, in the last six decades; agriculture still occupies a place of pride. The significance of agriculture in the national economy arises from the role it plays in India's national income, employment and export. To quote, it contributes 22% to total gross domestic product, 66% total employment, and 15% total exports of the country[7]. Anonymous (2006-07) Agricultural products-tea, sugar, oilseeds, tobacco, spices, etc.-constitute the main export items of India. Broadly speaking, the proportion of agricultural goods which were exported came to 50% of our exports, and manufactures with agricultural contents (such goods as manufactured jutes, cloth and sugar) contributed another 20% or so; and total comes to 70% of India's exports. Not only has that, with a view to develop agriculture on commercial basis, the New Agricultural Policy of India accorded agriculture the status of an industry. Added to this is the WTO's agreement on agriculture necessitating agricultural development to the global competitive level. By now, the signs of agricultural development are perceptible in marked shift from staples to cash crops. To quote, the area under coarse grains has gone down from 45 million hectares to 29.5 million hectares during 1960-61 to 1998-99. On the other hand, area under cotton and sugarcane has increased from 7.6 to 9.3 million hectares and from 2.4 to 4.1 million hectares respectively during the same period.

Horticulture

Horticulture is yet another agro-based important industry

improving the productivity of the land, generating employment, improving economic conditions of the farmers and entrepreneurs, enhancing exports and, above all, providing nutritional security to the people. Horticulture sector includes fruits, vegetables, spices, floriculture, and coconut, among others. It covers 17.2 million hectares of land in 2003-04 which accounts for 8.5% of the gross cropped area of the country. It contributes 30% of gross domestic production (GDP) from agriculture[6] (Anonymous 2003-04). With fruit production at 47.5 million tones in 2003-04, India accounted for about 10% of the global production of fruits from an area of 4.0 million hectares and ranked the second largest producer of fruits in the world. With 90 million tones of vegetable production, again in 2003-04, India ranked as the highest producer of vegetables in the world. Similarly, India occupied first position in the production of cauliflower, second in onion and third in cabbage.

It is a happy augury to mention that the Government of India has launched a National Horticulture Mission (NHM) with an objective to increase demand for nutritional security, improve income of farmers, add value to agriculture products, and increase availability of vegetables per person per day. As such, the NHM aims at doubling horticulture production to 300 million tones by 2011-12 and also enlarge the area under such cultivation to 40 lakh hectares.

Sericulture

Sericulture, also known as 'silk farming' is the rearing of silkworms for the production of raw silk. Although there are several commercial species of silkworms, *Bombyx mori* is the most widely used and intensively studied. Confucian text reports the discovery of silk cultivation around 2700 BC. Later it was introduced in Europe and other Asiatic countries. By now, sericulture has become one of the most important cottage industries in a number of countries like Japan, China, Republic of Korea, India, Brazil, Russia, Italy and France. Today, China and Japan are the two main producers, together manufacturing more than 50% of the world silk production each year. Sericulture industry is an oriental industry in India and is famous for its silk products worldwide.

Sericulture is an agro-based industry. It involves rearing of silkworms from the production of raw silk, which is the yarn obtained out of cocoons spun by certain species of insects. The major activities of sericulture comprises of food-plant cultivation to feed the silkworms which spin silk cocoons and reeling the cocoons for unwinding the silk filament for value benefits such as processing and weaving. The significance of sericulture agro-industry arises from its benefits such as its high employment potentiality, women friendliness, value addition, high potential for income and low gestation period. To quote, sericulture provides employment to as many as 60 lakh persons engaged in various sericulture activities in the country. It is estimated that sericulture has potential to generate employment @11 man days per kg of raw silk production (in on-farm activities) throughout the year. The employment potential is *par-excellence* and no other industry generates this kind of employment, especially in rural areas. Nearly three-fifth (57%) of the gross value of silk fabrics flows back to the cocoon growers. Thus, the large chunk of income goes back to the villages from the cities. As regards, gestation period, mulberry takes only six months to grow for commencement of silkworm rearing. Not only that, mulberry once planted will go on supporting silkworm rearing year after year for 15-20 years depending on inputs and management provided. As many as five crops can be taken in one year under tropical conditions. If stipulated packages of practices are adopted, a farmer can attain net income levels up to Rs. 30,000/0 per acre per year. Sericulture by employing 60% of women workers is women friendly. However, only about 0.1% of the arable land in the country is under mulberry cultivation.

Food Processing

Food processing involves set of methods and techniques used to transform raw ingredients into food or to transform food into other forms for consumption by humans or animals either in the home or food processing industry. Broadly, food processing industries include cannery, meat packing plant, slaughterhouse, sugar industry, vegetable packing plants, industrial rendering, etc. Food processing provides special benefits to the society. These include toxin removal, preservation, easing addition, all-season availability of many foods, easing marketing and distribution tasks, and makes many kinds of foods safe to eat by de-activating spoilage and pathogenic micro-organisms. Of late, more and more people live in the cities far away from where food is grown and produced. Increasing number of adults is living away from the families who gets little time for the preparation of food based on fresh ingredients. Not only that, the demand for nutritious food considering health conditions has also been increasing day by day. That there will be more and more demand for readymade or processed food in coming days is already indicated by the meteoritic growth of Mumbai's Dabbawala. Thus, food processing industry offers yet more opportunities for entrepreneurship development to establish and run food-based industries.

Animal Husbandry

Animal husbandry, also called animal science, stockbreeding or simple husbandry, is the agricultural practice of breeding and raising livestock. It has been practiced for thousands of years, since the first domestication of animals. The popular forms of animal husbandry are swineherd (for hogs and pigs), shepherd (for sheep), goatherd (for goat), and cowherd (for cattle). The industries that come under animal husbandry include aquaculture, beekeeping, cuniculture, dog breeding, horse breeding, poultry, breeder, and factory farming. Needless to mention, increase in demand for animal husbandry products has become *sine quo non* with increase in population. This, in turn, underlines the need for increase in supply of these products which, in turn, necessitates increase in number of animal husbandry based enterprises.

Biotechnology

An emerging area in agri-business is bio-technology. Global evidences confirm that agricultural bio-technology has a major impact on agricultural productivity. That is why increasing emphasis has been given to research and development in the agro-biotech sector with an aim to produce crops with high level of tolerance against cold, heat and salinity. A number of improved food products have also been developed. It is expected that with increase in investment in research and development in India, agro-bio technology will further develop and, in turn, Indian agriculture will.

An idea about the scope for developing agri-entrepreneurship can be had from looking at how much food is produced in India. This is borne by Table 7.2.

Table 7.2: Scale of Food Production in India

Food	*Production (million Tonnes)*	*India's Rank in the World*	*India's Share (%)*	*India's Share (%) in Exports*
Wheat	65	2	12	0.02
Paddy	124	2	22	18
Coarse grains like Maize	29	3	4	-
Milk	98	1	16	Negligible
Fruits	47	2	10	Negligible
Vegetables	82	3	10	Negligible
Edible Oilseeds	25	3	7	Import
Pulses	15	1	21	Import
Sugarcane	245	2	21	-
Tea	0.85	1	28	12

Source: Jha, Alok (2009)

Table 7.3: Level of Processing in Perishable Foods

Food Products	*Level of Processing (in %)*		
	Organised	*Unorganised*	*Total*
Fruits & Vegetables	1.4	0.8	2.2
Milk & Milk Products	13	22	35
Meat (Buffalo)	21	-	21
Poultry	6	-	6
Marine Products	8	-	8

Source: Jha, Alok (2009).

Given the above large size of food production, the level

of food proceessing especially processing of perishable foods is too low in India is indicated from the figures given in Table 7.3.

That India offers good and big opportunities for development of agri-entrepreneurship is well indicated from the following facts and figures:

Today, India accounts for:

- 41% of worl'ds mangoes
- 30% of cauliflower
- 28% of tea
- 23% of bananas
- 24% of cashewnuts
- 36% of green peas
- 14% of milk
- 10% of onion

[*Source*: Jha, Alok (2009)]

Challenges of Agri-business Entrepreneurship

Developing entrepreneurship in agri-business is as much useful is not so easy and simple. In fact, there are certain challenges before entrepreneurship development in agri-business as follows:

- Lack of required skilled manpower
- Lack of infrastructural facilities
- Problem of marketing
- Competition with medium and large-scale enterprises
- Lack of awareness and appreciation about career in agro-entrepreneurship.

Suggestions for Entrepreneurship Development in Agri-business

The evidences available suggest that there is ample scope for entrepreneurship development in agri-business sector in our country which, however, has so far not been exploited. The following suggestions may help develop entrepreneurship in agri-business in more effective manner:

- Creating awareness about agri-business entrepreneurship
- Development of required skilled manpower

- Development of infrastructural facilities
- Promotion and protection by the Government
- Announcement of separate industrial policy
- Development of agri-business special export zones
- Preparation of agri-business potential report.

Concluding Remarks

Developing entrepreneurship in agri-business sector is not an unmixed blessing. Both opportunities and problems exist in this endeavor. It is evidenced that beginning has already been made in this direction and impact has also been noticeable though not quite perceptible as yet. One way to develop entrepreneurship in agri-business sector is to make sincere efforts by all concerned in this endeavor. People have a tendency to shift their responsibility and blame others for ineffective performance or failure. This tendency needs to be given up and own the responsibility and sincerely perform one's job/duty. To conclude, I would like to cite N.R. Narayana Murthy's view in reply to a question on the debacle of the Indian cricket team in the World Cup tournament in the West Indies in March last. Referring to the corporate sins as applied to cricket, he said, *"The tragedy of India is that instead of seeing what is wrong with us and taking steps to correct it, we indulge in hysterics and look for scapegoats. Everyone is busy in blaming the coach and the captain. The real problem lies with the system. Not just in cricket but in virtually any walk of life we are unwilling to put in our sincere efforts."* We can succeed in every thing if only follow four cardinal principles: (i) adhere to genuineness/meritocracy, (ii) be willing to give our best effort, (iii) adopt best practices, and (iv) follow absolute discipline.

We must remember that just rhetoric does not work, action does. All those involved in the endeavor of developing entrepreneurship in agri-business need to sincerely put in their best efforts for the cause. Then only, entrepreneurship development will take place in agri-business sector and, in turn, agri-business will develop in the country.

8

Tourism Entrepreneurship*

What ticks economic development of an economy? The ultimate answer is the effective use of its all types of resources. Human resources, natural resources, and material resources are the major types of resources an economy has. Nonetheless, it is the human resources that make the utilization of other resources. India is endowed with resources of tourist attractions. However, this is not yet properly exploited for the economic benefits of the country. Developing tourism entrepreneurship is an effective manner to exploit its tourism attractions for the benefit of the country. It is against this backdrop, the present chapter makes an attempt to highlight the important aspects of tourism entrepreneurship in India.

Introduction

Before we define tourism entrepreneurship let us first understand the meaning of the term 'tourism.' Tourism as a word appeared for the first time in 1811 and was associated for 'mobility' for recreation (Lundberg 1972: 11). Lickorish and Kershaw (1958) consider tourism as analogous of travel industry and define it as "a part of national income, which

---

* This chapter draws from S. S. Khanka and Anjan Bhuyan: "Developing Rural Tourism Entrepreneurship in Assam (Its Problems and Prospects)," *IASSI Quarterly*, Vol. 23, No. 1, July-September 2004, pp. 112-131.

caters for the traveler, who is visiting the place outside the locality, where he resides or works." According to Sarkar and Dhar (1998), "Tourism is a multidimensional concept and implies many things to many people. For the tourists it is travel, relaxation, a holiday, an expose to other cultures and traditions. Those who 'sell' tourism naturally see things differently. To them, it is an industry, a source of income, especially of foreign exchange. Thus, conceptually it is an amalgam phenomena and relationships arising from the movement of people 'to' and their 'stay' in the different destinations. The 'journey' (a dynamic element) and 'stay' (a static element) are the two necessary constituents of the mass phenomenon called tourism." In terms of working definition, tourism is defined as visiting for at least one night for leisure and holiday, business and professional or other tourism purposes. Here, visiting means temporary movement to destinations outside the normal home and workplace not motivated by any lucrative activity (Tribe 1995: 1-6). The two terms leisure and recreation are very intimately related with tourism. Leisure usually refers to discretionary time. Discretionary time is the time remaining after working, commuting, sleeping and doing necessary household and personal chores which can be used in a chosen way. Recreation refers to pursuits undertaken in leisure time. Recreation pursuits include home-based activities as reading and watching television, and those outside the home including sports, theatre, cinema and tourism.

A tourist is any person traveling to a place other than that of his / her usual environment for less than 12 months and whose main purpose of the trip is other than the exercise of an activity remunerated from within the place visited ((UNWTO 2003: 53-56).

The Perspective

Ever since the emergence of the concept of tourism, tourism development has taken place with a very satisfactory pace and rate. By now, tourism has emerged as number one largest smokeless and fast growing industry in the world due to its ample promises and prospects. Presently, it accounts for 8% to the world trade and around 20 % of service sector in the world. Evidences indicate that many countries have progressed from backward to developing to developed mainly due to tourism development. For example, tourism industry contributes to more than 70 % of the national income of some of the countries like Malaysia and Singapore. The World Tourism Organization (WTO) predicts that the international tourism will grow at approximately 4% per year through the year 2010. Within 10 years period, tourism industry will provide 385 million jobs globally. If India also generates same level of employment as world average, 25 million additional jobs will be created.

That the level of tourism development in India has so far at a very low level is indicated by its paltry share to national income and to the world trade. While tourism contributes to more than 70% in the national income of some of the countries like Malaysia and Singapore, its share to the national income of India is still dismally low at 2.5%. Though India shelters around 15 % of the world population with its 2.5 % of the world territory, it accounts for only 0.40 % in the world tourism market. At present, India ranks 47th among the top 60 tourist destinations of the world. However, the prognostic picture of the Indian tourism is not because of lack of tourism potential, but because of unexploitation of the ample tourism potential she is blessed with. Recognizing the India's vast tourism development, the World Travel and Tourism Council (WTTC 2000) has predicted: "India has potential to become number one tourist destination in the world with the demand growing at 10.1% per annum." Nonetheless, tourism is India's third largest foreign exchange earner after gem and jewelry and readymade garments. There is certainly brighter side as well as regards tourism development in India. K. P. Singh , the then President of ASSOCHAM, in his 'Foreword' unfolds the tourism potential by mentioning: "Tourism is the most important civil industry in the world. The travel and tourism economy supports 18 million jobs in India or 5.9% of total employment and accounts for 5.6% of the gross domestic production (GDP). In 2010, this will rise to 25 million jobs or 6.8% of total employment. The travel and tourism demand in India amounts to Rs. 1200 billion and by 2010 will reach to Rs. 6,200 billion. It would grow at annual rate of 8.3%, more than double the global forecast of 4.1% (Singh 1999)." Tourism, in the twenty-first century, with its multi-sectoral spin-offs is believed to be the catalyst to bring about enhanced development and prosperity in India. India is a treasure trove for tourism development. She possesses long, unspoiled beaches of golden sands and swaying coconut trees; from winding trails that take you gently up the snowy slopes of a great mountain range like the Himalayas unfurling images of quaint, timeless communities; from sprawling forts and breathtaking palaces that hide in their bosoms so many tales of intrigue and ambitions, love and betrayal; from wild life sanctuaries and sea worlds, disneylands and shopping festivals .... There hardly appears to be a thing that is not worthy of some showering of tourist's attention and attraction.

Recognizing the potential for tourism development in the country, the Government of India has given ever increasing importance to tourism development. To mention, a tourism cell was created in the Department of Transport in 1949. This was the beginning of the process that culminated in the formation of a separate Ministry of Tourism under the charge of a Cabinet Minister in the sixties. Subsequently, a comprehensive tourism policy highlighting the objectives of tourism development in the country was promulgated by the Government of India in 1982. Tourism was declared as an industry in 1986 and became eligible for several incentives and facilities including tax incentives, subsidies and priorities in the sanctions of loans by the State Financial Institutions. In July 1991, tourism was also declared as priority sector for foreign investment (*Employment News* 2003). The Government of India has declared its recent Tourism Policy in 2002 to further boost the tourism in the country. India, like other Third World Nations, is off late laying stress on the tourism sector development due to two major aspects. *First,* tourism requires smaller capital investments and also does not require any industrial gestation period. *Second,* it can provide employment to a wider range of labour covering skilled to unskilled. Besides, tourism also offers multi and multiplier benefits. To list a few, it enables us to: (i) foster economic development; (ii) enrich our lives with new experiences; (iii) enjoy and to be educated; (v) to learn respect for other (foreign) cultures; and (vi) contribute to international cooperation and peace throughout the world, i.e. the most desideratum of the time.

Tourism Enterprise, Entrepreneur and Entrepreneurship

'Tourism enterprises' refer to the different forms of tourist related business ventures permitted within the National Constitution. Like any other enterprise, tourism enterprises are also business ventures having similar preparative principles, but working on a very wide scale. Sinclair and Stabler (1997) have defined the tourism enterprise as "a composition of products involving transport, accommodation, catering, natural resources, entertainment and other facilities and services, such as shops and banks and other tour operators."

A 'tourism entrepreneur' may be defined as a person or a group of persons producing and managing tourism products. In this process the entrepreneur must have the commonly prescribed entrepreneurial traits along with service sector specialties. As revealed by Shaw and Williams (2202), the service sector specialties involve two fundamental objects: "*One* concerns the commercial structure of the industry (especially the dominance of certain activity components and ownership groups), while the *second* relates to an understanding of the general organization of economic power structures."

As regards the definition of tourism entrepreneurship, we believe that the most useful and convincing way to define tourism entrepreneurship is to establish its congruence with entrepreneurship it has emanated from. Accordingly, tourism entrepreneurship can be defined as the professional application of knowledge, skills and competencies and/or of monetizing a tourism related new idea, by an individual or a set of people by launching an enterprise *de novo* or diversifying from an existing one (distinct from seeking self-employment as in a profession or trade), thus, to pursue growth while generating wealth, employment and social good. In other words, entrepreneurship in tourism, or say, tourism entrepreneurship refers to the activities of the major group of stake-holders of this service sector primarily designed for the effective and profitable interaction of demand for and supply of tourism products; at the same time assuring competitive professionalism and gainful socio-economic status. In simple words, it embraces all sorts of activities involved in creation and operation of a legal tourism enterprise. A legal tourism enterprise excludes all forms of tourism or tourism like activities which are against the generally accepted Laws of the Land. For example, in India, wildlife hunting, flesh-trading (prostitution), drug trafficking etc. are considered illicit and illegal.

Policy Measures for Tourism Development in India

The National Tourism Policy, 2002 earmarked considerable changes and policy inclusions in the Indian Tourism Industry. *'Incredible India'* campaign-fallout of the Policy insisted on worldwide publicity of Indian tourism. The most significant aspect of the new tourism policy rests on the coordinated efforts of public and private sectors in tourism planning and promotion. The new policy centers around six broad objectives **(Six Ss)** – Welcome (*Swagat*), Information (*Suchana),* Facilitation (*Suvidha*), Safety (*Suraksha*). Cooperation (*Sahyog*), and Infrastructure Development (*Samrachana*) which are the main areas of operation in the policy. However, the initial National Policy on tourism was declared in 1982, by amalgamating the discrete efforts of tourism promotion in the initial years of Indian Planning. By 1986 (during the 7th Plan), tourism was assigned the status of a service sector industry. By now some fourteen Indian states have declared tourism as an 'industry'. Some of the salient features of tourism promotion in India since 1991 are listed as follows:

- Tourism was made a priority sector for foreign direct investment in 1991 making it eligible for automatic approvals up to 51% of the equity.
- A National Strategy for Tourism Development was evolved in 1996 which advocated the strengthening of an institutional set up in human resource development, setting up of an Advisory Board of Tourism Industry

and Trade (which has since been set up), the integrated development of tourist destinations and the promotion of private sector in tourism development.

- Declaration of Export House Status to the tourism industry in 1998; specifically Hotels, Travel Agents, Tour Operators, and Tourist Transport Operators are given this status.
- Declaration of Ecotourism year 2002.
- Adoption of Single Window Clearance System for Tourism Entrepreneurs.
- Confederation of Indian Industry (CII) and the Task Force on Infrastructure for Tourism suggests in their reports that tourism should be declared as an infrastructure industry of the country.
- Sustainable policy determination, openness for foreign direct investments, financial assistance to the private tourism entrepreneurs etc. are also remarkable landmarks in the history of the tourism industry in India.

Eco-Tourism / Nature Tourism / Rural Tourism

By the end of the 20th century, tourism has become the largest industry in the world, and this is now considered as the most rapidly growing industry of the world. The World Tourism Organization (WTO 1996) predicts that international tourism will grow at approximately 4% per year through the year 2010. Until the start of the second last decade of the last century, tourism was seen as a profitable sector of business with no obvious constraints to growth, few barriers to entry to market, an almost universal welcome from governments, and few effective regulatory requirements to take the environment into consideration. Commercial organizations, be large or small, were acting on the 'Dowkin's Principle of Self Interest." With such wanton and rapid growth in tourism activity, it is no wonder that the impact of largely unplanned tourism development has been felt deeply as impending on environment, ecology, and on the people or the community. In the wake of these impacts, there is a need for the alternate tourism so that we can preserve tourism with its benefits for next generations also. And the outcome is the concept of eco-tourism. Thus, sustainable tourism development has become one of the essential elements of new tourism paradigm from "mass tourism" to "sustainable tourism." Ecotourism is now a major growth area in its own right. It is against this backdrop, the ASSOCHAM (1999: 24) organized an International Conclave on Tourism for Sustainable Development during December 10-11, 1999 at New Delhi. After three years, the United Nations declared year 2002 as the "*Year of Mountain and Eco-tourism*." The World Tourism Organization (WTO) declared the theme of the World Tourism Day to be observed on 27 September 2002 as "*Eco-Tourism: The Key to Sustainable Development*."

Though ecotourism assumes so much significance in the present context, it accounts for a small proportion of the global tourism market – current estimates vary between 3 to 7% only. Ecotourism is usually considered to be more than just tourism to natural areas. However, since the formal introduction of the term by Ceballos- Lascurain almost three decades ago, controversy over appropriate uses for the term and inconsistency in its application have hindered the development of the concept and its practical realization at specific sites. Those at the forefront of ecotourism research and development now provide definitions, which address the fundamental goals of conservation of natural areas and local development. For example, The Ecotourism Society defines ecotourism as "Purposeful travel to *natural areas* to understand the culture and the natural history of the environment; taking care not to alter the integrity of the ecosystem; producing economic opportunities that make the conservation of the natural resources beneficial to the local people."

The World Conservation Union's (IUCN) Commission on National Parks and Protected Areas (CNPPA) defines ecotourism as "Environmentally responsible travel and visitation to relatively undisturbed natural areas, in order to enjoy and appropriate nature (and any accompanying cultural features both past and present) that promotes conservation, has low visitor impact and provides for beneficially active socio-economic involvement of local population." One of the best definitions of ecotourism is that provided by the Australian National Ecotourism Strategy which states: "Ecotourism is nature-based tourism that involves education and interpretation of the natural environment and is managed to be ecologically sustainable." The above definitions indicate that ecotourism is a complex phenomenon, involving integration of many factors including tourists, resident peoples, suppliers, and managers and multiple functions. In ecotourism, natural areas and local population are united in a symbolic relationship through the introduction of tourism.

A sound ecotourism is characterized by the four key hallmarks that distinguish it from simple nature, wildlife or adventure tourism. The four hallmarks are that ecotourism projects should:

1. Be designed, built and operated so that they leave a "soft imprint";
2. Contribute money to the local economy and local community services;
3. Contribute financially to environmental protection; and
4. Educate visitors and members of the local community.

The definitions of ecotourism focus on three significant aspects viz. nature, tourism and local communities. It differs in a meaningful way from mass tourism that aims at consuming nature leaving it depleted on more than one front. *Conservation, sustainability* and *biological diversity* are the three interrelated aspects of eco–tourism. As a developmental tool, ecotourism can advance the three basic goals of the Convention on Biological Diversity:

1. Conserve biological (and cultural) diversity, by strengthening protected area management systems (Public or Private) and increasing the value of sound ecosystem;
2. Promote the sustainable use of biodiversity, by generating income, jobs and business opportunities in ecotourism and related business networks;

3. Share the benefits of ecotourism developments equitably with local communities and indigenous people, by obtaining their informed consent and full participation in planning and management of ecotourism businesses.

The strong orientation of the ecotourism field towards principles, guidelines and certification based on sustainability standard gives it an unusual position in the tourism field. Ecotourism is viewed, as a means of protecting natural areas through the generation of revenues, environmental education and involvement of the local people in such ways; both conservation and development will be prompted in a sustainable manner. While difficult to measure, ecotourism is believed to be the fastest growing tourism segment. Eco-tourism has recently come to be regarded as the panacea that enables us to aggressively seek tourism dollars with no obvious damage to ecosystems, since wild resources are not being harvested and there is no apparent associated development. As a concept, ecotourism has gained momentum recently in India, but as a way of life Indians have practiced ecotourism since times immemorial to nature and rich cultural heritage.

The main *Objectives* of Ecotourism are:

- Provision of socio – economic benefits.
- Provision of environmental services.
- Conservation of the natural areas.
- Provision of high quality experience.
- Promotion of environment advocacy.

Fundamental *functions* of Ecotourism include:

- Protection of natural area
- Generation of money
- Education
- Quality Tourism
- Local Participation

Success of Ecotourism

Unfortunately, ecotourism will not be successful without effective management and the framework, which has been presented, will be of little consequence in the absence of adequate institutional arrangements and administrative commitments. The development of positive relationship between people, resources and tourism is very unlikely to occur without implementation of effective policies, management strategies, and involvement of a wide range of organizations, including NGO's and other development agencies. To get success in ecotourism we should follow a process. The various steps of this process are:

- To assess its impact.
- To plan for tourism development on the basis of sustainability.
- To involve the local community.
- To assist and encourage the participation of the NGO's.
- To facilitate the functioning of the ecotourism development.
- To examine the developmental process.

Options for Revenue Collection

We know that tourism is an important economic tool, and is contributing for the development of the countries. But in case of the ecotourism we have to generate revenue to make theory a practice. And the success of the ecotourism depends upon the quality of tourism. And this depends upon the resource exploitation and the revenue generated. While developing the ecotourism, we can opt for several methods of revenue generation as follows:

1. Entrance fee
2. Facility use fee
3. License/permit fee

4. Sales, royalties
5. On-site donations
6. Collection from the Tour Operators
7. Collection from the other sources related to tourism.

We can say that ecotourism is neither a simple concept to define nor a straightforward phenomenon to implement and evaluate. Ecotourism should be regarded as being more than tourism to the natural areas and should be viewed as a means of combining the goals of resource conservation and local development through tourism in a synergistic fashion. This means that care should be taken to ensure that the goals of tourism development do not interfere with the goals of protecting natural areas and biodiversity. All the stakeholders in tourism development should safeguard the natural environment with a view to achieving sound, continuous, and sustainable economic growth geared to satisfying equitably the needs and aspirations of present and future generations.

Tourism in the Indian Economy: A Retrospect

Tourism development in India received little importance during the initial years of Indian planning. Indian planners did not put sufficient importance to tourism and made it a state subject. In the first Five Year Economic Plan (1951-56), no allocation was made for the tourism sector development. It has been only from the 7th Plan onwards, that considerable importance was given to the sector. However, the 'real take off' of Indian tourism started only in the mid nineties (see Table 8.1)

The increase in the outlay and expenditure in the Indian tourism sector have been less than sufficient in terms of its share in the total plan outlay over the years. A look at the Five Plans shows that in the Third Plan (1961-1966), year tourism got approx Rs. 8 crores. This was only 0.11% of the total Plan outlay. In the Eighth Plan, (1992-1997) also, it was less than 1% of the total plan outlay.

Table 8.1: Plan Outlays and Expenditure on Indian Tourism

(Rs. in Crores)

Plan Period	*Outlay*	*Expenditure*
1st (1951-56)	Nil	Nil
2nd (1956-61)	NA	NA
3rd (1962-66)	8.00	5.00
7th (1985-90)	394.00	432.00
8th (1992-97)	806.00	1088.00
9th (1997-02)	2481.00	NA

Source: Different Plans

At present, India ranks 47th among the top 60 tourist destinations of the World. The share of India in the global tourism market is only 0.38 percent which has remained stagnant for decades. Moreover, the trend on international tourist flow has also not been encouraging in the Indian tourism market in the recent period. During 2002, an estimated 715 million tourists crossed international frontiers out of which only 2.4 million tourists came to India while 80 million went to France followed by 50 million each to the United States and Spain. Even smaller Third World countries like Malaysia and Thailand received more than 10 million tourists in the same year.

In the mid nineties, Indian tourism received proper dynamism of growth with the adoption of the policy of economic liberalization and with the Indian ratification of the agreement to set up a World Tourism Organisaiton unit in the country. Things have changed more rapidly in the aftermath of these happenings. Some of the positive symptoms are:

Rural Tourism and Rural Tourism Entrepreneurship

Rural tourism has been a comparatively new concept in Indian tourism. This form of tourism has become popular in many parts of the world with the growing need for super segmentation of the tourism market. Officially, the Ministry of

Tourism has yet to define 'rural tourism.' However, the Ministry has already promoted *'heritage tourism,' 'religious tourism', 'eco-tourism'*, etc., which include rural tourism. 'Rural tourism', 'agri-tourism', 'green tourism' and 'eco-tourism' are interrelated terms. Available literature on the subject, including some from the European Community, gives two main clusters of definitions of rural tourism. These are:

- **Based on the percentage of tourism:** Each of the above mentioned categories is a derivative of the subsequent one, forming concentric circles. Rural tourism benefits the entire rural community in terms of total revenue generation while agri-tourism benefits only the farmers.
- **Based on the various constituent elements of supply**: Tourism is termed, "rural tourism" when rural culture is a key component of the product on offer.

Entrepreneurship development in rural tourism is community based focusing on:

a. Trusteeship of local communities,

b. Use of individual and community owned assets, and

c. Expansion in choices of rural livelihoods.

The underlying idea behind rural tourism should be to create, preserve, and enhance the stake of local communities over locations for common good, and not for the benefit of any individual or firm. Rural tourism in this sense encompasses all the activities that cater to national and international tourists through facilities that are owned, managed, and serviced by members of the village community and run essentially as a community based initiative.

The emergence of rural tourism will help in boosting a range of activities, services and amenities provided by farmers and rural people to attract tourists to their area to generate extra income. According to Shrivastava and Thakur (2002), "The basic concept of rural tourism is benefit to the local community through entrepreneurial opportunities, income generation, employment opportunities, conservation and development of rural arts and crafts, investment for infrastructure development and preservation of the environment and heritage."

The Federation of Indian Chambers of Commerce and Industry (FICCI) has initiated the promotion of the concept of rural tourism in India and abroad. Specific areas and centres were identified as potential areas for rural tourism in India such as heritage sites of Rajasthan, Gir forest in Gujarat, backwaters of Kerala, hills of UP, Shanti Niketan in West Bengal, dances and musical instruments of Orissa, Nithyagram of Karnataka, Tribals of Bihar, scenic beauty of Meghalaya, folk dances of Andhra Pradesh, wooded valleys of Himachal Pradesh, Teej festival of Haryana and mask dances of Sikkim. Since most tourist sites are located away from the urban centres, the trend is towards an increase in the share of tourism outside the well known urban centres. In rural India a variety of Indian lifestyles are experienced where more than 74 percent of Indians live with the treasure of craft, performing arts and rich traditional values.

Why Rural Tourism Entrepreneurship?

Rural tourism entrepreneurship needs to be focused on the Indian perspective for six important reasons:

1. To facilitate the use of local resources (both human and non-human).
2. To create additional scope of employment for every type of rural labour.
3. To achieve a better standard of living and increased income sources.
4. To explore the possibilities of forward and backward linkages through vertical and horizontal integration of labour.
5. To preserve and maintain the traditional culture and value system along with refinements on these via the assimilation process of tourist linkages.

6. To grow consciousness of eco-bio diversity.

Future Strategy for Developing Rural Tourism Entrepreneurship

The Annual Report of the Ministry of Tourism, 1999-2000 states that tourists invariably seek a pleasant and delectable experience on their trips. The most desired tourism product should consist of (a) an environment of peace and stability, (b) an assurance of safety and security, (c) an affable host society, (d) an industry and a government that provides the requisite service with a smile, (e) absence of extortion and hostility, and (f) accessible tourist attraction.

Considering all these aspects, the rural tourism entrepreneurship generation should be a prime objective of the governmental initiatives. The following steps are advocated for the same:

1. A Government Policy of Rural Tourism development is a prime necessity with a well designed policy framework.
2. Establishment of education and training institutes for tourism studies in coordination with all state Governments.
3. Preparing tourism products to attract specific categories of tourists in consonance with the determination of the carrying capacity of a tourist location.
4. Declaration of circuits for rural tourism.
5. Development of general as well as tourism infrastructure.
6. An effective tourism publicity drive should be adopted involving local as well as outside media to bring to the limelight the potentials of rural tourism in the country.

Concluding Remarks

The development of tourism entrepreneurship in India is still at a very low level. However, considering its tremendous economic impact and social contributions, it must be promoted as a sector of national importance for which the county offers ample promise. The task is certainly challenging, but the costs of inaction will far outweigh those of action. With the right policies in place, India can become a much more important travel and tourism destination. Therefore, development of tourism entrepreneurship and, in turn, tourism development warrants a thoughtful policy framework. The sooner that is done; the better will be tourism entrepreneurship development in the country.

9

Social Entrepreneurship

Introduction

That our understanding about social entrepreneurship will be better strengthened by looking into its roots, let us begin with defining the original term 'entrepreneur.' Economic literature reveals that the term 'entrepreneur' has a rich history and has been used loosely to mean different meanings from time to time. For example, Richard Cantillon (1971:2) who used the term 'entrepreneur' for the first time in economics during the seventeenth century, associated it with the function of 'risk-bearing'; Jean Baptiste Say (1827: 285-286), during the nineteenth century, associated his definition of entrepreneur with the function of coordination; and in the twentieth century, Joseph A. Schumpeter (1939: 103) described entrepreneur as the 'innovator' who drives the creative-destructive process of capitalism. According to Schumpeter, entrepreneurs can perform the function of innovation in *five* ways: "by exploiting an innovation or, more generally, an untried technological possibility for producing a new commodity or producing an old one in a new way or opening up a new source of materials or a new outlet for products, by reorganizing an industry and so on." In the Schumpeterian sense, entrepreneurs are the change agents in the economy. By introducing innovations, they move the economy forward. Though other economists have also used this term with various connotations and nuances, the Schumpeterian sense of entrepreneur as innovator has so bar been serving as the foundation for the contemporary use of this term in economic context.

Now that we have defined the original term 'entrepreneur', we can profitably describe and define the terms 'social entrepreneur' and 'social entrepreneurship.'

Social Entrepreneurship Defined

We believe that the most useful and convincing way to define social entrepreneurship is to establish its congruence with entrepreneurship it has emanated from. Entrepreneurs are innovative, highly-motivated, and critical thinkers. When these attributes are combined with the drive to solve the social problems, a 'social entrepreneur' is born. Social entrepreneurs are individuals with innovative solutions to society's most pressing and daunting social problems. They are ambitious and persistent, tackling major social issues and offering new ideas for wide-scale change. Throughout history, such individuals have introduced solutions to seemingly intractable social problems, fundamentally improving the lives of countless individuals by changing the way critical systems operate (Yunus 1997: 9-24, Emerson 1996 and Mizan 1994). Dees (2001) gives a very detailed definition of a social entrepreneur. According to him, the social entrepreneur plays the role of a change agent in society by:

- Adopting a mission to create and sustain social value;
- Searching for and pursuing new opportunities to serve that mission;
- Continually innovating, adapting, and learning in pursuit of the mission;
- Acting boldly without consideration of resources current in hand; and
- Being accountable for outcomes of activities.

Florence Nightingale and Maria Montessori offer two prominent historical examples. Muhammad Yunus, recipient of the 2006 Nobel Peace Prize, is a more recent example. In nutshell, social entrepreneurs are pioneer of innovations that benefit humanity at large.

Following are some historical examples of leading social entrepreneurs across the world:

Vinoba Bhave (India): Founder and leader of the 'Land Gift Movement', he caused the redistribution of more than 7,000,000 acres of land to aid India's untouchables and landless.

Satyan Mishra (India): Founder and Chief Executive Officer (CEO) of the Indian Company, 'Drishtee', with its over 4,200 Drishtee-trained entrepreneurs provides economic opportunities to the poor by facilitating access, generating employment and delivering essential services in an affordable way. In this way, Drishtee is enhancing access and empowering rural communities by creating significant cost and time savings to sell a range of products and services.

Bunker Roy (India): Bunker Roy created the Barefoot College in rural communities in India to train illiterate and semi-illiterate men and women, whose lack of educational qualifications keeps them mired in poverty. Today, Barefoot College graduates include teachers, health workers, and architects, who are improving communities across India.

Muhammad Yunus (Bangladesh): Established the 'Grameen Bank' to offer micro loans to impoverished people in Bangaladesh in 1976, thereby empowering them to become economically self-sufficient. His proven micro-credit model has now been replicated around the world.

Maria Montessori (Italy): Developed the Montessori approach to early childhood education.

Florence Nightingale (U. K.): Founder of modern nursing, she established the first school for nurses and fought to improve hospital conditions.

What common element found in case of above illustrative social entrepreneurs is that they are mass recruiter of local change makers-a role model proving that citizens who channel their passion into action can do almost anything (Lovell 1992). Here the view of Bill Drayton Founder and CEO of Ashoka about social entrepreneurs, seem worth citing:

"Social entrepreneurs are not content just to give a fish or teach how to fish. They will not rest until they have revolutionized the fishing industry (*www.skollfoundation.org*)."

In sum and substance, social entrepreneurship is defined considering the three approaches of combining commercial enterprises with social impacts, innovating for social impact, and catalyzing social transformation. The present chapter is particularly interested in the perspective that emphasizes social entrepreneurship as a catalyst for social transformation. Putting more specifically, this study focuses on social entrepreneurship that creates innovative solutions to immediate social problems and also mobilizes the ideas, capacities, resources, and social arrangements required for long-term sustainable social transformation.

Difference between Business Entrepreneurship and Social Entrepreneurship

Having understood the meaning and perspective of social entrepreneurship, it becomes curious to know what distinguishes social entrepreneurship from its for-profit cousin. As a matter of fact, various parameters differentiate the two sets of entrepreneurs from one another as shown in the following Table 9.1.

Social entrepreneurs are characterized by the following key attributes:

- **Ambitious:** Having high ambition is one of the major characteristics of the social entrepreneurs. They are the reformers and revolutionaries with a social mission. They are the ambitious people tackling major social issues and offering new ideas and solutions for wide-scale change. Such entrepreneurs are found in all walks of life and all kinds of organizations: innovative non-profits, social purpose ventures such as for-profit community development banks, and hybrid organizations that mix elements of non-profit and for-profit organizations.

Table 9.1: Difference between Business Entrepreneurship and Social Entrepreneurship

Bases	*Business Entrepreneurship*	*Social Entrepreneurship*
Motive	Their motive is profit.	Their motive is social impact.
Driving Force	They are spurred by money. They are driven by altruism.	
Change Agent	They change the face of the business.	They act as change agents for the society by creating sustainable solutions for the social problems.
Satisfaction	They feel satisfied by establishing a new business and/or creating a new market for their product.	Social entrepreneurs feel satisfied by generating value in the form of sustainable and transformational change that benefits disadvantaged people in the society.
Offering	A business entrepreneur may create entirely a new industry.	Social entrepreneur offers new solutions to social problems and, then, implements them on a large-scale for the benefit of the humanity at large.
Value Creation	Profit is the gauge of value creation.	Social impact is the gauge of value creation.

- **Missionaries:** The life-histories of successful social entrepreneurs reveal that their mission, i.e. the ultimate purpose is not creating just wealth, but most importantly, generating as much as possible social value. Yes, wealth creation may be the part of effort, but is not an end in itself. As a matter of fact, promoting systematic social change and impact is the real and ultimate purpose of social entrepreneurs. It is this mission that gives them strength, fortitude, and courage to tackle with major social issues seemingly intractable social problems.

- **Strategic:** Like the successful business entrepreneurs, social entrepreneurs also search and identify the major social issues what others miss. They use these as opportunities to improve the existing social systems, create solutions, and invent new approaches that create social value (Yunus 1999).
- **Resourceful:** Social entrepreneurs function in a social framework, not within the business world. As such, they have limited resources because of their limited access to capital and traditional market support systems. Given such conditions, they need to be skilled enough to muster and mobilize human, financial, and political resources required to solve the social problems.
- **Result Oriented:** Ultimately, social entrepreneurs are driven to produce measurable results to make perceptible dent on the society. These results change even transform the existing equilibriums, realities, and create new pathways for the benefits of the disadvantaged and downtrodden people of the society. They have the skill to unlock and harness the potential society has to effect social change (Jain 1994: 1363-1377).

The Perspective of Social Entrepreneurship

The preceding description suggests that social entrepreneurship is like a responsive cord combining the passion of a social mission with business-like disciplines of innovation and determination. The time is witness that many governmental and philanthropic efforts to solve some of the daunting social problems have fallen far short of our expectations (Dees 1998: 55-67 and Bhatt 1989). Many social institutions are accordingly viewed as inefficient, ineffective, and even unresponsive. Given such unfortunate stable situation, the time seems certainly ripe for entrepreneurial approaches to solve the social problems (Rose 1992). Thus, social entrepreneurship as a phrase has emerged well suited to our times.

Economic history is witness that the language of social entrepreneurship may be new, but the concept / phenomenon not. We have always had social entrepreneurs, even if we did not call them that. Yes, it has certainly gained renewed currency in a world characterized by a growing divide between the haves and have-nots. Given this heightened visibility, individuals have come forward to help the down-trodden and have-nots of the society. These are solution-minded pragmatists who are not afraid to tackle any big problem for the cause of poor people in the society. They have uncanny knack to recognize the tremendous potential the billions of poor people possess. They are absolutely committed to helping them use their talents and abilities to harness their potential for their improvement and upliftment (Sreenivasan 2000). . For doing so, they use inspiration, creativity, courage, fortitude and, most importantly, direct action, to create a superior but stable equilibrium that results in enduring social benefits and a better future for society. These individuals, or say, social entrepreneurs introduce solutions to seemingly intractable social problems for improving the lives of countless marginalized, disadvantaged and disenfranchised people who are weak and poor in financial means and political clouts.

Social Entrepreneurship in Practice

Below we are presenting three cases of social entrepreneurship and subsequently comparing them on three aspects of their experiences with an objective to glean out the core elements required to become successful in social entrpreneurship.

Bangladesh Rural Advancement Committee (BRAC)

The BRAC was established in 1972 by Fazle Abed, a Bangladeshi corporate executive, in the aftermath of the Independence War. Over the past 30 years, BRAC has focused on breaking the cycle of poverty in Bangladesh. Starting as a relief and resettlement organization, BRAC pioneered the development of comprehensive, locally organized approaches to rural development and poverty alleviation. It provides a range of services – rural capacity-building, education, health services, and micro-credit – to 2.6 million rural people, and it has been exceptionally successful in developing projects that contribute to its own financial sustainability.

- *Essential Innovation:* Focuses on local constituent needs and capacities through a systemic approach to poverty alleviation that emphasizes systematic learning at many levels. Instituted rapid scaling up of the organization while ensuring sustainability.

- *Scope:* Operates in 60,000 of the 86,000 villages in Bangladesh. Organizes the poor for self-help and builds local capacities for economic development, healthcare, and education. Focuses on working with women and other oppressed groups. Seeks to change local attitudes and culture for landless poor, and shift economic circumstances.

Source: *www.brac.net*

The Grameen Bank (GB)

The GB was established in 1976 by Muhammed Yunus, a Bangladeshi economic professor, and his colleagues. Convinced that poor borrowers might be worthwhile credit risks, they demonstrated that landless women in mutually accountable borrower groups achieved very high repayment rates. The Grameen Bank forms small groups of five people to provide mutual, morally binding group guarantees in lieu of collateral. Past participants have proven to be reliable borrowers and astute entrepreneurs; as a result, they have raised their social status, lessened their dependency on their husbands, improved their homes, and provided better nutrition for their children. These borrowers developed the social development guidelines known as the "Sixteen Decisions," which have formed the basis of village group meetings throughout the Grameen system. Today, over 90% of the millions of micro-credit borrowers around the world are women.

- *Essential Innovation:* Provides group lending for poor people without collateral. Succeeded in expanding organizational capacity to serve millions of small borrowers.
- *Scope:* Provided small loans to 2.3 million very poor borrowers. Created 12 other businesses (e.g., fisheries, hand loom factories, renewable energy plants) to serve the poor. Expanded poor women's roles in income generation, as well as in micro-credit theory and practice around the world.

Source: www.grameen-info.org

The Self-employed Women's Association (SEWA)

The SEWA was founded in 1972 by Ela Bhatt, is a trade union of women who earn their livelihoods in three broad occupational categories that, historically, have been very difficult to organize: Hawkers and vendors, home-based producers, and manual laborers and service providers. Their initial programs focused on improving members' working conditions through influencing the actions of local police and policy makers. Later, SEWA provided a variety of services that were otherwise unavailable to their members. With approximately 315,000 members, SEWA is the first and largest trade union of informal sector workers. In addition to its unionizing activities, SEWA has several "sister" institutions, including a bank that provides financial resources, an academy that provides teaching, training and research, and a housing trust that coordinates housing activities for its members. SEWA has become an international force, working with women's and labor movements worldwide.

- *Essential Innovation:* Organizes groups of women that are atomized and have little reason to cooperate for political change, or otherwise address economic, social, and health issues. Builds local leadership capacity to scale up organization and movement.
- *Scope:* Organized 315,000 self-employed women as union members. Improved working conditions, access to health care, credit, and savings for the more than 90% of India's self-employed/unorganized, female laborers. Influenced the creation of self-employment labor division in the Indian government. Influenced the International Labor Organization (ILO) to pass standards for home workers (including minimum wage and working conditions). Co-founded international network to support the work of women in the informal sector (Women in Informal Employment Globalizing and Organizing, WIEGO).

Source: www.sewa.org

Now, the above cases are compared on three aspects: the nature of innovations they have articulated, the characteristics of their leaders, and the paths chosen for scaling up their impacts.

Nature of Innovations

	Core Innovation Pattern	*Mobilizing Assets and Capacities of Poor*	*Emphasis on Continuous Learning*
BRAC	*Build Local Capacity:* Create village groups that can solve local problems and provide a variety of services and supports for village development.	*High*: Shift from relief and service delivery to building local organizations and capacities for self-help, with particular attention to women.	*High:* Embrace commitment to being a learning organization very early: establish systems for "learning for experience" for benefit of individuals, programs, and the organization as a whole.
Grameen Bank	*Micro-credit Package*: Provide group loans for poor and marginalized people to develop income-generating activities; follow up with other development programs.	*High:* From the start, focus on improving the capacity of poor and marginalized people, especially women, to participate in small businesses.	*Medium:* Make systematic investments in learning of participants and staff; invest less in formal learning processes at the organizational level.
SEWA	*Build Local Movement*: Mobilize self-employed women to campaign for policies to support work activities and to develop services adapted to their work and overall welfare needs.	*High:* Focus on building capacities of poor, self-employed women to organize and secure economic and legal rights.	*High:* Help members learn new skills and develop political leader-ship capacities: make long-term commitment to organiza-tional learning and growth in a changing political context.

Entrepreneurial Characteristics

	Bridging Capacity	*Adaptive Leadership Capacity*
BRAC	*High:* Founder was international business executive who committed himself to reducing poverty in his country. Developed close contacts with grassroots communities and activists as well as with government officials, business leaders, donors and development NGOs.	*High:* Founder has led organization for 30 years and guided transition from doing relief work to serving as a grassroots development catalyst, partnering with government and international coalitions, and developing into a successful market competitor. Founder understands political context and utilizes key political relationships effectively.
Grameen Bank	*High:* Founder was an economics professor who grew up in Bangladesh and completed graduate education in the United States. Over the years, has built strong and lasting relationships with business leaders, government officials, donors, academics, and poor villagers, both men and women.	*High:* In place for 30 years, founder has led expansion from small, local experiment to nation-wide organization with branches in other countries, twelve different businesses, and close ties to government and international donors.
SEWA	*High*: Founder born into high caste and trained as a lawyer in social activist family (e.g., India's independence movement). Maintained relationships with elite officials, professionals, and social activist while convening disparate groups of very poor, self-employed women around common issues.	*High:* Founder led organization for 25 years to be successful local and national movement. Facilitated rise of new leaders and international association. Utilized relationships with key political leaders and government officials to support campaigns and to overcome challenges from opposing constituencies.

Scaling Up Path

	Scaling up Strategy	*Transformation Leverage*	*Overall Impact of the Initiative*
BRAC	• Develop programs for village development. • Expired coverage by expanding organization.	**Cultural:** Organize village capacity for action on development problems. **Economic:** Establish micro-credit for business.	**Reach** High **Transformation:** Economic – High Political – Low Cultural – High
Grameen Bank	• Create and test micro-credit package. • Expand coverage via large organization. • Follow-up with support functions.	**Economic:** Provide capital for small business development. **Cultural:** Support women in new economic and business roles.	**Reach:** High **Transformation:** Economic – High Political – Low Cultural – Medium
SEWA	• Mobilize members for policy influence campaigns. • Provide support services otherwise unavailable to members.	**Political:** Empower poor women for voice on harassment. **Economic:** Improve business climate for self-employed women. **Cultural:** Legitimate new roles and choices for poor women.	**Reach:** High **Transformation:** Economic – High/Medium Political – High Cultural – High

What common elements emerge from above comparisons of three social entrepreneurs can be summed up as follows:

Social entrepreneurs identify and target unfortunate but stable equilibriums that cause the neglect, marginalization, or suffering of a segment of humanity; they bring to bear on this situation their inspiration, direct action, creativity, courage, and fortitude; and they aim for establishing a new stable equilibrium that secures permanent benefit for the targeted group and society at large.

Boundaries of Social Entrepreneurship

As mentioned earlier, social entrepreneurship is a new term but old concept. There is no denying the fact that the concept of social entrepreneurship is gaining increasing popularity, yet its meaning is so far blurring. It means different things to different people. While some associate social entrepreneurship exclusively with not-for-profit organization starting for profit, others use it to describe anyone who starts a not-for-profit organization. There are yet others who use it to refer to those business owners who integrate and discharge social responsibility in their business. This makes what social entrepreneurship really means much confusing and quite baffling. No doubt, there may be some activities highly meritorious and socially valuable, but do not fit the definition of social entrepreneurship. Our view is that a clear definition of social entrepreneurship will aid the development of the field. This, therefore, underlines the need for drawing boundaries of social entrepreneurship to understand the subject more meaningfully.

There are two primary forms of highly meritorious and socially valuable activity: *Social Service Provision and Social Activism*. These are considered the cousins of social entrepreneurship which need to be distinguished and excluded from social entrepreneurship (Martin and Osberg 2007: 36-38). As regards social service provision, a courageous and committed individual identifies an unfortunate stable equilibrium, initiates some initiatives to address it, but fails to establish a new superior long-lasting equilibrium. For example, a courageous person identifies the illiteracy problem of slum children (of Silampur in Delhi) and starts a school to teach them. The school may help some slum children become literate and transform themselves. But unless it is designed to achieve it in a large scale or is so compelling as to launch legions of imitators and replicators, it is not likely to lead to a new superior and sustainable equilibrium in the society. Several such organizations abound around us with good in their intensions, noble in purpose, and exemplary in execution. Since they remain confined and constrained to limited frame, they should not be mingled and confused with social entrepreneurship. Thus, social entrepreneurship is different from social service provision not in initiation, but in the outcomes. In fact, it is mainly the large-scale social impact of one's activity that anchors one as a social entrepreneur

The second type of socially valuable activity is '*social activism*.' In this case also, the motivation (i.e., unfortunate stable equilibrium) behind activity and characteristics of the actor (i.e., inspiration, creativity, courage, and fortitude) are the same as of the social entrepreneur. But what is actually different from social entrepreneur is the nature of the actor's action orientation. Unlike social entrepreneur, the social activist does not take direct action but takes indirect action through others like governments, NGOs, workers, etc. Yes, the successful social activism can also result in improvement over the existing equilibrium and even establish a new equilibrium. Nonetheless, the very nature of social activism is distinct in its emphasis on ultimate influence rather than on direct action. It is due to this vein only; Mahatma Gandhi, Martin Luther King, and Vaclav Havel present the historical examples of social activism. Hence, they cannot be called as social entrepreneurs because it would baffle the very concept of social entrepreneur, on the one hand, and would also cause confusion to the concept of social activism, on the other.

In sum and substance, social entrepreneur takes direct action and generates a new superior and sustained equilibrium; the social service provider takes direct action to improve the outcomes of the current equilibrium; and the social activist influences others to generate a new and sustained equilibrium. This difference between the three terms, viz.; social entrepreneurship, social service provision, and social activism, is also depicted in the following diagram:

Pure Forms of Social Engagement

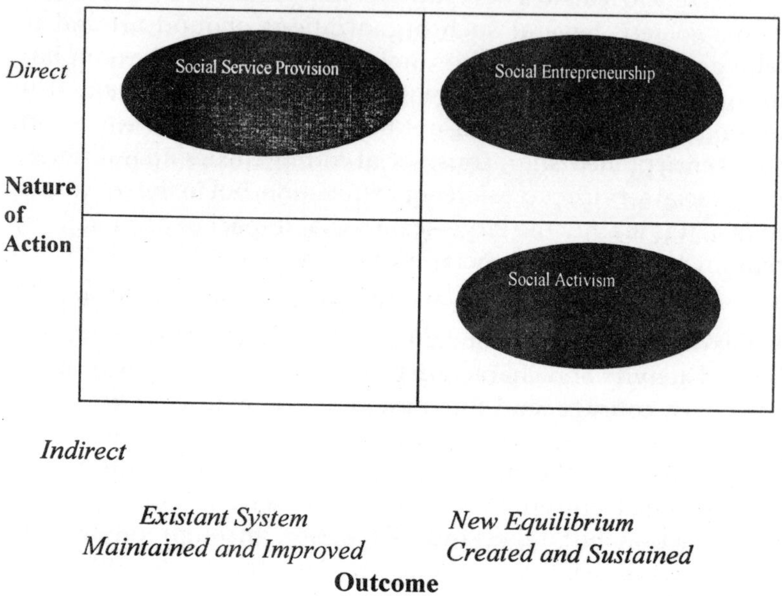

Concluding Remarks

Social entrepreneurship transforms the society to a superior and stable equilibrium. Hence, social entrepreneurship needs to be seeded, nurtured, and developed for the benefit of the society by all concerned- be it the individuals or governments or social institutions or non-governmental organizations (NGOs). Being an evolving concept, social entrepreneurship needs to be studied and researched in its various dimensions like that of business entrepreneurship to understand it in clear meanings. The term social entrepreneurship needs to be defined in its exact and precise meaning to develop the subject. Just like business entrepreneurship, one way to develop and better our understanding about social entrepreneurship will be to sponsor and undertake research studies on the subject. Sooner it is done, better will be social entrepreneurship.

10

Ethical Entrepreneurship*

Business, or say, entrepreneurship and society have been coeval since time immemorial. Both are inter-dependent on each other. One can not survive and thrive without other. Both cooperate with each other on reciprocal manner. Society gives inputs in terms of men, material, and money to the business which, in turn, reciprocates by offering goods and services to the society for meeting its needs. This relationship between business and society, quoted by Raj (2001), is appreciated in *Rigveda* also: "Corporate should work like a honeybee, which takes the nectar of a flower without the flower being losing its shape and fragrance and provides honey for the wellbeing of the society." The management guru Peter Drucker (1954) also states that the relationship between business and society is "like the relationship between a ship and the sea which engirds it and carries it, which threatens it with storm and shipwreck which has to be crossed but which is yet alien and distant." Drucker (1968) further reiterates, "Even the most private enterprise is an organ of society and serves a social function." Business enterprise, be small or large, earns profits from society by offering goods and services to it. Hence, it has also some responsibilities towards the society". In other words, business by its operations has to add some good to the society. This calls for a business to be

*This chapter draws heavily from S. S. Khanka: Ethical Entrepreneurship: Challenges and Rewards, ***Yojana***, Volume 47, No. 7, July 2003, pp. 19-22.

run in a fair and just manner. Acting in a fair, just, and transparent manner is called *'ethics.'*

Before we discuss, in detail, ethical entrepreneurship or ethics in entrepreneurship, it seems pertinent to define ethics and related principles in eloquent terms.

What is Ethics?

The word 'ethics' used as *'ethicus'* in Latin, and *'ethikos'* in Greek, means character or manner. In this sense, ethics is a code of conduct. Another word 'morality' is also used to mean ethics. Morality means behaviour. However, the two terms 'character' and 'moral' mean two different things. Character is internal to a man. As Swami Vivekananda also said, "eternal principle of truth marks ethics or character". In this sense, ethics/character is essentially a matter of concern of the inner contents of individual. Behaviour is relatively external; i.e., the response one makes at the interface of interactions with others. Character is externalized via behaviour. In other words, the character of a person is expressed in terms of actions, which when taken together, can be termed as 'good' or 'bad', 'right or 'wrong' or 'moral' or 'immoral'. Thus, ethics also implies moral judgments about human behaviour.

Here is an example of ethics, i.e. moral judgement as good or right:

> There was one situation in Karnataka where an officer wanted us (Infosys Technologies) to bribe him. He told us to pay him Rs. 4 lakhs or pay the Government Rs. 40 lakhs. We paid Rs. 40 lakhs. One's clear conscience is the softest pillow to sleep (Chary 2002: 85).

Nonetheless, ethics and morality are interchangeable terms. Therefore, what is ethical is moral and conversely, what is unethical is immoral. Here it is important to mention that ethics and / or morality go well beyond etiquette, procedure, protocol, and even mere observance of the laws of the land. Thus, the question is not whether an act is legal or illegal but whether the act is good or bad. This is because at times a legal act may not necessarily be morally good act. For example, all the acts committed at the Nuremberg trials were legal but were not morally good acts. Just conversely, all illegal acts may not necessarily be morally bad. For example, the snatching and stealing act of Robin Hood from the haves and distribute the same among the havenots was illegal but morally good. Thus, the essence of an act being ethical or not depends on whether it adds to good or welfare of the society or not.

Depending on occurrence of behaviour ethics may be of two types: Empirical Ethics and Eternal Ethics.

Empirical Ethics: Empirical ethics examines human behaviour at the time of its occurrence. It considers things in isolation. In other words, while considering the empirical ethics, the background and surrounding relationships are not considered at all.

Eternal Ethics: Eternal ethics makes transcend in the dimension of the ethicality. It makes retrospection of the happenings and places these at the stream of flow of accidents over the period of time. In other words, eternal ethics considers things or actions in a holistic manner considering all related to the action.. Then, judging things as ethical or unethical becomes very clear.

The essence of the entire *Mahabharat War* exemplifies the both types of ethics. How?

- Kunti parts with Karna by placing him on a raft floating along the river current.
- Krishna influences Kunti to ask Karna to give his life-saving gem.
- Krishna motivated Arjun to fight with his real brother, i.e. Karna.
- Arjuna attacked on Karna when his chariot was stuck and was armless.

If we just consider all above activities as these happened, each one seems unethical and wrong. Kunti violates the honour of motherhood, Krishna is found violating the divinely qualities, and Arjuna violates the principle of war, i.e. not to rage war on the armless. Thus, these conduct become empirical ethics. But, if we look at these activities placing them at the stream of flow of mischief committed by Duryodhana and Karna over the period, these activities are found right to remove evil and restore truth on the earth. Then, these activities become eternal ethics.

A morally good act has three parts of factors:

(a) The objective of act itself;

(b) The subjective motive of the actor; and

(c) The situation or circumstances in which the act is done.

These are exemplified as follows:

(a) To act justly is an objectively good work, just as to murder is an objectively evil/bad act.

(b) The actor must also have good intentions. For example, giving donations to charitable institutions to avoid paying tax is not a good intention on the part of donor/ actor.

(c) The situation or circumstances must also be considered. For instance, giving alms to the poor is a morally good act. But refusing alms to the poor who you know would spend it on his alcoholic addiction is equally a morally good act.

Ethical behaviour is, in a sense, the normative behaviour based on a set of code of conduct. Based on normative plane, the normative ethical theories are categorized as deontological theories and teleogical theories.

Deontological Theories: In this theory, the performance of action is considered to be inherently either right or wrong. The ethicality of the action does not depend upon its consequences, whatever these are. The moral rules derived from the Ten Commandments would be an example of 'deontological theory of ethics'. Here is one example of deontological theory of ethics of Sri Aurobindo.

> Sri Aurobindo passed the ICS final examination in August 1892 and only one more formality left was that of passing the 'riding test.' Between August and November 1892, Sri Aurobindo had four different chances of appearing for this test and, on each occasion, he failed to put in an appearance. Evidently, he had made up his mind not to go in for the ICS. When he was asked: 'Why did you appear at all for the ICS? Was it on account of some (yogic) intuition that you did not go for the riding test.' 'Not at all, 'he replied, **'I knew nothing of yoga at that time. I appeared for the ICS because my father wanted it** (Nirodbaran 1990: 18).'

Teleological Theory: Just contrary to deontological theory, the ethicality, or say, morality of the action depends upon its consequences. An example of teleogical theory is utilitarianism, i.e., an action is considered to be good or right if it produces the greatest good for the greatest number of people.

Some scholars have understood ethics in the sense of altruism. Altruism is defined (by sociologists) in two senses. *First,* one's willingness to sacrifice his/her welfare for the sake of others (Krebs 1982: 55). *Second,* one's manifest behaviour and its consequences without any reference to his/her dispositional intentions (Worchel et.al. 1988: 394), i.e., regardless of the intention of the help provider.

The first sense refers altruism as an internal state, the second refers to it as a behaviour with consequence. Since it is often difficult to identify the help provider's dispositional intension, researchers have preferred to define altruism in the latter sense, i.e., overt behaviour of the help provider.

What Makes Ethics?

What makes one behave in a just manner? Though one can list a number of elements that make ethics, the following are the major ones:

- Truthfulness
- Transparency
- Righteousness

- Morality
- Sacrifice/Giving

As per *Bhagawad Gita*, the following elements help form ethics:

1. Truthfulness
2. Purity
3. Compassion
4. Forgiveness
5. Poise
6. Patience
7. Cooperation
8. Fearlessness
9. Giving/Sacrifice
10. Commitment of Divine
11. Restraint Welfare of Others
12. Renunciation
13. Simplicity
14. Peace
15. Cleanliness
16. Non-Injury
17. Angerless
18. Non-Greedy
19. Non-Cruelty
20. Non-Egoistic
21. Non-Fault
22. Respectful
23. Courageous
24. Commitment to
25. Impersonalisation

An ethics is applicable to every human being, so is to entrepreneurs also. This is popularly known as 'business ethics'. Simply stating, business ethics means conducting business activities in a just and fair manner. Similarly, ethical entrepreneurship means performing entrepreneurial functions in a just, fair, and righteous manner. We shall discuss in the following pages how entrepreneurs can function ethically so as to add good to the society as a whole.

Aspects of Ethical Entrepreneurship

Plato made one observation over 2000 years ago: "The unexamined life is not worth living". In fact, this profound observation is valid today as well. It is applicable to all walks of human life, be a common man or administrator, professional or businessman/entrepreneur. In case of human organization like business, its essential purpose of being in existence, better call it *'the raison d'etre'* of human organization, is to add some good to human beings. Viewed from this angle, Drucker (1968: 461) opines that the entrepreneurs need to consider whether their activities, policies and procedures are likely to contribute and promote the societal good, its stability and strength. No one will deny that entrepreneurs need to achieve their objective of earning profits. But what is the matter of concern is the manner in which these are achieved need to be consistent with the interest of the society. After all entrepreneurs earn profits by serving the needs of the society. Alternatively speaking, along with achieving his/her objective, i.e., earning profits, the entrepreneur has also responsibility to the other stakeholders in the enterprise, for example, consumers, employees, government, suppliers and local communities. This calls for the ethical behaviour on the part of the entrepreneurs. We examine the ethical aspects of the entrepreneurial behaviour in relation to some of these stakeholders in the enterprise.

Entrepreneur and Customers

One cannot imagine about enterprise without its customers. The existence and survival of any enterprise or business depends on customers. Hence, the purpose of an enterprise in order to exist and survive is to create and keep its customers (Leavitt, 1986: 19). However, these are not so easy. Because, activities involved in creating and keeping customers at times raise issues relating to ethics. How? An entrepreneur may have two options before him like either to respond to market demand or create demand. As regards creation of demand, some consider it essential because the change in technology and, in turn, product makes it difficult, even impossible for customers to know the products and the benefits they offer unless these are sold to them. Hence, the need for persuasion of customers by using psychological ploys and techniques arises. But, here some raise questions like: Is it ethical to create unnecessary demands for products for the sole benefit of the enterprise? Is it ethical to use psychological ploys and maneuvering to disturb the customer's freedom of choice? Certainly, it is not ethical or righteous work.

Ethical issues may also arise while deciding how to keep or retain the customers. What do customers want? They want quality products and services at reasonable prices. But, we do not find this actually happening always. Instead, knowing their impact on bottom line, compromising decisions on these are taken which is detriment to the customers. Also, these practices might not be illegal, but certainly these might not be considered ethical or moral also.

Entrepreneur and Employee

Customers get products and services what the employees manufacture. An enterprise is unthinkable without employees. Hence, entrepreneur's have obligations towards employees. However, ethical issues may arise depending on how they treat or view employees' work. For example, they might view employees work in terms of social exchange theory. Under this theory, work is treated as a commodity, owned and sold by the employee in return of wages and salaries. Thus, in this view, the employer views employees as a means of production only and then treats accordingly. Allied to this are other ethical issues like unfair payment, irregular payment, false payment, etc. to the employees.

Entrepreneur and Government

As an enterprise is a social organ, it is related to several parties including the Government. In other words, there is an interface between the entrepreneur and government. Experience suggests that in course of interface between the entrepreneur and the government agencies, several ethical dilemmas may surface, these might be as follows:

1. Given the situation of rampant bribery and corruption, should the entrepreneur yield to such situations, i.e., illegitimate demands made by corrupt officials because refusing to do so would have adverse even detrimental effects on business?

2. Knowing the practices, should the entrepreneur go for tax evasion?

These are real ethical issues involved in interface between the entrepreneur and the Government.

Why Ethical Entrepreneurship?

Researches have established that if entrepreneurs function ethically, it rewards. This is substantiated subsequently. As mentioned earlier, ethical behaviour is very much aligned with moral altruism. To envision and develop a keen social conscience, to perform selfless acts, and to place the interest of others before that of one's together form moral altruism. The moral altruism is founded on four cardinal values, namely, *prudence, fortitude, justice,* and *temperance.* The practice of these values is critical to successful entrepreneurship. Let a brief mention of what these values mean be given.

Prudence means to avoid undesired consequences or circumspect. In other words, prudence means appropriate and sound judgment made in the light of a given environment. *Fortitude* implies courage required to act positively and surmount the odds and obstacles to do what is right and just. *Justice* is to give others what is due to them. *Temperance* means one's abstinence from self-indulgent and adherence to what is genuine and justified.

The regular, or say, habitual practice of these virtues of prudence, fortitude, and temperance results in moral strength. The practice of prudence, for example, enables the entrepreneur to consider in his or her decision all related and relevant aspects of a given problem/situation. Such an assessment of situation facilitates proactive behaviour. Fortitude enables an entrepreneur to acquire the coverage required to take great risks for the cause that is noble and worthwhile. Added to this is that fortitude enables the entrepreneur to preserve against great odds. Here, Leavitt's (1986: 95) view seems quite worth noticing: "Determined people try to make it happen because they believe in it, not because the odds are on their sides." According to Mendonca and Kanungo (1998: 209), "Through the habitual practice of above virtues, the entrepreneur develops the courage and ability to identify the deficiencies in the *status quo,* to scan the environment, and be alert to and exploit opportunities for the growth and expansion of the enterprise. Vision without action is wishful thinking; vision with action constitutes a powerful combination for change. Prudence provides the foundation for "vision"; fortitude generates the necessary strength for action." The practice of temperance checks the entrepreneur from swinging in his behaviour. In other words, temperance facilitates the entrepreneur to maintain the emotional balance which helps regulate ones feelings and emotions tempted by changing situations.

The yet another reward ethical entrepreneurship brings for entrepreneurs is achievement motivation. McClelland and Winter (1969) consider 'need for achievement' (*n-ach)* as a premium mobile force in entrepreneurship developments. The practice, in particular, of the virtues of prudence and fortitude facilitates and fosters entrepreneur's need for achievements. To illustrate, prudence enables the entrepreneur to conspicuously examine his or her environment and then set goals as per his or her ability to achieve these goals. Fortitude prepares the entrepreneur to make efforts towards the goals and also be prepared to accept the success as well as failure.

Concluding Remarks

There is no denying the fact that small business is crucial to India's economic and social development. Ethics, or say, moral altruism contributes to the efficient and effective performance of the entrepreneurial behaviour which is critical to the success of the business enterprise. Success includes more than economic returns. It also includes the moral growth of the employers which, in turn, benefits the employees, entrepreneurs, and the society at large. Hence, earlier the entrepreneurs behave ethically, better it will be for the success of business, in particular and social-economic development of the country, in general.

PART II
THE EMPIRICAL EVIDENCE

11

Entrepreneurship Development in North-East India*

Introduction

The 'Seven Sister States' of India viz. Arunachal Pradesh, Assam, Manipur, Meghalaya, Mizoram, Nagaland, and Tripura constitute the North Eastern Region (NER) of India. The entire NER is spread over 2,55,089 sq. kms. area which is 7.8 per cent of the total geographical area (3,287,263 sq. kms) of the country. As per the Census of India 2001, the total population of North East India is 3,65,00,108 persons which is 3.5 per cent of the total population of India. Alternatively speaking about 3.5 per cent population of India lives in her 7.8 per cent area in the North East India. Now Sikkim is also included in the NER.

The NER enjoys a unique geographical location. While China and Bhutan fall on its North and North – West, Myanmar and Bangladesh on its East, South and South West. Thus, the NER is characterized by its unique geo- political entity. It shares quite longer border (98 percent) with these four neighboring countries than with India (2 per cent). It is connected with ' mainland' India by a very narrow land corridor often called

* An earlier version of this chapter appeared as "Entrepreneurship Development in the North Eastern India: Experiences and Prospects", *Sedme*, Volume 32, No. 3, September 2005, pp. 55-71.

'Chicken Neck' having an approximate width of 33 kms on the eastern side and 21 kms on the western side. As such, the narrow corridor is bound to be overburdened and constricted. Such geo-political situation of the NER is very important from two standpoints. One is strategic and two is the feeling of alienation. The NER is not only geographically far from the mainland India, but also lagging far behind in economic development from the mainland India. The entrepreneurial context of the NER constituted by various components as indicators is outlined in Table 11.1 with an objective to reflect its position in relation to country as a whole.

It is clearly revealed from the figures in Table 11.1 that NER is not only geographically far from the mainland India, but also lagging far behind in economic development from the mainland India. In other words, the NER has not as favourable environment for entrepreneurship development as the country as a whole. The economic backwardness of the NER has given genesis to the feeling of alienation which has got manifestations in the forms of militancy and terrorism. These problems over the years have become a headache, or, say, cancer for the whole country. Because poverty anywhere is dangerous for prosperity everywhere, therefore, the problem warrents earliest solution.

Then, the million dollar question arises is what is the solution to the problem? The obvious answer to this question is to remove economic backwardness of the region by judicious harnessing of available resources in the region. Evidences abound in both at world and national levels confirm that entrepreneurship development by harnessing resources promotes economic development. The regions/ states like Gujarat, Maharashtra, Panjab and Haryana where entrepreneurship has developed are economically developed. On the country, the regions/ States like Bihar, Madhya Pradesh and North Eastern States with lack of entrepreneurship development have remained economically backward. Economic history is witness that entrepreneurship development is pre-requisite for industrial / economic development. That is why it is said, *"an economy is the effect for which entrepreneurship is the cause."*

Table 11.1: NER Still Lags Far Behind the Country

Sl. No.	*Indicators*	*NER*	*India*
1.	Literacy Ratio, 2001	68.63	65.38
2.	Urban Population (in %), 2001	15.51	27.78
3.	Sex – Ratio (Females per' 000 Males), 2001	937	933
4.	Population Density (Persons per sq. km.), 2001	147	324
5.	Percentage of Workers engaged in Household Industries to Total Workers, 2001	3.48	4.07
6.	Percentage of Gross Cultivable Area to Total Geographical Area, 2001	25	59
7.	Land – Man Ratio (hac/ man), 2001.	0.66	0.32
8.	Percentage Utilization of Agricultural Land, 2001	58.74	73.05
9.	Per Hectare Use of Chemical Fertilizers (in kg.), 2001	26.59	87.12
10.	Food grain Production (kg per Hectare), 2001	1367	1630
11.	Average Population per Bank (in' 000), March, 1999.	19	15
12.	Credit- Deposit Ratio (in %), 2001	28.31	57.20
13.	Percentage of Electrified Villages to Total Villages. 1999 – 2000.	80.87	86.30
14.	Length of Roads per 100 sq km. Area (in kms), 1997	54.80	74.90
15.	Percentage of Pucca Roads to Total Length of Roads, 1997	24.96	58.68
16.	Area Per Post Office (in Sq. Km.), 2001	41.96	22.33
17.	Per Capita Income (At Current Prices in Rupees), 2000-2001	12,202	16,487

Source: *Basic Statistics of NER* , E & M Cell, Government of India, North Eastern Council Secretariat, Shillong, 2002.

It is evident that the NER is endowed with various resources such as forests, minerals, oil, water, medicinal plants, huge bio-diversity, natural beauty, human resources, etc. But it is unfortunate that, the NER even after five decades of country's freedom, is plagued by the predicament of *"poverty amidst plenty."* Given such condition, entrepreneurship development can play a very significant role in removing poverty and unemployment by utilizing available local resources. Keeping these in view, an attempt has been made in this chapter to delineate the entrepreneurial context of the NER. For the convenience of presentation, the topics considered coalesced around three main themes: i) Entrepreneurship Development Programmes in India: A Historical Perspective, ii) Entrepreneurship Development Programmes in the NER: Efforts and Experiences, iii) Development of Small- Scale Industries in the NER: An Overview.

Entrepreneurship Development Programmes (EDPs) in India: A Historical Perspective

It will not be less than correct to say that India got the political freedom on 15th August 1947, but not the economic freedom. And attainment of economic freedom i.e., emancipation from poverty and unemployment was the biggest challenge before the country. The war for economic freedom started in 1950 in the form of planned development. Then, it was realized that the way to get rid of poverty and unemployment lies in the effective exploitation of hidden potential in the country. For this the policy makers started advocating the promotion and development of small – scale industries in the country. As a result, small – sector was recognized as employment- oriented sector during the early sixties. The employment – oriented thinking for small sector underwent changes by the end of sixties and now small- sector was recognized as an effective instrument to utilize the entrepreneurial potential remained hitherto dormant in the country.

Realizing the various problems faced by the entrepreneurs in establishing enterprises, the Government decided to offer promotional package to the entrepreneurs. Promotional package included financial help and incentives, infrastructural facilities, and technical and managerial guidance provided through various supporting organizations of the Central, State and local levels. This experience made the planners and policy makers realize that facilities and incentives are, of course, necessary for establishing enterprises, but are not sufficient to solicit adequate response from the entrepreneurs. Hence, now it was realized that emphasis on human development is a necessary condition for entrepreneurship development. As such, the serious thinking on entrepreneurship development began from here.

Entrepreneurship development in India started with the establishment of Small Industry Extension and Training Institute (SIET) in 1962 in Hyderabad. SIET got an opportunity with support from Harvard University to do pioneering work in entrepreneurship development in India. SIET in collaboration with Prof. David C. McClelland of Harvard University conducted 03 months' training and research programmes in Rajamundi, Kakinada and Vellur towns of Andhra Pradesh and Tamilnadu. McClelland proved that, through proper education and training, the vital quality of an entrepreneur, which McClelland called 'need for achievement' (n'ach) can be developed (McClelland 1969). The fact remains that McClelland's this successful experiment proved to be a seed for entrepreneurship development in India which has become popular today as EDP (Entrepreneurship Development Programmes).

It is against this background now the Government and financial institutions started thinking to develop entrepreneurship in the country through training programmes. It was the Gujarat Industrial Investment Corporation (GIIC) who for the first time started a three month training programme on entrepreneurship development in 1970. This programme was designed to unleash the talent of potential entrepreneurs and some selected entrepreneurs. Special emphasis was given on three aspects : 1. Establishment of a small – scale enterprise, 2. Its management, and 3. To earn profits out of it. By the latter half of 1970s' the news of GIIC's EDP spread to the other parts of the country also. As a result, SIET and Small Industry Development Organisation (SIDO) through Small Industry Services Institute (SISI)and Industrial Development Bank of India (IDBI) through

Technical Consultancy Organisations (TCOs) started organising EDPs. The encouraging results of these efforts culminated to the establishment of 'Centre for Entrepreneurship Development (CED), Ahmedabad in 1979. Here, it is noteworthy that CED, Ahmedabad was the first centre of its kind wholly committed to the cause of entrepreneurship development. Inspired and influenced by the success of CED, Ahmedabad, the national level financial institutions such as IDBI , IFCI, ICICI and SBI with active support from the Gujarat Government sponsored a 'Nation Resource Organisation', called 'Entrepreneurship Development Institute of India (EDI), Ahmedabad, in 1983. This institute was entrusted with the responsibility of extension and institutionalization of entrepreneurship development activities in the country which the Institute has been discharging successfully. Almost at the same time of establishment of EDI in 1983, the Government of India established 'National Institute for Entrepreneurship and Small Business Development' (NIESBUD) to coordinate entrepreneurship development activities in the country. In course of time, some State Governments with the support from national level financial institutions established state-level Center for Entrepreneurship Development (CED) or Institute of Entrepreneurship Development (IED). By now, the twelve States, viz., Bihar, Goa, Gujrat, Himachal Pradesh, Jammu & Kashmir, Karnataka, Kerala, Madhya Pradesh, Maharashtra, Orissa, Tamil Nadu , and Uttar Pradesh have established CED or IED. EDPs in these states were conducted by the TCOs before the establishment of CEDs or IEDs. According to the study of NIESBUD, some 686 organisations are involved in conducting EDPs in the country which have imparted training to thousands of people by conducting hundreds of EDPs. Today, India operates the oldest and largest entrepreneurship development programmes in any developing country and EDP has emerged as a nation-wide campaign in our country.

EDPs in the NER: Efforts and Experiences

The relatively more backward NER has been attracting the attention of development advocators of India since Independence. However, the first sincere effort for economic development of the NER took place with the establishment of the North Eastern Council (NEC) in 1972. The main objective of the NEC was to promote economic development of the NER through inter-state plans and bring the NER to the mainstream of the country, This is a matter of great satisfaction that the NEC has since been seriously involved in its task of regional development. Two more significant efforts were initiated in 1973 with an objective to remove the economic backwardness of the region. *One*, the establishment of the North Eastern Industrial and Technical Consultancy Organization (NEITCO) to impart training on entrepreneurship development, and *second,* the establishment of the Entrepreneurial Motivation Training Centres (EMTCs) in Assam in its six district headquarters of Kokrajhar, Mangaldai, Diphu, Dhimaji, Jorhat and Silchar.

Since EMTC was one of the oldest and noblest initiatives taken in the field of entrepreneurship development in the country, some mention about the same seems pertinent. The State Planning Board of the Government of Assam, under the dynamic leadership of the then Chief Minister, took the initiative in requesting SIET Institute, Hyderabad to be associated with training and research in the field of entrepreneurship development in Assam with specific focus on self -employment for the educated unemployed youth of the State. In response to it, the SIET Institute organized two training programmes for three weeks duration each in 1973, for the officers of Government of Assam. *One* training programme was focused on entrepreneurship development for a selected band of officers from the departments of industry, agriculture, animal husbandry, public works and other departments and financial institutions of the Government of Assam. The training programme included inputs like various methods and techniques of identification and development of prospective entrepreneurs, development of entrepreneurial personality, and identification of economic opportunities for setting up small-scale enterprises in the State. Functional areas of management for establishing and operating small enterprises on sound lines were also included in the training programmes. *Second* the another simultaneous training was imparted to the another group of officers of the industries department to encourage people to establish small scale industries, undertake industrial potential surveys, select growth centres, plan infrastructure facilities and develop business profiles. Integrated entrepreneurship development model and plan were evolved as a result of SIET's experience and realisation that entrepreneurship development is a multi-disciplinary task, and the long range plan should be executed through well coordinated and orchestrated institutional suppol1 (Nagayya 2000: 36-38).

The integrated model of entrepreneurship development proposed by SIET included five main components, namely, (i) local organization to initiate and support potential entrepreneurs till the break-even stage, (ii) inter-disciplinary approach, (iii) strong information support, (iv) training as an important intervention for entrepreneurial development, monitoring and evaluation, and (v) institutional financing.

Initially EMTCs were established in six centres in Assam under the State Planning Board, which were monitored by 26 officers trained by SIET in May 1973. The team in each centre consisted of multi - disciplinary talents. It is learnt that in 1979, after a comprehensive evaluation of the performance of EMTCs by SIET Institute, the programme was transferred from the State Planning Board to the Industries Department. Three more centres were added to the earlier six locations. The nine EMITCs where the programme is being implemented were as follows:

Mangaldoi (Darrang District), Silchar (Cachar District), Diphu (Karbi Analong District), Jorhat (Jorhat District), Dhemaji (Dhemaji District), Kokrajhar (Kokrajhar District), Dibrugarh (Dibrugarh District), Nalbari (Nalbari District) and Nagaon (Nagaon District). The first six cnetres were started in May 1973 and the remaining three in 1979.

Within a period of two years, 1550 persons were trained in the six centres by March 1975.

As many as Two-thirds of them were ready with their project reports. The required plant training was arranged in respect of 581 entrepreneurs (37.5%). Actual financial sanction was obtained for 310 proposals (20.0%), 278 units were established (17.9%). Most of the units were set up between July, 1974 and March 1975. A recent study of IIE has shown that from 1973 to 1997, in all over 30,000 persons were trained by nine EMTCs in Assam. Out of this number, during 1983-87, the percentage of trained persons was 24.6, during 1988-92, it was 30.1 and during 1993-97, it was 22. In the first ten years, it was a total of 23.3 per cent. On an average, per year more than 1000 persons were trained and helped to become self-employed. Though the seriousness with which the programme is being implemented in recent years is not up to the expectations, the efforts put in by EMTCs, certainly deserve compliments from everyone concerned. This experiment carried out in Assam has proved the effectiveness of the pre-training, training, and post-training mechanism at the field level covering a few districts, with one EMTC as the overall coordinator of the programme for the region consisting of a few districts.

In other states of the North East, other than support institutions for stimulating industrialization, there was no mechanism for organizing entrepreneurship development efforts. The impact of EMTCs has established their special contribution for promoting entrepreneurship if a comprehensive and wide ranging mechanism is evolved for the purpose in every state/ region. Stimulatory, support and sustaining roles of various agencies including entrepreneurs need to be well orchestrated and pursued vigorously over a few decades to ensure the growth of entrepreneurship for small, tiny and micro enterprises in less developed regions, in particular.

With an objective to bring the EDPs in the NER at par with the national level, the North Eastern Regional Centre of SIET was established in Guwahati in 1979. The main task of this regional centre was to develop and promote entrepreneurship and small – scale industries in the NER. The name of SIET was also changed as the National Institute of Small Industry Extension and Training (NISIET) in 1984 and the Regional Center of SIET in Guwahati became the North Eastern Regional Centre (NERC) of the NISIET. The NISIET has played a significant role in the regional development of the NER. In 1984, the NERC of NISIET was converted into a full-fledged Institute, named, Indian Institute of Entrepreneurship (IIE), Guwahati. The IIE, Guwahati has been seriously involved in the entrepreneurship development in the Region and has by now emerged as one of the premier Institutes in entrepreneurship in the country.

Having discussed the Government approach toward entrepreneurship development, now it seems pertinent to delineate the so far progress made and experiences gained in the field of entrepreneurship development in the NER.

Human development is essential condition for economic development. Recognizing this fact, the NEC has shown keen interest in human development in the NER and has done some appreciable job in this regard. For example, the NEC sponsored one study on *"Entrepreneurial and Managerial Needs of the North East Region"* to the SIET in 1976. The study was completed in 1978. The SIET combined this study along with the similar efforts going on in another six countries. Thus, by integrating the researches of eight institutions in seven countries, SIET under the auspices of the 'Asian Association of Development Research and Training Institute' published a significant publication titled *"Small Industry Development in Selected Asian Countries"* (Sharma 1979). For the NER, a separate detailed study was brought out by the SEIT in 1978 (Sharma and Akhouri 1978). Among other aspects, this study perspicaciously analyzed the existing and potential entrepreneurship development in each state of the NER and also suggested a working strategy for entrepreneurship development in the region. The NEC has since beginning taken the onerous responsibility of entrepreneurship development in the NER. The EDPs sponsored by the NEC are oriented towards three directions: 1) Create awareness about entrepreneurship development, 2) Organize EDPs for 6-8 week duration, and 3) Organize some special EDPs for the existing entrepreneurs. Nonetheless, development of new generation entrepreneurs has been the main foci of the EDPs conducted by the NEC.

The NEC set a target to impart EDP training to develop some 5,000 entrepreneurs during the seventh plan period. However, the NEC through four training organizations, could impart training to 3609 candidates only as against its target of 5,000 candidates (Mali and Bandopadhyay 1993). From April 1990 to March 1996, the NEC, in collaboration with the SIDBI and the IDBI, sponsored a total of 212 EDPs to five training organizations. The number of EDPs with their types and number of participants is given in Table 11.2.

Table 11.2: Training – Organisation-wise EDP's Number and the Participants

Training Organisation	*General EDPs*	*Women EDPs*	*Rural EDPs*	*Total*	*Number of Participants*
NISIET	**24**	**4**	**10**	**38(18%)**	**940**
IIE	12	4	8	24(11%)	591
NEITCO	41	11	13	65(31%)	1,715
NSIC	16	4	6	26(12%)	524
NECON	30	7	22	59(28%)	1,605
TOTAL	123(58%)	30(14%)	59(28%)	212(100)	5,375

Source: North Eastern Council, Shillong

It is seen from figures in Table 3.2 that the maximum number of EDPs organised are general ones, but women EDPs have also been given importance, As regards organization- wise EDPs, NEITCO(41) and NECON(30) have organised the maximum number of EDPs.

The state-wise distribution of these EDPs is presented in Table 11.3.

Table 11.3: State-wise Number of EDPs and Participants

State	*Number of EDPs*	*Number of Participants*
Arunachal Pradesh	**23(10.8)**	**598(11.0)**
Assam	74(34.9)	1,807(33.6)
Manipur	27(12.7)	693(12.9)
Meghalaya	26(12.3)	653(12.2)
Mizoram	13(6.1)	350(6.6)
Nagaland	27(12.7)	694(12.9)
Tripura	22(10.5)	580(10.8)
Total	212(100.0)	5,375(100.0)

Note: Figures in parentheses denote percentages to total.

As seen from Table 11.3, Assam has conducted the maximum EDPs and Mizoram the minimum (6%). The three states of Manipur, Meghalaya and Nagaland have conducted 13% EDPs each.

In fact, entrepreneurship development is a dynamic activity that needs to be revised and improved as per the requirement of the target group. Since conducting EDPs involve much resources such as money, time and human efforts which are always scarce in supply, it becomes imperative to know whether the EDPs are beneficial or not. In other words, whether the objectives for which EDPs are conducted are achieved or not or achieved to what extent, is known by studying the effectiveness of EDPs . So far, several studies have been conducted on the effectiveness of EDPs in the country (Awasthi and Sebastian 1996; Gaikwad et.al. 1974; and SBI 1978). Such studies on the effectiveness of EDPs are conducted in the NER also (SIET 1974; NISIET 1990; and NEITCO 1991). One such recent evaluation study titled *"A Critical Study of the Effectiveness of Entrepreneurship Development Programmes in the North East"* was conducted by the IIE, Guwahati for the aforesaid 212 EDPs conducted under the auspices of the NEC, Shillong. Here, a mention about the main results on the effectiveness of EDPs as reported by the said study seems pertinent.

In the first phase of the study, structural questionnaires were sent by mail to a total of 2,717 trainees which resulted in response from, 1097 (40%) participants only. Due to quite low response received, it was decided to obtain some more responses by sending investigators to the different states of the NER. This effort could generate response from 2,616 trainees. Thus, the study could cover a total of 3,713(69%) trainees out of 5,375 trainees. The main reasons for intractability of around 31 per cent were non-availability of proper address, migration to other places, inaccessibility etc. The study revealed that only 935 (25%) trainees could establish any industry out of 3,713 EDP participants (Table 11.4).

Table 11.4: Success Rate of EDPs

Sl No.	*Items*	*Number*	*Per cent*
1	Total Number of Trainees	5,375	100.0
2	Respondents:		
	(a) Contacted via Mailed Questionnaire	1,097	20.4
	(b) Contacted Directly	2,616	48.7
3	Total Number of Respondents	3,713	69.0
4	Successful, i.e. who established industry	935	25.2

Note: Rate of success calculated on the basis of 3,713 respondents.

According to a national-level study on effectiveness of EDPs, the success rate of EDPs is reported at 25.95 % (Awasthi and Sebastian 1996). Relatively speaking, out of every 10 trainees, only 3 started their enterprises.

In its above study, the IIE classified its respondents into three categories: achievers, dreamers and duds. Here, it is worth mentioning that obtaining such information through mail was virtually impossible, hence the above classification relates to 2,616 trainees only those who were contacted directly. Their category- wise distribution is given in Table 11.5.

Table 11.5: Category-wise Number of Respondents

Sl. No.	*Classification*	*Number*	*Per cent*
1	Total Number of Trainees	5,375	
2	Respondents contacted directly	2,616	100.0
3	Achievers contacted directly	569	21.8
4	Dreamers	541	20.6
5	Duds	1,506	57.6

It is startling to note that of the 78 percent trainees who did not start their enterprises, 58 percent were duds, i.e. who have altogether given up the idea to establish any enterprise. In other words, training interventions could not motivate around three-fifths of trainees at all to start their enterprises. This, in turn, underlines the relevance of training interventions to motivate people to become entrepreneurs. Attempt was also made in the study identify the reasons for not establishing enterprises by the trainees. Following were the major reasons reported.

Table 11.6: Reasons for Not Establishing Enterprises

Reasons	*Dreamers*	*Duds*
Problem of fund	483(89.2)	1,107(73.5)
Lack of Encouragement	192(35.4)	286(19.1)
Government Policy	206(38.0)	—
Legal Formalities	168(31.0)	—
Problem of Marketing	173(32.0)	182(12.1)
Family Problems	—	560(37.3)
Problem of Row Material	143(26.4)	156(10.4)
Problem of Electricity	152(28.00)	—
Factory Land /Shed	100(22.00)	218 (14.5)

Note: Most of the respondents reported more than one reason for not establishing their units.

It is seen from figured in Table 11.6 that problems of fund, raw material, government policies, family problems, and legal formalities are the major reasons in that order deterring the trainees to start their enterprises.

Development of Small-Scale Industries in the NER: An Overview

Entrepreneurship precedes enterprise. Thus, entrepreneurship gets its reflection on small –scale enterprises. Hence, in any discussion on entrepreneurship development, a mention about the development of small-scale industries is inescapable. In fact, development of industries is already limited in the NER, but much more limited is the availability of data on whatever industries exist there. Nonetheless, based on available data, an overview of development of industries in the NER is presented in the following Table 11.7.

Table 11.7: Industrial Development in the NER (An Overview)

States	*Large and Medium Scale*	*Small-Scale Enterprises*
Arunachal Pradesh	**17(9.55)**	**4,520(10.22)**
Assam	129(72.48)	23,637(53.47)
Manipur	12(6.74)	6,000(13.58)
Meghalaya	10(5.62)	2,629(5.92)
Mizoram	1(0.56)	4,333(9.80)
Nagaland	7(3.93)	982(2.23)
Tripura	2(1.12)	2,114(4.78)
Total	178(100.00)	44,207 (100.00)

Source: Indian Institute of Entrepreneurship, Guwahati, 2000.

The already very small number of industrial units is highly unevenly distributed among the states in the NER (Table 11.7). For example, while around 54 percent industrial units are concentrated in Assam alone, industrial activity in Nagaland and Tripura is almost in non-existence. Manipur and Arunachal Pradesh come next to Assam in terms of number of industrial units working over there. Figures in Table 11.7 like that of Table 11.1 also indicate that the entrepreneurship, or say, industrial development is still at a very low level in the NER.

This is also a matter of great concern that not only the number of industrial units is small in the NER, but most of them (53 per cent) are plagued by sickness also. In most of the cases, the sickness has advanced to such an extent that it has rendered them unviable. To quote, in March 1999, out of a total of 23, 506 sick small –scale industries in the entire North-East Region, as many as 19,766 units (85 per cent) were termed as non-viable. Speaking alternatively, out of every 10 sick small-scale industries, 8 were non-viable. These are at the brink of their death. Sooner or later their closure is sure. The scenario of state-wise sick small –scale industries in the NER is presented in Table 11.8.

Table 11.8: State-wise Sick Small-Scale Industries in the NER (March 1999)

States	*Viable*	*Non-viable*	*Viability not Decided*	*Total Sick Units*
Arunachal Pradesh	6	102	8	116
Assam	581	9,003	705	10,289
Manipur	391	4,367	479	5,237
Meghalaya	21	401	25	447
Mizoram	—	40	0	40
Nagaland	3	160	3	166
Tripura	549	5693	672	6,914
Total	1,551	19,766	1,892	23,209

Source: Indian Institute of Entrepreneurship, Guwahati.

The main evil effects of industrial sickness on an economy have been locking up the economy's financial resources, wastage of scarce capital assets, loss of production, and loss in employment or increase in unemployment (Khanka 1992). Thus, sickness benefits none and industrial sickness is a bane on the Indian economy. According to a study of the Indian Institute of Entrepreneurship, Guwahati, about 24 per cent of small-scale industries have already been closed by now in the entire NER and another about 85 per cent are at the brink of their closure (see Table 11.8). Then , it is sure that it is going to aggravate the already prevalent mass unemployment hovering in the region. The fact remains that the problem of unemployment has been the root cause of disturbances in the NER whose manifestation in various forms has become a threat for the NER and the country as well. Increasing incidence of industrial sickness also presents an unhappy example for the prospective entrepreneurs that there in no scope for career for them in industry. Possibly, this is one of the important reasons why the local unemployed youth are not coming forward to start their enterprises in spite of the Government's pronouncements to offer various incentives and concessions to establish industries in the NER. Here, it seems pertinent to make a mention about the various incentives and concessions the Government offers to entrepreneurs to establish industries in the NER.

It is evident by now that whatever industrial development has so far taken place in the NER, it is mainly concentrated in Assam. Hence, it seems pertinent to make a mention of the incentives and concessions offered by the Government of Assam to the entrepreneurs to establish industries in the State.

The Government of Assam has so far announced its five Industrial Policies in 1982, 1986, 1991, 1997 and 2003. The Industrial Policy 2003 is effective from 1st October 2003 and will be valid for a period of 5 years i.e. up to 30th September 2008 unless modified/terminated whichever is earlier. The Government has announced a 10-year new policy with nomenclature the *North East Industrial and Investment Promotion Policy (NEIIPP), 2007* that would include Sikkim for the first time under its ambit. The very nomenclature itself indicates its departure from the old one in so far as its scope and subsidy-contents are concerned. The NEIIPP 2007 includes the following twelve main features:

(i) Under NEIIPP 2007, all new units as well as existing units which go in for substantial expansion, unless otherwise specified and which commence commercial production within the 10 year period from the date of notification of NEIIPP, 2007 will be eligible for incentives for a period of 10 years from the date of commencement of production.

(ii) The incentives under the NEIIPP, 2007 will be available to all industrial units, new as well as existing units, on their substantial expansion, located anywhere in the North Eastern Region. Consequently, the distinction between 'thrust' and 'non-thrust' industries made in NEIP, 1997 will be discontinued from the date of notification of NEIIPP 2007.

(iii) Under NEIIPP 2007, incentives on substantial expansion will be given to unts effecting 'an increase by not less than 25% in the value of fixed capital investment in plant and machinery for the purpose of expansion of capacity/modernization and diversification' as against an increase by 33 ½ % prescribed at present.

(iv) Under NEIIPP 2007, 100 % excise duty exemption will be continued as at present on finished products made in the North Eastern Region. However, in cases, where the CENVAT paid on the raw materials and intermediate products going into the production of finished products (other than the products which are otherwise exempt or subject to nil rate of duty) is higher than the excise duties payable on the finished products, ways and means to refund such overflow of CENVAT credit will be separately notified by the M/O Finance.

(v) 100 % income-tax exemption will continue under NEIIPP, 2007 as at present.

(vi) Capital investment subsidy will be enhanced from 15% of the investment in plant and machinery to 30% and the limit for automatic approval of subsidy at this rate will be Rs. 1.5 crore per unit as against Rs. 30 lakhs at present. Such subsidy will be applicableto units in the private sector, joint sector, co-operative sector as well as the units set up by the State Governments of the North Eastern Region. For grant of capital investment subsidy higher than Rs. 1.5 crore but upto a maximum of Rs. 30 crore, there will be an Empowered Committee.

(vii) Interest subsidy will be made available @ 3 % on working capital loan under NEIIPP 2007 as at present.

(viii) Under NEIIPP 2007, new industrial units as well as the existing units on their substantial expansion will be eligible for reimbursement of 100 % isurance premium under the Comprehensive Insurance Scheme (CIS).

(ix) To include tobacco and tobacco products, pan masala,

plastics carry bags and goods produced by refineries, in a host of industries which would not be eligible for incentives under NEIIPP, 2007.

(x) To provide incentives to service sector, bio-technology and power generating industries.

(xi) To continue North Eastern Development Finance Corporation Ltd. (NEDFi) as the nodal agency for disbursal and subsidies under NEIIPP, 2007.

(xii) In order to ensure that genuine industries come up in the region, the policy disallows concessions to goods in respect of which only peripheral activities take place. In order to have proper coordination and monitoring, a high level committee and an Advisory Committee along with an Over Sight Committee (OSC) will be set up.

The provisions of the NEIIPP, 2007 would provide the requisite incentives as well as an enabling environment to speed up the industrialization of the North Eastern Region which is otherwise less than 4 % p.a. against a national average of 8 %.

Concluding Remarks

As indicated by the various components, i.e. indicators of environment, in Table 11.3 the entrepreneurial environment of the North East India cannot be considered as favourable or conducive. That the environment for entrepreneurship development in the NER is unfavourable is also evidenced by the less number of small-scale industries established so far, on the one hand, and a large number of sick industries among the already less number of industries in the region, on the other. No doubt, the Government has made concerted efforts to create a favourable environment for entrepreneurship and enterprise development in the NER by offering special economic package, incentives and concessions to start small-scale enterprise, and the most recent effort is the Government of India's new industrial policy entitled *"North East Industrial and Investment Promotion Policy (NEIIPP), 2007"*. But, no perceptible improvement in the entrepreneurial scene of the region is, thus, suggestive of the fact that an environment becomes favourable or conducive for entrepreneurship and/or enterprise development only when it integrates all the required components of it. Unfortunately, like some other regions in the country, this is not the case in the NER. For example, fiscal and financial assistance can no way compensate for the lack of infrastructural facilities like transport, communication, marketing facilities, etc.

12

The Micro Study

Introduction

Entrepreneurship as one of the factors of production has, by now, assumed *primum mobile* role in industrial and economic development of a country. A cross-country examination reveals that entrepreneurship development precedes industrial and economic development and, thus, the development of latter has become *sine qua non* with the development of the former. The vital role that entrepreneurship development plays in an economy's economic development is best put as *"an economy is the effect for which entrepreneurship is the cause"*. That is why ever increasing emphasis has been given to entrepreneurship development everywhere in the world including India. India is the number one country in Asia which operates the largest initiatives for entrepreneurship development. The wide differences in levels of economic development of different regions within India are attributed mainly to differences in their levels of entrepreneurship development. The North Eastern Region (NER) of India presents one such case of low level of entrepreneurship development and, in turn, industrial and economic development (see Table 11.1). The poverty and unemployment stalking in the NER corroborate the notion that "poverty anywhere is dangerous for prosperity everywhere". Hence, the demand of the situation is to foster and promote economic development in the NER at the earliest possible. And entrepreneurship development has been considered as the most effective means to foster economic development through entrepreneurship development in the Region. The same underlines the need for and importance of undertaking a research study on entrepreneurship development in the NER of India.

Objectives, Hypotheses and Methodology

Rationale

The rationale of the present research study is imbued with mainly two justifications, namely, Economic Rationale and Academic Rationale.

Economic Rationale: Given the continuously increasing number of job seekers/unemployment, on the one hand, and continuous shrinking of jobs in the Government sector, on the other, there is a need to convert job seekers into job –providers to reduce and / or remove large –scale unemployment hovering the Region. The underlying belief is that just as 'self- help' is considered as the 'best-help', so is 'self–employment' considered as the 'best- employment'

Academic Rationale: No doubt, the literature on entrepreneurship by now is replete with various models and/ or theories of entrepreneurship development. Nonetheless, the significance of practical experiences gained in a particular context to the body of existing knowledge and new learning can be, by no account, contested on mainly two counts. *First*, proceeding from the general to the particular is more often than not perilous because authenticating the particular from the general, that too based on secondary sources, may not fit in a particular context. *Second*, the secondary sources often offer contestable interpretations and alternate views. Therefore, the context-specific actual experiences assume relevance and significance in search of new learning of the phenomenon of entrepreneurship.

Added to these is evidence to believe that limited is the level of entrepreneurship development in the NER, but much more limited is the availability of data on whatever entrepreneurship development exists there. Not only that, whatever data is available on entrepreneurship development is too much scanty, scattered and unsystematic. As such, due to the lack of reliable and systematic data on entrepreneurship development in the NER, some strong predilections of the policy-makers and certain assumptions made about the various aspects of entrepreneurship development, and often such assumptions have been treated as if they hold good for entrepreneurship development in different regions also. For example, it has been assumed that the entrepreneurs are born; that the entrepreneurs come from business family background; that the entrepreneurs' experience in business helps them perform better; and that incentives and concessions attract people to become entrepreneurs. Admittedly, a development strategy and a programme based on these assumptions would obviously fail to stimulate entrepreneurship development if the conditions prevalent in a region are found to be different (Papola 1985: 18).

There are reasons and evidences available to believe that the entrepreneurial scene in the country and for that matter in the NER is not necessarily characterized by above mentioned features, i.e assumptions. McClelland's "Kakinada Experiment in Andhra Pradesh (1961) which became basis for India's Entrepreneurship Development Programmes (EDPs) and his other motivational studies (1965) establish that the entrepreneurial ability which he calls ' need for achievement' can be developed. There is research evidence (Sharma 1975) to show that the entrepreneurs coming from non- business background has higher degree of entrepreneurial orientation and commitment to entrepreneurial function than the entrepreneurs coming from the business background. As regards the effectiveness of different kinds of promotional measures to promote entrepreneurship, research studies (Papola and Tiwari 1981) report, interestingly, that incentives and concessions are not necessarily the most effective measures for entrepreneurial promotions; they cannot, in any case, adequately compensate for the deficiencies of infrastructure. In the especially backward areas like the NER, their effectiveness may even be more doubtful in view of the serious problems of accessibility and linkages with markets outside the NER.

In the ultimate analysis, given the scanty, scattered and unsystematic data on entrepreneurship development in the NER, our knowledge of the NER in this matter has been far from adequate. Thus, any serious attempt at drawing plans for the entrepreneurship development of the NER is hampered by the non-availability of comprehensive, reliable and systematic data and information on this vital subject. This is an area in which not much research work has been done so far in the NER of India. The present study is, therefore, a pioneering attempt to make a modest contribution based on rare primary data in understanding entrepreneurial phenomenon in the NER.

Objectives

The main objective of the present research study is to delineate entrepreneurship development in the NER of India. However, the issue of entrepreneurship development, especially in a backward region like NER, is highly complex and intricate. It is difficult, if not impossible, to examine the issue of entrepreneurship development in its entirety in an individual study. The objective and scope of the present study are, therefore, inevitably limited to some major aspects of entrepreneurship development in the NER. The specific objectives we have set for ourselves in the present study are:

- That like other developments, entrepreneurship development is also context specific, hence, the first objective of the study is to delineate the entrepreneurial context of the NER.
- That the entrepreneurs belong to the distinct class of the society, therefore, the second objective we have set for ourselves is to present the entrepreneurial profile to know who they are.
- That there are certain driving forces that make a person entrepreneur, the next objective set is, accordingly, an excursion into the various driving forces involved in the making of an entrepreneur.
- That there are certain attributes that influence the entrepreneurial behaviour or performance, the next objective is set to ascertain the nature of relationship between the entrepreneurial attributes and their performance.

- That every context contains the promises and problems for development, the penultimate objective set for the study is to configure the major problems that impede the effective and vigorous display of the entrepreneurial role in the study region and also highlight the potential the NER holds within its fold for entrepreneurship development.
- That the ultimate objective of any research lies in recommending solutions to solve the identified problems, therefore, the last objective is set to submit suggestions and recommendations how to develop entrepreneurship in a more effective manner in the NER of India.

Hypotheses

The present study intends to test the following hypotheses which, except the last one, are drawn from the findings of earlier studies conducted in the subject.

(i) The entrepreneurs are likely to be drawn from varied socio-economic stratum particularly when specific incentives and facilities are provided to establish enterprises.

(ii) Entry into entrepreneurship particularly from non-business backgrounds is due to academic effulgence and prior work experience.

(iii) There are more than a motive or reason for an individual to plunge into entrepreneurship.

(iv) Entrepreneurial motivation undergoes change in pursuant to the entrepreneurial experience.

(v) The migrant entrepreneurs are likely to be more successful than the local ones.

(vi) The formal education and specific training positively influence the entrepreneurial performance.

(vii) The married entrepreneurs are more successful than the unmarried ones.

(viii) Entrepreneurs with the internal locus of control perform better than those with external locus of control.

(ix) One's business background helps perform better in business.

(x) Both awareness about various schemes and facilities offered for entrepreneurship development and attending entrepreneurship development programmes (EDPs) positively affect the entrepreneurial performance.

Major Concepts Used

It seems appropriate to put the technical things in a simple and non-technical way, because those who are actually to be benefited from technical writings may not have right kind of knowledge to grasp and understand the particular discipline. Keeping this fact in view, the major terms used at length in the present study, viz, Entrepreneur, Entrepreneurship, Enterprising Culture, and Small-Scale Industry, need to be conceptualized explicitly at the outset. Other concepts and terms have been defined wherever those are used in the study.

Entrepreneur: A person who creates some new venture, organizes factors of production, undertakes risks and handles economic uncertainty involved in enterprise/ venture. In other words, an entrepreneur is a person who undertakes a wealth creating and value adding process, through incubating ideas, assembling resources and making things happen.

Copreneurs: Copreneurs are entrepreneurial couples who work together as co-owners of their businesses. Unlike the traditional "Mom and Pop" (Pop as "boss" and Mom as "subordinate"), copreneurs are creating a division of labour that is based on expertise as opposed to gender." Studies show that companies co-owned by spouses represent one of the fastest-growing business sectors.

Entrepreneurship: Entrepreneurship is a set of attributes that and entrepreneur possesses and practices to establish and run the enterprise. It is the process of doing something new and / or something different for the purpose of creating wealth for the individual and adding value to society.

Intrapreneur: A person who pursues an innovation from within the security of his or her organizational position. He /

she is also termed as "intra-corporate entrepreneur."

Enterprising Culture: Enterprising culture is a commitment of the individual to the continuing pursuit of opportunities and developing an entrepreneurial endeavour to its growth potentials for the purpose of creating wealth for the individual and adding value to society.

Small–Scale Industry: An industry with fixed investment in plant and machinery up to the limit of Rs. 1.0 crore.

Tiny Enterprises: An enterprise with fixed investments in plant & machinery up to Rs. 25 lakh.

Micro Enterprises: An enterprise with fixed investment in plant & machinery up to Rs. 50 lakh.

Medium-Scale Industry: An industry with fixed investment in plant & machinery between Rs. 1.00 crore to Rs. 5.00 crore.

Large-Scale Industry: An industry having fixed investment in plant & machinery above Rs. 5.00 crore.

Export-Oriented Unit: Any small-scale industrial undertaking in which the investment in fixed assets in plant & machinery does not exceed Rupees one crore and the unit that exports at least 30 per cent of its annual production by the end of third year from the date of its commencement of production will be called **'export-oriented unit.'**

Family-Owned Business: Family business is one which is substantially controlled and/or managed by members of family and is succeeded by the next generation.

Scope and Methodology

Recognizing that the true display of the entrepreneurial role and attributes can well be seen only in case of the small entrepreneurs , i.e. the owners of the small–scale industries, the present study has, therefore, deliberately been limited to the small-scale industries for studying the phenomenon of entrepreneurship development. After selecting the industry for study, the next task was to choose a region, a state and districts subsequently for identifying suitable place for conducting this study. The three considerations that (i) the NER of India has been one of the most backward regions in India, (ii) the various studies undertaken so far on entrepreneurship development in India do not cover the NER entrepreneurs for indepth investigations.; and (iii) the maximum number of industries in the NER(around 54 % of small-scale industries and around 74 % of large and medium scale industries) are located in Assam alone followed by Manipur (see Table 11.7), became the important bases for selecting Assam and Manipur as the universe of the present study for survey purpose. Considering the dispersal of small-scale industries across the districts in the two states viz., Assam and Manipur, finally in all six districts- 05 districts, namely, Sonitpur, Kamrup, Nagaon, Dibrugarh, and Jorhat from Assam and 01 district namely, Imphal from Manipur were selected as the survey universe for the study.

The present study is based on both the secondary and primary data, yet mainly on the primary data. The major sources of secondary data are population statistics, annual survey of industries, basic statistics of NER, government websites, published and unpublished data from the district industry centers, etc. Besides, it also makes a fairly extensive use of the varied arguments and evidences advanced in earlier research studies and other relevant publications irrespective of their scope and coverage.

In order to make an excursion into the various aspects of the entrepreneurial phenomenon for which secondary data are either not available or too inadequate, we undertook a sample survey of small-scale industries (SSIs) in the six districts to collect relevant data on entrepreneurship development. For this, a structured questionnaire was prepared to collect data at enterprise level. For survey purpose, firstly, an up –to-date list of the registered SSIs was obtained from the office of the General Managers, District Industry Centers of the 06 sample districts. Then the two criteria were formulated to satisfy one's inclusion in the sample to suit the main objectives of the study. The two criteria formulated were:

(i) The entrepreneurs must be the first generation entrepreneurs, i.e. the entrepreneurs must have started their own enterprise even though they might have family business background. Thus, the entrepreneurs who were just running and managing the ancestral units have been excluded from the study.

(ii) Both manufacturing and service units running for at least last three years were included in the sample study.

For arriving at the actual size of the sample units, two approaches could have been employed. *The first* approach would have been to have a preliminary survey of all the small-scale industries working at these six districts collecting information regarding the two criteria mentioned earlier and, then, excluding those units which did not satisfy any one or both the conditions listed as criteria for selection. This process would have given the total units for the study and the size of the sample could have been drawn from this number. *The second* approach would have been to select more units than the desired sample size and then exclude those units that do not satisfy any one or both the conditions for their inclusion in the sample. Here, it was assumed that there is a random distribution of such units that are discarded from the total units. The first approach for the selection of the sample could not be employed because it would have involved the cumbersome preliminary survey of all the units situated at the six selected districts to adjudge the above mentioned two criteria for selection. Thus, the second approach was found to be more suitable and feasible for selection of sample in the present study.

In this approach, in the beginning a 75 percent sample size was drawn from the total number of SSIs working at the six districts, as reported by the respective District Industry Centers, by a simple random procedure using lottery method of selection. Then, those units which either did not respond or did not satisfy the two criteria set for one's inclusion in sample study were excluded from the total number of 75 per cent. Thus, questionnaires were put to those entrepreneurs who satisfied the two basic criteria formulated for this purpose.

In this way, 243 small–scale entrepreneurs (45 percent) were finally selected to collect the required data with a common schedule of questionnaire canvassed personally. Because of English language difficulties and reading and writing deficiencies, it was decided that the interviewer would ask the questions and fill out the responses of the interviewee. This was done for all the respondents. Interviewers were trained by the researcher through role-playing the administration of the questionnaire. A pre-test was made where the interviewers administered the questionnaire to a number of respondents. They rehearsed the process of asking the questions and filling in the responses. The survey work was conducted during June–October 2004. These 243 entrepreneurs represented seven categories of industries which appeared that all the categories have been well represented in the sample. With regard to the personal information (bio-data) of the entrepreneurs, in case of a partnership enterprise, bio-data of the most active partner who also initiated the promotion of the enterprise has been collected. Similarly, in case of private limited type of units, bio-data of the managing director, who also was the promoter of the company, has been collected. Thus, the information collected for 243 enterprises contain information of 243 entrepreneurs spread over headquarters of six districts.

No doubt, our sample covers entrepreneurs running seven categories of enterprises in six districts, but the region covered is a specially and typically backward one and has certain special characteristics of its own. Therefore, the findings may have only a limited validity in regions which have witnessed a relatively higher level of development and which have different contextual settings in terms of different endowments. Moreover, the sample is not necessarily representative of the structure of enterprises existing in the NER. The selection of enterprises is again purposive with a view to covering enterprises of diverse nature, each of which has a sizeable number of enterprise units operating in one or more districts. In fact, the focus has been on enterprise/industrial categories rather than on the area.

13

The Entrepreneurial Profile

Introduction

Before we delineate the profile of our sample entrepreneurs to trace out where they do emerge from, it seems in the fitness of the context to give an overview of the emergence of the entrepreneurs in historical perspective.

In fact, the emergence of entrepreneurs has been a hyperactive area in entrepreneurship research. Many researchers have studied the entrepreneurial background they emerge from. To cite, (Weber (1930) traced out the Prostestant Christianity as a source for the emergence of entrepreneurs. Sayigh (1962), Alexander (1964) and Carrol (1965) provided empirical evidences from Lebanon, Greece, and Phillippines respectively to argue that entrepreneurs do emerge from people with higher level of education. Other researchers like Kunkel (1970) and Young (1971: 139-49) reported that entrepreneurial talent is not equally distributed among population across societies and regions. Sharma (1980) identified particular social groups such as Marwaris and Paunjabis in India having high entrepreneurial talent. Nath (2000) has reported the emergence of entrepreneurs by regions and social groups in India. According to Ronstadt (1983), entrepreneurs mainly emerge from between the ages of twenty-five and forty-five. Hisrich and Peters (1995) identified one's past experience in business as a source of emergence of entrepreneurs.

Apart from the socioeconomic background of the

entrepreneurs, some researchers have also laid considerable emphasis on entrepreneurs' personality characteristics to know better who these people are. From this point of view, the two influential theoretical viewpoints are that of Schumpeter (1967) and Rotter (1966). In Schumpeter's opinion, persons with innovative nature are more likely to emerge as entrepreneurs. According to Rotter, persons with internal locus of control, i.e. those who believe that the most part of their future lies in their hands, have more tendency to assume the entrepreneurial career.

Having being given an overview of entrepreneurial emergence in historical perspective, now it will be interesting to trace out where the entrepreneurs of our study emerge from.

There is evidence and research to believe that the entrepreneurs form a distinct class in the society and all are not and cannot become entrepreneurs. Although the entrepreneurial history is replete with successful entrepreneurs, yet no one is typical entrepreneur. As such, there is really nothing as a "true entrepreneurial profile". Entrepreneurs come from a variety of educational backgrounds, family occupations, age-groups, and work experiences. Therefore, a potential entrepreneur may presently be a student, housewife, soldier, unemployed, secretary, salesperson, mechanic, manager, or engineer. A potential entrepreneur can be male or female and of any race, religion, region, or nationality. Hence, it seems pertinent, to first identify who they are before making probe into what and how they perform as entrepreneur. Hence, the delineation of the entrepreneurial profile.

The term 'entrepreneur' is defined differently by different thinkers and writers. Because of different meanings given to the the term 'entrepreneur', Kilby (1971: 40) has likened the entrepreneur with an animal called 'Heffalump' haunted by many individuals, but all unable to capture him/her. The early literature (for example by Richard Cantillon 1755, Jean-Baptiste Say, 1827: 285-286, Joseph A. Schumpeter 1934) associated entrepreneur with a person, often a risk-taker, business organizer, innovator, and profit seeker. We, in our study, adopt a more dynamic view of looking at entrepreneur and entrepreneurship as a person undertaking activities concerned with the discovery and exploitation of profitable opportunities (Stevenson and Jerillo 1990: 23, Venkataraman 2000: 217).

The entrepreneurial performance depends on the entrepreneurial responsiveness to the entrepreneurial functions. Research studies conducted in different countries have shown that host of factors including both the external such as material resources, industrial climate, and responsiveness of the political system and the internal factors such as entrepreneur's demographic characteristics, family background, psychological attributes, etc. exert their influence on the entrepreneurial responsiveness to the entrepreneurial functions (Kristiansen 2001: 43-60, Khanka 1990: 37-83, McClelland 1971, and Glade 1967). While the external factors have already been delineated in the preceding chapter, the internal factors are dissected and discussed in the present chapter.

The profile of entrepreneurs covered in the present study is submitted into the two broad categories:

I. Entrepreneurial Origin

II. Entrepreneurial Characteristics

ENTREPRENEURIAL ORIGIN

Periodic Origin

So far as the origin of the entrepreneurs is concerned, it is found that the most of the units covered in this study are relatively new/young. As seen from Table 13.1, nearly

Table 13.1: Enterprises by Period of Establishment

Period of Establishment	*Number of Units*
Prior to 1947	3 (1.22)
1948-1970	4 (1.64)
1971-1990	55 (22.71)
1991-2000	149 (61.30)
2001-2003	32 (13.13)
Total	**243(100.00)**

three-fourths of units were started during the post-liberalization period 1991 onwards. Till 1970, there were only 07 units established.

Thus, the industrial activity in Assam and for that matter, in the NER is of a recent origin mainly due to the Government's various incentives and concessions offered to establish small-scale industries, on the one hand, and expansion of entrepreneurial education and training in the recent years creating awareness about the entrepreneurial career among the local people, on the other.

Geographical Origin

Nearly half of the entrepreneurs (48.56%) are with their local origin and around one fourth (24.69%) are from the other districts of the state. The corresponding numbers of women entrepreneurs are expectedly quite larger, i.e. 66.67% and 25.00% respectively (see Table 13.2). The dominance of entrepreneurs with local origin is understandable in terms of what is called as ***"Homeland Factor"*** in the location of the industries (Weber 1910), i.e. one's familiarity with the local environment, market, government officials, nexus with family, friends and relatives which make it easier to establish and run the enterprise. It is interesting to note that not a single entrepreneur has come from other states within the NER. This is suggestive of the two things. **One,** unlike agriculture, industrial enterprise is not a freely mobile factor, willing to move any place for only marginal advantage. **Two,** the fiscal concessions and financial assistance offered on soft terms and conditions to establish industries cannot possibly compensate for the lack of inadequacy of infrastructural facilities like transport, communication, and marketing services (Papola and Tiwari 1985, Khanka 1990:131).

The choice of location of enterprise / industry has been a subject of research interest since the seminal work of Weber (1910) on **"Theory of Location of Industry".** Over the century, this research has resulted in a prodigious volume of publication. However, research on the changes related to location of industries also called 'the spatial distribution of industries' has mainly relied on two broad aspects: enterprise and territory. In the

Table 13.2: Geographical Origin of the Entrepreneurs

Geographical Origin	*Sonitpur*		*Kamrup*		*Nagaon*		*Dibrugarh*		*Jorhat*		*Imphal*		*Total*		
	M	*F*	*M*	*F*	*M*	*F*	*M*	*F*	*M*	*F*	*M*	*F*	*M*	*F*	*F*
Local	18	10	18	01	11	04	28	06	08	01	11	02	94 (45.41)	24 (66.67)	118 (48.56)
Beyond the	01	02	13	03	01	—	04	—	01	—	31	04	51 (24.64)	09 (25.00)	60 (24.69)
Local but within the State															
Beyond the state but within the NER	-	-	-	-	-	-	-	-	-	-	-	-	-	-	-
Beyond the NER	18	-	25	-	04	-	07	02	07	01	01	-	62 (29.95)	03 (8.33)	65 (26.75
Total	37	12	56	04	16	04	39	08	16	02	43	06	207 (100)	36 (100)	243 (100)

M=Male F = Female

first case, the attention focused on factors that determined the location choice of an industrial unit. In the second, the attention shifted to the nature of the industrial development in a specific region.

Of late, consequent upon the modification of the competitive milieu in the globalised economy, the considerations related to industry/enterprise location, among other things, have also been modified, and even changed. The choice of location of industry has, therefore, assumed significance in the entrepreneurial decision-making activity. Keeping this in view, we also tried to know the factors considered by our sample entrepreneurs while selecting a specific location for their enterprises.

In order to know the influence of factors in the choice of location, we asked the entrepreneurs in our questionnaire whether or not he or she had taken into account the location of factors. The degree of influence of various factors was measured in terms of the percentage of positive answers obtained by the factors in relation to all 243 entrepreneurs. For the convenience of analysis, we further classified all the influencing factors into three categories- (i) qualitative (e.g., strategic considerations, agglomeration economies and market features); (ii) subjective (e.g., the entrepreneurs' bondage in the area on account of personal circumstances); and (iii) regulation factors (e.g., factors related to state subsidies and regulations).

Table 13.3 gives the factors that influence the location choice of our sample entrepreneurs in aggregate.

It is seen from Table 13.3 that the subjective factors have the most influence (65.60%) in the choice of enterprise location for which reasons are not difficult to seek. Running enterprise at one's native place provides inevitable advantages like knowledge about the market, nexus and rapport with the various organizations to be dealt with while running the enterprise and, moreover, enjoying the psychological confidence of being the *"son of the soil"*. The female entrepreneurs, like else where in the country (Sethi 1999: 193), are more inclined to locate enterprises at the place of their residence so as to be able to simultaneously attend to their domestic responsibilities. Next come qualitative

Table 13.3: Aggregation of Factors Which Influenced the Location Choice

(in %)

	Qualitative Factors	*33.69*
1.	Low costs of Labour	10.32
2.	Availability of skilled labourers	28.67
3.	Availability of land at low cost	21.00
4.	Existence of basic infrastructural facilities	55.38
5.	Availability of raw material	40.62
6.	Availability of financial services	31.93
7.	Climate and environmental conditions	18.56
8.	Economic, social and political milieu	32.76
9.	Proximity to densely populated areas	38.39
10.	High number of customers in the area	63.43
11.	Low number of competitors in the area	29.56
	Subjective Factors	**65.60**
12.	Location coincides with the entrepreneur's residence	69.62
13.	Location belongs to the neighbourhood of the entrepreneur's residence	61.58
	Regulation Factors	**12.30**
14.	Availability of incentives, concessions and subsidies	9.38
15.	Availability of tax exemptions and concessions	8.94
16.	Labour and industrial laws	11.23
17.	Bureaucratization of the administration	19.68

factors (33.69%) in influencing one's choice of industrial location. Market; infrastructural facilities; raw material; population size; economic, social and political milieu; and financial services rank in that order in influencing the choice of enterprise location. The regulation factors are, however, found the least influencing the choice of enterprise location (12.30%). The likely reasons attributable to it are the entrepreneurs' awareness of the government regulations, complex and cumbersome procedure involved in availing of the facilities like subsidies and exemptions, and lack of infrastructural facilities making the government schemes ineffective.

It is worth mentioning that the subjective and objective (qualitative) factors are likely to undergo change in their influence on the choice of enterprise location. In pursuant to the entrepreneurial maturity, the subjective considerations like family/ community/ personal contacts become weaker and that of qualitative/economic imperatives grow stronger. The entrepreneurial maturity equips one better to avail of entrepreneurial opportunities wherever they arise (Raghupati 1995: 33-37).

Occupational Origin

While looking at the entrepreneurs in terms of their family occupational background, it is found that, like elsewhere in India, entrepreneurs still tend to come from business background (60.49%) and, thus, only a few are drawn from non-business background, i.e. farming (11.52%) and profession (27.99%) (see Table 13.4). This is because having an entrepreneurial / business family background provides a strong inspiration for becoming an entrepreneur. Besides, the independent nature of flexibility of self-employment exemplified by the entrepreneur father is ingrained in the mind of child at an early age. This is duly validated by one of our sample entrepreneur who stated: *"My father was so consumed by the venture he started and provided such a strong example, it never occurred to me to go to work for any one else."* This feeling of independence is often further enforced by an entrepreneurial mother. In this way, one's business background is found to serve as a cushion to opt for entrepreneurial career. However, there is also evidence to believe that, as a result of government initiative to develop entrepreneurship across regions and sections of the society, the entrepreneurship is becoming broad-based as increasing number of people belonging to non-business background are branching out into business / entrepreneurship (Nair and Pandey 2006: 52).

Table 13.4: Family Background of the Entrepreneurs

Districts	*Entrepreneurs' Family Occupation*			*Total*
	Farming	*Trade & Industry*	*Profession*	
Sonitpur	07 (14.28)	35 (71.44)	07 (14.28)	49
Kamrup	01 (1.67)	41 (68.33)	18 (30.00)	60
Nagaon	01 (5.00)	11 (55.00)	08 (40.00)	20
Dibrugarh	02 (4.26)	26 (55.32)	19 (40.42)	47
Jorhat	01 (5.56)	11 (61.11)	06 (33.33)	18
Imphal	16 (32.69)	23 (46.94)	10 (20.41)	49
Total	28 (11.52)	147 (60.49)	68 (27.99)	243

An examination of the entrepreneurs' last occupation / status before entering entrepreneurship reveals that nearly one-fourth (23.46%) shifted from paid / salaried job to business (see Table 13.5). Nearly 30% of the entrepreneurs came directly to their present venture either after completing their studies or undergoing some period of unemployment. One-fifth of the entrepreneurs who joined entrepreneurship with unpaid family workers as their previous status also might be either unemployed

Table 13.5: Previous Occupation / Status of the Entrepreneurs

Districts	*Previous Occupation/Status of theEntrepreneurs*				
	Business	*Paid Worker*	*Unpaid Family Worker*	*Student/ Unemployed*	*Total*
Sonitpur	7	13	16	13	49
Kamrup	22	10	07	21	60
Nagaon	4	6	3	7	20
Dibrugarh	18	9	11	9	47
Jorhat	5	9	1	3	18
Imphal	7	10	3	19	49
Total	65 (25.92)	57 (23.46)	51 (20.99)	72 (29.63)	243 (100)

Note: Figures in parentheses denote percentages to total.

or disguisedly unemployed. One-fourths of entrepreneurs (25.92%) were engaged in trading before coming to their present enterprises. On the whole, nearly 70% of the entrepreneurs were engaged in some activity before they entered into entrepreneurship.

Occupational Mobility

Occupational mobility denotes movement or changes in occupation which may take place in two forms. It may be a movement of a son / daughter from the principal occupational of his / her father or it may be a drift in one's own occupation during his / her occupational career. The first type of movement is called *inter-generation occupational mobility* and the latter type of movement is called *intra-generation occupational mobility*. The mobility is called horizontal when it takes place between the occupational classes of the equal rank or vertical when it occurs between classes of the unequal rank. Several factors like one's freedom of choice, motivation, efforts of an individual and opportunities available in the society determine one's occupational mobility.

Keeping this fact in view, an attempt has been made to trace out the occupational mobility from paternal grandfathers to the fathers of the entrepreneurs in the region of our study. It can be noticed from Table 13.6 that there is some evidence of occupational inheritance or stability, i.e. the tendency to follow one's own father's principal occupation. To cite, out of 228 grandfathers, 148 (65%) of the entrepreneurs followed their fathers' occupation. And, this inheritance is very much evident in the traditional occupations. For example, of the 102 business / industry owner grandfathers, 76 (75%) stayed in their fathers' occupation. Likewise, the occupational inheritance is also well observed in other occupations, i.e. farming and profession.

In spite of above observed occupational stability, there is definitely some degree of occupational mobility as well. For example, of the 73 farmer grandfathers, three-fifths (60%) have drifted from their fathers' main occupation. At the same time, a comparison of the 102 business / industry grandfathers with their 121 business / industry owner sons clearly reveals that the sons of farmer and professional grand-fathers have drifted to business and industry occupation. Thus, the change in occupation is from the primary to the secondary occupations.

Table 13.6: Inter-Generation Occupational Mobility of Entrepreneurs

Occupation of the Entrepreneurs' Fathers	*Occupation of the Paternal Grandfathers*				
	Farming	*Prfession*	*Business and Industry*	*Not Known*	*Total*
Farming	29	-	15	-	44 (18)
Profession	19	43	11	5	78 (32)
Business and Industry	25	10	76	10	121 (50)
Not Known	-	-	-	-	-
Total	73 (30)	53 (22)	102 (42)	15 (6)	243 (100)

Note: Figures in parentheses denote percentages to total.

Entrepreneurial Characteristics

Demographic variables are the hyperactive areas of behavioural research. Over the past half century and above, this research has resulted in a prodigious volume of literature. However, the entrepreneurial research as a relatively young field, it has been rife with controversy, breakthroughs and multiple paradigms. The question of how the entrepreneurial characteristics can affect the entrepreneurial roles has, however, been posed and pursued relatively infrequently. This underlines the need for identifying the entrepreneurial characteristics in a research study like the present one.

Sex

The sex-composition of our sample entrepreneurs is presented in Table 13.7. Like elsewhere in the world and India, the number of women entrepreneurs is far less that that of male entrepreneurs in the North-east India is indicated by over four-fifth proportion (85.19%) of the latter in the total sample size (see Table 13.7). The reason for such male dominance is not difficult to seek. As Birley (1989) notes, entrepreneurship is an activity that is situationally and culturally bound. The role of women has traditionally been seen by both men and women – to be that of wife and mother. Women bear the reproductive roles of childbearing and rearing, caring elders and, home management, and these responsibilities often lead to work-family conflicts. These, combined with problems arising from the lack of business experience, adequate education and training, spousal and / or family support, role models, inaccessibility to funds due to lack of collaterals, funders' perception of women's weak repaying capacity, difficulty in gaining the confidence of suppliers and clients, etc. have bearing on women in initiating, running and succeeding in business (Haq 1992: 195-203), Ghosh, Gupta and Dhar 1998: 159, Stevenson 1986 and Kanikar and Contractor 1994). The non-acceptance of women in business in an orthodox, traditional, and socio-cultural driven society of the North East India is yet an additional reason that explains the lesser number of women entrepreneurs in the region. On the whole, these, perhaps, are the main reasons why there are quite less studies and books published in India on women entrepreneurs than male entrepreneurs.

Table 13.7: Sex-Composition of Entrepreneurs

Districts	*Entrepreneurs*		*Total*
	Male	*Female*	
Assam: Sonitpur	37 (75.51)	12 (12.49)	49
Kamrup	56 (93.33)	4 (6.67)	60
Nagaon	16 (80.00)	4 (20.00)	20
Dibrugarh	39 (82.98)	8 (17.02)	47
Jorhat	16 (88.89)	2 (11.11)	18
Manipur: Imphal	43 (87.76)	6 (12.24)	49
Total	207 (85.19)	36 (14.81)	243

Note: Figures in parentheses denote percentages to total.

Marital Status

It is seen from Table 13.8 that more married persons than unmarried ones joined the entrepreneurial careers. This finding is similar to those found in other nations also (Rutten and Upadhya 1997: 1-13). This is suggestive of the fact that, people join entrepreneurship mainly due to 'push factors', or say, 'economic reasons' which Patel (1987) nomenclatures as *'forced entrepreneurs'*. However, this finding is contrary to the findings of earlier study carried out by the present researcher (Khanka 1990: 109) in Kumaun Division of Uttaranchal (earlier Uttar Pradesh) in which more unmarried persons (two-thirds) than married ones were found joining entrepreneurship. Most possibly, the contextual differences between the two regions explain the differences in findings. For example, Kumaun Division has been characterized by high degree of out-migration of married males from hills to plains in search of jobs (Khanka 1990).

Table 13.8: Marital Status of Entrepreneurs

Districts	*Marital Status of the Entrepreneurs (At the time of entry into entrepreneurship)*					
	Married		*Unmarried*		*Total*	
	Males	*Females*	*Males*	*Females*	*Married*	*Unmarried*
Assam:						
Sonitpur	28	7	9	5	35	14
Kamrup	54	4	2	-	58	2
Nagaon	16	4	-	-	20	-
Dibrugarh	33	6	6	2	39	8
Jorhat	11	2	5	-	13	5
Manipur:						
Imphal	37	5	6	1	42	7
Total	**179 (86.47)**	**28 (77.78)**	**28 (13.53)**	**8 (22.22)**	**207 (85.10)**	**36 (14.82)**

Looking at the sex-wise marital status of entrepreneurs, less number of married women (77.78%) than married men (86.47%) joined entrepreneurship for the understandable reasons as the former are to discharge the roles as mother, wife, and home manager maker.

Age

A break-up of entrepreneurs by age shows that, like elsewhere in India, the entrepreneurs are mostly young to middle aged (with average age of 41 years) with around 70% being within 30-50 years of age-bracket. This proportion is as high as 86% in case of women entrepreneurs (see Table 13.9). Further, those women entrepreneurs are comparatively younger to their male counterparts is well indicated by quite lower average age (37 years) of the former than that of the latter (42 years). This is explained by the fact that women, due to their reproductive roles in the later ages of marriage, find difficult to enter business. This finding is, however, contrary to the findings of other studies (Das 1999: 152) carried out in the Southern India (Kerala) in which larger number of women was found entering entrepreneurship during the later years of their middle age. This is, very possibly, because of Kerala's highest sex-ratio (1050) and the 100 per cent literacy rate of both male and female as against the Assam's one of the

Table 13.9: Age-Composition of Entrepreneurs

Age-Composition	*Number of Entrepreneurs*		*Total*
	Men	*Women*	
20-30	21 (10.14)	5 (13.89)	26 (10.70)
31-40	68 (32.86)	22 (61.11)	90 (37.04)
41-50	75 (36.23)	9 (25.00)	84 (34.57)
51-60	43 (20.77)	-	43 (17.69)
Total	207 (100.00)	36 (100.00)	243 (100.00)
Average Age	**42 Years**	**37 Years**	**41 Years**

Note: Figures in parentheses denote percentages to total.

lowest sex-ratio (932) and female literacy rate (46.7%). On the whole, the urn-shaped age-composition of the entrepreneurs is suggestive of the fact that the propensity to assume the entrepreneurial role, i.e. risk-taking role becomes the maximum in the prime of working age which tends to decline with the advancement in age.

In an attempt to find out if the birth-order has any effect on an individual's becoming an entrepreneur, more entrepreneurs (129 out of 243) in our sample were found to be the firstborn. There has so far not been any study conclusively establishing the relationship between the birth-order and entrepreneurs, nonetheless at least two reasons are attributed for such relationship in the present study. *One*, being the first born or an only child is postulated to result in the child receiving special and warm attention and thereby developing more self-confidence. *Second*, the first-born or only child is inevitably asked to do some petty-petty type of works relating to family matters including business matters which mould and tune the child unnoticingly towards doing / achieving attitude, i.e. the essential element, according to McClelland (1961), for becoming an entrepreneur.

Education

That the formal education is not a necessary condition for starting business enterprise is well evidenced from the success of high school drop-outs as Andrew Carnegie, William Durant, Henry Ford, William Lear, and Dhirajlal Hirachand Ambani (Dhirubhai Ambani). Nonetheless, it is interesting to note that around two-thirds of the entrepreneurs (65%) are either holding university degrees or technical diplomas (see Table 13.10), thus, the number of the entrepreneurs with school level of educational qualification is low (35%). This is suggestive of the fact that the propensity or willingness to take risk tends to increase with increase in level of education and vice versa (Nafziger 1979: 350-358). This is because education enlarges one's horizons of knowledge, helps deal with people and communicate clearly in written and spoken word which are important in any entrepreneurial activity. The smaller number of technical diploma and/or degree holders in spite of their more likelihood to make

Table 13.10: Educational Qualification of the Entrepreneurs (At the time of starting the enterprise)

Level of Education	*Assam*										*Manipur*		*Total*		
	Sonitpur		*Kamrup*		*Nagaon*		*Dibrugarh*		*Jorhat*		*Imphal*				
	M	*F*	*M*	*F*	*M*	*F*	*M*	*F*	*M*	*F*	*M*	*F*	*M*	*F*	*P*
Upro High School	20	10	5	2	9	-	5	2	4	1	20	3	63 (30.43)	18 (50)	81 (33.33)
Intermediate	4	-	-	-	-	-	1	-	-	-	-	-	5 (2.42)	-	5 (2.06)
Graduation and Post-Graduation	13	2	35	2	6	4	25	6	9	1	21	3	109 (52.66)	18 (50)	127 (52.26)
Technical Education (Diploma or Degree)	-	-	16	-	1	-	8	-	3	-	2	-	30 (14.49)	-	30 (12.35)
Total	37	12	56	4	16	4	39	8	16	2	43	6	207 36 (100)	(100)	243 (100)

M = Male, **F = Female, P = Person**

Note: Figures in parentheses denote percentages to total.

debut into manufacturing ventures is understandable in terms of much less number of such institutions imparting technical education in the region.

Concluding Remarks

Now, it can be concluded that entrepreneurs certainly form a distinct class in the society. This class may consist of any person with any educational, occupational background, age, with or without work experience, etc. He / she can be male or female, belong to any race, religion and nationality. Thus, entrepreneurs belong to the highly heterogeneous backgrounds. Hence, it becomes interesting to know what makes them move to become entrepreneur with such heterogeneity. A modest attempt is made in the next Chapter 14 to probe into the same.

14

The Entrepreneurial Motivation*

Introduction

We have seen in the previous chapter 13 who and what an entrepreneur is. We found an entrepreneur is *inter alia* a risk bearer who embarks on a different journey of starting and running an enterprise. Then, a few obvious but important questions arise: What prompts people to embark on such a difficult journey like entrepreneurship? Or, what motivates people to start their own business enterprise? The answer to this question, based on our sample study, has been attempted in this chapter.

Much concern is shown in the form of increasing attention focused on encouraging small business development, or say, entrepreneurship development in India by providing financial incentives, creating infrastructure, and deregulating restrictive legislation. Nonetheless, there does not seem expected and perceptible dent in entrepreneurship and small business development in the countryside. There are reasons and evidences to believe that both start-up and success of a small enterprise also depend on the initiative and motive of the individual entrepreneur to create and run a viable business (Vijaya and Kamalanabhan 1998). Therefore, discovering the factors that motivate the individual to embark on establishing a business enterprise assumes significance in developing entrepreneurship. Research evidence suggests that there has so far not been any

* This chapter draws heavily from S.S. Khanka, "Motivational Orientation of Assamese Entrepreneurs in SSE Sector," *The Journal of Entrepreneurship*, Vol. 17, No. 1, Jan. June, 2009.

detailed and systematic study in the NER discovering the individual's motivation to start their own business enterprises.

Why to Study Entrepreneurial Motivation?

Since long, there has been a debate, of course, inconclusive, about what causes entrepreneurship or creates enterprise: Whether environment or entrepreneur and which one is more important in that? Some hold the view that, like other developments, entrepreneurship development or enterprise creation are also contextual (Dana 1992: 126-130). Environment consisting of factors like government policies, market conditions, availability of inputs and resources etc. constitutes context for entrepreneurship development or enterprise creation. According to the supporters of this view, it is due to the changes in context or environment, enterprise development varies from context to context, or say, from place to place. But, there are other researchers also who argue that the person i.e. entrepreneur is in no way less significant in entrepreneurial or enterprise pursuit (McClelland 1961; Manimala 1986: 43-67). In an attempt to resolve the debate on whether entrepreneur –related factors are more or less important than environment-related factors, some researchers (Mac Millan & Block 1985 : 184-196) have brought in the analogy of horse and jockey in a race to say that both are equally important. They say it is important to note that while the jockey is not the creator of his horse, the entrepreneur is to a large extent responsible for the creation of his/her enterprise (Manimala & Pearson 1995). There is pre-eminence of the entrepreneur in the process of enterprise or venture creation. There is no denying the fact that the start up of a new enterprise would depend on many factors other than the entrepreneur, such as market, capital, inputs, technology, and the like. But, it is also true that these factors would create nothing unless they are coordinated by the entrepreneur. He/ she spots the opportunities, chooses the appropriate products and markets, arranges the required funds, selects the right people for right tasks, and so on. It then appears that the entrepreneur is an important factor in the process of enterprise creation. Then, the natural question arises is why he/ she is doing it. In other words, what motivates the entrepreneur to do all what is required to create and run his / her enterprise.

In fact, entrepreneurial motivation has emerged as a hyperactive area of behavioural research. Over the past half –century, this research has resulted in a prodigious volume of publication . A major thrust of this line of research came from the work of David C. McClelland (1961) which showed that the entrepreneurial person was characterized by high level of achievement motivation, a psychological construct originally proposed by Murray (1938) and measured by projective techniques such as Thematic Apperception Test (TAT). Murray's achievement motive was multi-dimensional and a combination of several motives, namely:

> To accomplish something difficult. To master, manipulate, or organize physical objects, human beings, or ideas. To do this as rapidly and independently as possible. To overcome obstacles and attain a high standard. To excel one's self. To rival and surpass others. To increase self-regard by the successful exercise of talent (Murray 1938: 164)

Let us try to examine the entrepreneurial (Achievement) motive as proposed by Murray with the help of a sequel to the story of the fox and the sour grapes as narrated by one entrepreneurs while talking about the motives of entrepreneurs (Manimala & Pearson 1998: 140-141). The fox in the story was being watched by his friends who were teasing him at his failure to get the grapes. This made the fox to prove himself and began to practice on regular basis for days together. At long last, the fox ultimately managed to bite off the grapes, only to confirm that they were really sour. But it was not so easy to admit that (sour) to his friends. Therefore, he pretended that they were sweet and went on eating more and more of them regularly. The ultimate result was the " high achiever" died of a peptic ulcer.

Though the story carries a lighter vein, it well highlights the important role that motive plays in promoting entrepreneurial behaviour. In this story, the underlying need of the fox was of ' ego need' which Murray referred to as "*self –regard*" in his list of the components of achievement motivation. Similarly, Murray's mention of the desire to achieve ' independently' refers to a separate motive called " the desire for independence."

An excursion into the available research reveals that the individual's decision to become the entrepreneur is the combined result of interaction of various factors. To cite, Collins and Moore (1964) report that there is empirical support for the fact that the need for independence, need for achievement, prior work experience, and being marginalized are dominant motivators for entrepreneurs. Similarly, in an attempt to review the literature, Vijaya and Kamalanabhan (1998) found that a number of motivational factors have been identified in entrepreneurs. These include the values placed on innovativeness, independence, outstanding performance, and respect for work.

It is against such backdrop of motives of entrepreneurs, it becomes quite legitimate for us to empirically look for the entrepreneurial motivation, i.e. ' why' of entrepreneurial behaviour of our sample entrepreneurs.

Motives of the Entrepreneurs of the Study

Motive implies the psychic force that ' moves' a person. Motivation too, like force, is a vector concept, i.e. it has both magnitude and direction. Magnitude of motive is understood in terms of its presence / absence or relative strength or degree of keenness. As regards direction of motivation, it can be understood in terms of multiplicity of goals or motives of one's behaviour. We have chosen in our study the 15 statements on motives on the basis of prior research on human motives. We have measured the keenness i.e. the degree of response of the entrepreneurs on each of the 15 statements using a Likert type five point scale as follows:

Degree of Response	*Numerical Value of the Degree*
Not at all	1
A Little Bit	2
To Some Extent	3
To a Large Extent	4
To Full Extent	5

The entrepreneurs' responses to the 15 motivating factors are shown in Table 14.1.

Table 14.1: Motivating Factors for Entrepreneurial Plunge

The Statements	*Mean Scores* *
1. Money motive	4.52
2. Independence / one's own boss	4.47
3. Provide greater comfort to family	4.39
4. Do something new and path-breaking	4.32
5. Reputation and recognition	4.16
6. Preside over a big business	4.05
7. Take family business to new heights	3.93
8. Do business because it is one's duty	3.85
9. Express one's creativity and ingenuity	3.76
10. Make optimum utilization of one's ability	3.66
11. Temperament fit between self and business	3.61
12. Contribute to the good of society	3.50
13. Desire to give financial security to one's kins	3.21
14. Flexibility of balancing work and family life	3.07
15. Enjoyable work	2.85

* Measured on a five point scale: 1= ' Not at all ' to 5 = ' To full extent'

Table 14.2: Average Response to Statements on Entrepreneurial Motivation

Type of Response	*Average Number of the Statements Checked by the Respondents*
No Response	4
Some Response	11

When we asked our respondent entrepreneurs to check the motivating factor for their entrepreneurial plunge or initiation, each of them checked more than one factors, of course, some of them in the same and other in varying degrees. On an overage, out of 15 close-ended statements, a respondent checked 11 of them (see Table 14.2).

Noticing more than one motivating factor checked by the respondents is not unlikely. The reason being , except in extreme cases of deprivation, human beings seek simultaneous satisfaction of different desires. This finding is enough evidence to uphold our hypothesis (iii):

" There is more than one motivating factor for an individual's entrepreneurial plunge."

Rather than interpreting each of the 15 statements individually, for the convenience of analysis, we have grouped all these statements into six major factors as shown in Table 14.3.

Table 14.3: Factor-wise Classification of Entrepreneurial Motives

	Factors	*Mean Score*
I.	**Self- Actualization Motive**	
1.	Money/ Economic motive	4.52
4.	Do something new and path-breaking	4.32
9.	Express one's creativity and ingenuity	3.76
10.	Make optimum use of one's ability	3.66
II.	**Nature of Work Motive**	
12.	Contribution to the good of society	3.50
15.	Enjoyable work	2.85
III.	**Autonomy and Power Motive**	
2.	Desire for Independence	4.47
6.	Preside over a big business	4.05
11.	Temperament fit between Self and business	3.61
14.	Flexibility of balancing work and family life	3.07

IV. Status Motive		
5.	Reputation and Recognition	4.15
7.	Take family business to new heights.	3.93
V. Affiliation Motive		
3.	Provide greater comfort to family	4.39
13.	Desire to give financial security to one's kins	3.21
VI. Deontic Motive		
8.	Do business because it is one's duty	3.85

Now, let us dwell on our interpretations and inferences about the motives of these 15 statements under six factors convey.

I. Self -Actualization

The term 'self-actualization' was coined by Kurt Goldstein (1939). According to Goldstein, self-actualization is an individual's motive to transform his/ her perception of self into reality Abraham H. Maslow (1954: 22) cited this term 'self-actualization' in explaining his popular ' Need – Hierarchy Theory of Motivation'. Maslow viewed that self –actualization is the acme of human motivation to become or achieve what one can. However, the kind of achievement that is implied in Masclow's sense is somewhat different from the achievement concept as proposed by McClelland (1961). Achievement of targets and standards is just one component of self-actualization concept as defined above, whereas the ' achievement concept' as defined by McClelland has two-hold focus (i) as desire to achieve one's own targets, and (ii) a desire to excel in comparison with others.

As for the self-actualization or achievement motive as defined by our data, there are four components in it in the order of their mean scores. The highest mean score of money/ economic motive (4.52) is understandable as the economic theory itself postulates " maximization of profits" as the business's objective or motive. Even in common perception, entrepreneurial motivation more often than not is described by the economic motive: "*money makes the mere go*". The classical economists like Adam Smith (1776) and Miltan Friedman (1962) also viewed the profit as the only motive of doing business. McClelland (1961) was also of the view that economic concern of entrepreneurs is, in fact, the symptom of strong achievement concern, since profitability provides the best and simplest measure of success. Peter Drucker (1970: 77) viewed profits as the necessary cost of being in and staying in business. Thus, these all support the existence of strong ***a priori*** reasons for an economic motive in business for an entrepreneur. Profit is oxygen to business.

The next component of this factor is desire to do something new and path breaking. Some researchers (Khandwalla 1985) have considered it as a separate and different motive compared to the desire to achieve high standards (McClelland 1961) on routine and humdrum tasks. Desire to express one's creativity and ingenuity and make optimum use of one's ability are yet another components under this factor which are very similar to the concept of self- actualization as enunciated by Kurt Goldstein (1939) and Abraham H. Maslow (1954).

II. Nature of Work

The second factor relates to the nature of work which is loaded by two components, namely, desire to contribute to the good of society and enjoyable work. There is research evidence (Sherrif 1958: 349-358) to believe that an entrepreneur's perceived contribution he/ she makes to the society becomes his /her super –ordinate goal to be achieved. This, in turn, enhances the unsefulness of his/ her endeavour. Enjoyable work implies one's intrinsic interest in his / her work. For example, job enrichment may make the work enjoyable and interesting to the entrepreneur. This factor is suggestive of the fact that the achievers would like to work on those tasks they would like and enjoy, and not one tasks just assigned to them. The same fact also suggests that not all individuals even with a high need for achievement motive are likely to become entrepreneurs.

III. Autonomy and Power Motive

There are four components loaded on this factor i.e. two each under autonomy and power. Autonomy implies freedom to decide about one's own matters. The two components, or say, variables indicating the autonomy are " desire for independence" and ' temperament fit between self and business' Research evidence suggests that desire for independence (read as autonomy) is the prime motivator of entrepreneurial behaviour. The two variables in the ' power component' are 'desire to preside over a big business' and ' flexibility of balancing work and family life'. Yet, there were some entrepreneurs categorical in saying that being a better business person was more important to them than becoming a big business man. In this regard, some would like quote N.R. Narayana Murthy (2001:10):" It is better to lose money than to act in ways that may make one lose a night's sleep."

IV. Status Motive

Social status implies standing or place of people in their society. Or say, it refers to esteem enjoyed by people from their society they belong. A measure of one's perception about one's status could, thus, be the prestige or esteem enjoyed among the equals and from those lower in status. We have sought to infer status motive of our entrepreneurs along these lines only. In our study, there are two components to this factor, namely desire for reputation and recognition' and 'desire to take family business to new heights'

Though both power and status motives form what is described by Maslow (1954) as 'ego' or ' esteem' needs. But, it appears that power and status motives need not always go together. The reason is not difficult to seek. For example, the reputation recognition and status attained by achiever's like artists (Satish Gujral), poets (Revindra Nath Tagore), writers (Khuswant Singh), etc, need not be accompanied by personal or positional powers. Similarly, even a top position or status need not always have powers with it. Ceremonial status / position with little power are examples of such cases. Converse may also be true. The people with power may have low status in the society. So to say, apparently there can be power without status and status without power.

There is a distinction between *'ascribed'* and *'achieved'* status. For example, entrepreneurs as a community may be having a particular position or status in the society. But, for an individual entrepreneur, the recognition and reputation among the entrepreneurial fraternity may have a greater motivational valence and value than the status simply by virtue of being a member of the (entrepreneurial) community. Entrepreneur's status is characterized by or say accoutrements, certain symbols, like attractive office, travel by air or car, stay in standard hotel, and image conscious while dealing with client and customers.

V. Affiliation Motive

Affiliation implies, among other things, a tendency of the people to confirm to the wishes and norms of those whom they value. In the entrepreneurial context, affiliation refers to belongingness which is something different and more than the ' Need for Affiliation' of McClelland (1961) and "Social Needs" of Maslow (1954). Belongingness implies one's obligations, commitment toward the people he/ she values. We have sought to infer the affiliation motive of the entrepreneurs studied in the present study along the same lines.

There are two components of the affiliation motive in the present analysis. They are the 'desire to provide greater comfort to the family' and ' desire to give financial security to one's kins'. This is understandable as per the Indian philosophy to make personal sacrifice for others' gain.

VI. Deontic Motive

Deontic motive is the last factor in our analysis which is defined by a single component, namely, ' to do business because it is one's duty.' It is worth mentioning that this kind of motive is rarely mentioned and discussed in the existing body of literature on motivation. The inclusion of this motive in the questionnaire was prompted largely by the response observed in case of some entrepreneurs during the survey work.

The Greek word *'deont'* means ' duty'. Accordingly, deontic motive implies one's (read as entrepreneur) duty or obligation or commitment to assume (entrepreneurial) task and responsibility for others cause or purpose. Manimala and Pearson (1998: 147) define deontic motivation as one arising from a sense of duty and / or a feeling of obligation. In other words, deontic motive can be defined as "working (becoming entrepreneur) because it is one's duty." We have inferred the stands of deontic motive of the entrepreneurs of our study along similar lines.

In the deontic sense, one may assumes entrepreneurial role both as by choice and compulsion. Plunging into entrepreneurship by one's choice makes it, what McGregor (1960) asserts, as enjoyable as play. At the same time, researchers like Schwartz (1983 : 203-214) unfold the other side of the same coin mentioning that a large majority of works have unpleasantness associated with them, yet people do them. For example, all people doing the tasks like cleaning toilets or reading the proofs of a telephone directory, do not like the same. Similarly, people who do not like their work would not like to stop it even if they are financially well-off. Joining family business without one's liking to keep on family business and identity alive may be one such example. All these point to the existence of some internals compulsions for the individual to work (to do business), which may be called the ' deontic motivation' for them.

Change in Motivation in Pursuant to Entrepreneurial Experience

Finally, an attempt has also been made to delve into the motivational dynamics of our sample entrepreneurs mainly based on two cues. ***One,*** human needs, as suggested by Abraham Maslow (1954), follow a hierarchical order from lower to higher order needs. ***Second,*** motivation to start a business enterprise and to remain there could be different. For example, Stanworth and Curran (1973:89-128) have elaborated how the entrepreneurial goal succession i.e., motivation in terms of the changing entrepreneurial roles change in response to diverse factors such as the firm's internal and external developments and the entrepreneur's perception of these. For example, as the business grows, the entrepreneur is required to play the role more of an 'implementer' i.e., manager rather than that of a 'doer' i.e., workman. Likewise, competitive situations may compel the entrepreneur to assign more consideration for achievement of business results than enjoy the personal autonomy. In other words, the entrepreneur needs to embroider his actions and roles in such a way as to suit to both the individual and organizational goals. Such a shift in entrepreneurial roles is called entrepreneurial transition from 'role playing' to 'role making'. It, thus, shows that the change in goal succession results in change in entrepreneurial motivation, also called ***'motivational dynamics.'***

Based on such background, we also tried to know the change in the motivation of our sample entrepreneurs. Table 14.4 bears out this information.

Table 14.4: Change in Entrepreneurial Motivation in Pursuant to Experience

At Start	*Pursuant to Experience*
Self-Actualization	Self-actualization
Nature of Work	Status
Autonomy and Power	Nature of Work
Status	Deontic
Affiliation	Affiliation
Deontic	Autonomy and Power

As seen from Table 14.4, some significant changes in entrepreneurial motivation pursuant to entrepreneurial experience are worth noticing. Two motives, namely, self-actualization and affiliation out of six motives have not changed, i.e. retained their ranks what were at start. This is quite understandable in the sense that an entrepreneur always needs to earn certain income to discharge his economic responsibilities. This is particularly so in view of serious threats by business environment posed to the survival of small enterprises. The recent Competition Bill of the Government of India, for example, has become deterrence of small-scale enterprises. As such, small enterprises have to earn minimum revenue for their survival.

Status and deontic motives move up two steps each. There is research evidence (Maslow 1954) to believe that once a need is satisfied, it ceases to remain as a need and then a higher order and altogether different need emerges. Having fulfilled economic requirements, it is expected that entrepreneur may perceive need for status and recognition and also may have feeling to perform his duty of running the business for the benefit of others, i.e. family members. Therefore, upward movement in motives like status and deontic seem well in order (Saxena 2005: 171). What is most worth noticing is a complete metamorphosis in autonomy and power motive moving down from third rank at start to the last rank 6 in pursuant to the entrepreneurial experience over the period. This is very possibly due to the reason, as reported by Stanworth and Currant (1973) also, that when business expands and grows in due course of time, the entrepreneur needs to play the role of implementer rather that of doer. The reason is obvious and simple. Operation of business becomes more and more complex with growth in business. The entrepreneur himself finds it difficult to deal with different and complex type of matters. Hence, he/she goes for decentralization of decision making through delegation of authority. This feature is quite evident in the family business in India like Tata, Birlas and Ambanis.

In view of above noticed dynamics of entrepreneurial motivation, we uphold the hypothesis that:

"The entrepreneurial motivation changes in pursuant to entrepreneurial experience."

Concluding Remarks

The present chapter was guided by the objective of examining motivational factors among entrepreneurs in Assam. Based on the findings we arrived at, it can be concluded that the major motivational factors for entrepreneurs to start their own enterprises were survival, financial independence and security, personal growth, and recognition. Based on factor analysis, it can be concluded that the following factors were common to entrepreneurs: Self-actualizaion, nature of work, autonomy and power, status, affiliation, and deontic.

Following are some tentative inferences based on our findings:

- The achievement motivation (n'ach) is expressed by an entrepreneur's need for realizing oneself through work and developing and exploiting one's full potential.
- The 'esteem' or 'ego' needs as designated by Maslow seem to be a combination of two motives, namely 'the power motive' and 'the status motive'. It also seems that there can be power without status and vice versa.
- Affiliation motive is reflected by getting support from and accepted by those who value for one (read as entrepreneur).
- Deontic motive arises from a sense of duty and / or a feeling of obligation to others one (read as entrepreneur) cares for.

15

The Entrepreneurial Performance

Having investigated into the entrepreneurial profile and motivation in the preceding chapters 13 and 14 respectively, an excursion into the performance of our sample entrepreneurs seems logical sequence in the study. Hence, the present chapter dwells on the entrepreneurial performance. Before we empirically examine the performance of our 243 sample entrepreneurs, it seems pertinent to first give a theoretical perspective on entrepreneurial performance.

The Entrepreneurial Performance: A Theoretical Perspective

What is performance? In general connotation, performance is outcome or result from an activity in relation to its determinants such as efforts and inputs. Sometimes, some people use the two terms 'performance' and 'rewards' as synonymous and use interchangeably. However, these two terms refer to two different meanings. Performance refers to tangible outcomes like profit earned or loss incurred, percentage of marks obtained, number of units produced, etc. But reward refers to pay- offs, also expressed as recompense from an activity. Thus, reward includes both tangible (for example, financial) and intangible (for example, psychic) incomes or outcomes. A reward may inhere in the activity itself such as the joy of playing cricket, its successful completion i.e., scoring century or even outside these in the form of an accolade, i.e., 'the man of the match', or 'the man of the series'.

As regards the entrepreneurial performance, it relates to both performance (economic) and reward (psychic) incomes. Research findings report that psychic income matters more than economic performance to sustain the entrepreneurial pursuit (Storey 2000: 242-286). They also advance the thesis that entrepreneurs differ in their thresholds of performance, and survival and exit are determined by whether economic performance stays above or falls below that specific threshold. This is well validated by our finding also (see Table 14.2) that entrepreneurial motivation changes from economic, which Abraham Maslow (1954) nomenclatures as 'lower level motivation', to non- economic, again in Maslow's words 'higher order motivation' in pursuit to entrepreneurial experience or survival. This can also be interpreted as the entrepreneurs who assign more importance to psychic income to their endeavours are expected to accept a lower level of economic performance or even, to some extent in some cases, negative performance. Family business in India presents one such example where business is not carried out mainly as a source of income but mainly as an embodiment of family's pride and prestige. In view of above, it would be interesting to see as to how the entrepreneurs of our sample study are performing.

For the purposes of our study, we have investigated into the economic performance only of our sample entrepreneurs mainly due to three reasons. *One,* the most of our entrepreneurs did not respond to our questions in pilot survey relating to their psychic reward/performance perhaps because of their lack of perception and understanding about their psychic performance/ income. *Two,* assessment of psychic income involves quite complex methodology. *Three,* the psychic performance ultimately boils down to the economic performance.

The entrepreneurial performance can theoretically be assessed based on various parameters using different tools and techniques. However, our study is circumspect in this regard also because of either no or highly inadequate response from the entrepreneurs to many of questions inserted in our questionnaire. Given the fact that the effect of various performance parameters is ultimately reflected in the form of profitability, i.e. profit or loss, we have, therefore, conveniently tried to assess the performance of our sample entrepreneurs in terms of the single and sole parameter of 'profitability'.

What determines profitability or entrepreneurial performance? Different researchers have reported different determinants of entrepreneurial performance. For example, Davis (1977) viewed entrepreneurial performance as a function of motivation and ability. As for the determinants of entrepreneurial performance, some researchers substitute 'motivation' and 'ability' by 'willingness' and 'opportunity'. They consider the 'individual preferences for the special features of self employments' and 'available outside options and their perceived attractiveness' as the determinants of entrepreneurial willingness and, in turn, performance (Praag and Ophen 1995: 513-540). There are other researchers who consider entrepreneurial performance as a function of entrepreneurial constellations, also called 'entrepreneurial domain' or 'context'. Accordingly, they postulate the entrepreneurial performance = f (Entrepreneurs' Social Backgrounds, Motivational Forces, Knowledge and Abilities, Financial Strength and Environmental Variables). It is against this backdrop, we can now profitably examine the performance of our sample entrepreneurs in relation to various determinants.

THE ENTREPRENEURIAL PERFORMANCE

Place of Origin

Table 15.1 bears information on entrepreneurs' performance in relation to their place of origin in terms of local (native and outsider (migrant) entrepreneurs.

Table 15.1: Entrepreneurial Performance in Relation to Place of Origin

Place of Origin	*Profit*	*No Profit*	*Total*
Local	140 (61.9)	86 (38.1)	226
Outsider	04 (23.5)	13 (76.5)	17
Total	144 (59.2)	99 (40.8)	243

N.B.: Figures in parentheses denote percentages to total.

$$E_{11} = \frac{144 \times 226}{243} = 133.97$$

$$E_{12} = \frac{99 \times 226}{243} = 92.07$$

$$E_{21} = \frac{144 \times 17}{243} = 10.07$$

$$E_{22} = \frac{99 \times 17}{243} = 06.93$$

$$X^2 = \frac{(140-133.93)^2}{133.93} + \frac{(86-92.07)^2}{92.07} + \frac{(04-10.07)^2}{10.07} + \frac{(13-6.93)^2}{6.9}$$

$= 0.275+0.400 + 3.658 + 5.317$

$= 9.650$

Table value of X^2 at 1 d.f. at 5 % = 3.841.

Thus, calculated value is > Tabulated value.

Thus, it establishes the significance of the place of native origin in the entrepreneurial performance.

Besides, that the native place as the entrepreneurial origin bears more impact on the entrepreneurial performance is well indicated by an exceedingly large number of native entrepreneurs (61.9%) earning profit than their outsider counterparts (23.5%). Thus, our hypothesis that the migrant entrepreneurs are more successful than the local ones does not hold true. This is mainly due to *"the son of the soil"* factor. That is, the local entrepreneurs enjoy some obvious advantages like awareness about the market and personal, family, and community rapport with people and organizations in the area/ location which help them get their things done more easily as compared to outsider (migrant) entrepreneurs who are new and strangers to the area in several respects.

Location of Enterprise / Industry

Location of enterprise / industry and its impact on enterprise performance has been a hyperactive area of industrial or entrepreneurship research since way back in 1909, when Alfred Weber enunciated the *"Theory of Industrial Location"*. Hence, a brief mention about theoretical perspective on location of industries seems pertinent.. As per the early theories of industrial location, entrepreneurs locate their industries at the place where the cost of production comes to the lowest, at least, at the time of establishing the industries. Therefore, the early theories of industrial location carried out the analysis on a simple framework where the locational and spatial diversification where simply determined by an adjustment between location and weight distance characteristics of inputs and outputs. The reason is that the then industrial structure was heavily dominated by the natural resource base and consumer-oriented industries. But, over the period, the very consideration for locating industries in a particular region has undergone a considerable change so the early theories of industrial location have become improper to explain location. Consideration of natural resources in the choice of industrial location has declined and the industries are likely to be established even in those areas with poor natural endowment. This holds especially true in the case of industries that are not heavily biased in favour of raw materials resources for their location. It is seen that such industries i.e. light in input weight and high in value, are gaining increasingly greater importance in the industrial map of India during the recent decades (Papola & Tiwari 1981:21).

Looking at the performance of our simple entrepreneurs in relation to their location of industries, it is found (see table 15.2) that the entrepreneurs who established their enterprises at the home place have been more successful (78 percent) than those who established outside the home place (44%). That the location of enterprise at the home place bears significant impact on entrepreneurial performance is also confirmed by a very high calculated value (82.81) at 1 d.f. at 5%. This is mainly due to *two reasons* as is revealed earlier in the Table 13.3 also. *One,* running enterprise at one's home place provides certain inevitable edges like knowledge about the market, nexus and rapport with the various organizations to be dealt with while running the enterprise, and moreover, enjoying the psychological confidence of being the *"son of the soil."* This is more so in case of women entrepreneurs for the obvious reasons.

Table 15.2: Entrepreneurial Performance in Relation to the Location of Enterprise

Location of Industry	*Entrepreneurial Performance*		*Total*
	Profit	*No Profit*	
At Home Place	85	24	109
Outsider Home Place	59	75	134
Total	144	99	243

$$E_{11} = \frac{144 \times 109}{243} = 64.59$$

$$E_{12} = \frac{99 \times 109}{243} = 44.41$$

$$E_{21} = \frac{144 \times 134}{243} = 79.41$$

$$E_{22} = \frac{99 \times 134}{243} = 54.59$$

$$X^2 = \frac{(85 - 64.59)^2}{64.59} + \frac{(24 - 44.41)^2}{44.41} + \frac{(59 - 79.41)^2}{79.41} + \frac{(75 - 54.59)^2}{54.59}$$

Second, unlike agriculture, an enterprise is not a freely mobile factor willing to move to any place for only marginal advantage in comparison to more disadvantages like unawareness about the market and people in a new place i.e., outside the home place. There is research evidence to believe that, more often than not, entrepreneurs who move to the outside home place to establish their enterprises to avail of incentives and concessions incur more disadvantages in terms of, for example, lack of infrastructural facilities. This, in turn, leads to loss and even the closure of the unit.

Sex

In the recent times, the increasing number of women entering entrepreneurship has attracted the increasing attention of researchers in behavioral sciences to know the differences, if any, between male and female entrepreneurs in their entrepreneurial behaviour (Hisrich and Peters 2002: 74-77). In view of this, we do also made an attempt to find out if the gender serves as a significant variable in entrepreneurial behaviour or performance (see Table 15.3)

Table 15.3: Entrepreneurial Performance in Relation to Sex

Sex	*Entrepreneurial . Performance*		*Total*
	Profit	*No Profit*	
Male	118 (58)	86 (42)	204
Female	26 (67)	13 (33)	39
Total	144	99	243

N.B. : Figures in parentheses denote percentage total.

$$E_{11} = \frac{144 \times 204}{243} = 120.89$$

$$E_{12} = \frac{99 \times 204}{243} = 83.11$$

$$E_{21} = \frac{144 \times 39}{243} = 23.11$$

$$E_{22} = \frac{99 \times 39}{243} = 15.89$$

$$X^2 = \frac{(118-120.89)^2}{120.89} + \frac{(86-83.11)^2}{83.11} + \frac{(26-23.11)^2}{23.11} + \frac{(13-15.89)^2}{15.89}$$

$$= \frac{(-2.89)^2}{120.89} + \frac{(2.89)^2}{83.11} + \frac{(2.89)^2}{23.11} + \frac{(-2.89)^2}{15.89}$$

$$= \frac{8.3521}{120.89} + \frac{8.3521}{83.11} + \frac{8.3521}{23.11} + \frac{8.3521}{15.89}$$

$$=0.0690884 + 0.1004945 + 0.3614063 + 0.5256198$$

$$= 1.056609 \text{ or } 1.06$$

Table value of x^2 at 1 d.f. at 5 % is 3.841. Thus, calculated value < Table value. Thus, the result is insignificant at 5 % establishing that sex does not matter in the entrepreneurial performance.

This is, to some extent, understandable in the sense that men in India enjoy better position in terms of education, experience, and economic background. Nonetheless, a mere count of the number of female entrepreneurs does not rule out their performance. That around two-thirds of total female entrepreneurs (67%) earning profits as against nearly three–fifths (58%) of total male entrepreneurs is suggestive of the better performances of the former than the latter. This is attributable to two reasons. *One,* females by nature are less ambitious than their male counterparts. This holds true in the entrepreneurial pursuits also (Sexena 2005: 198). *Two,* while the male entrepreneurs mainly run manufacturing enterprises, female entrepreneurs run service-related enterprises and researchers report that the latter type of enterprises are less risk-oriented than those of former ones.

Education

Like sex, the education of the entrepreneurs has also received significant research attention. This is because education opens and enlarges entrepreneur's horizons of knowledge and learning which, in turn, help him/ her deal with people and communicate effectively in written and spoken words which are considered important in any entrepreneurial activity. Alternatively speaking, education helps the entrepreneur better understand and cope with the problems he/ she confront. Keeping this in view, we also tried to see whether education has a bearing in influencing the entrepreneurial performance. However, the education is not found playing any significant role in the performance of our sample entrepreneurs (see Table 15.4) as is well indicated by far lower calculated value (0.733) than tabulated value (3.841).

Table 15.4: Entrepreneurial Performance in Relation to Education

Education	*Entrepreneurial Performance*		*Total*
	Profit	*No Profit*	
General/ Technical	102 (61.08)	65 (38.92)	167
Other	42 (55.26)	34 (44.74)	76
Total	144	99	243

N.B.: Figures in parentheses denote percentage total.

The evidence given in Table 15.4 does not lend much support to the view that educated entrepreneurs perform better. Two reasons can be attributed to our finding. *One,* that like pursuing the political career, the formal education is not necessary for starting and running an enterprise. Our finding is duly supported by the remarkable success of some of the illiterate and / or high school dropout entrepreneurs world over like Andrew Carnegie, Henry Ford, Thomas Edison Alwa, William Durant, William Lear, and Dhirajlal Hirachand Ambani, fondly known as 'Dhiru Bhai Ambani'. The fact remains that it is not the entrepreneur's education, but his/ her entrepreneurial acumen that matters in the performance and makes all the difference in the entrepreneurial performance. *Two,* research evidence shows that the education i.e., technical and professional education, suitable for running business enterprises influences the entrepreneurial performance (Nair and Pandey 2006: 55). But, in our sample study of 243 entrepreneurs, there were only 3% entrepreneurs with technical education and that too with ITI and polytechnic level. There were as many as 40% entrepreneurs with education up to school level only and remaining (57%) with degree level in general stream (see Table 13.10). Thus, academic effulgence is found insignificant in influencing the entrepreneurial performance. This our hypothesis that the formal education influences the entrepreneurial performance does not hold true.

Marital Status

Table 15.5 gives the classification of entrepreneurial performance on the basis of their marital status.

Table 15.5: Entrepreneurial Performance in Relation to Marital Status

Marital Status	*Performance*		*Total*
	Profit	*No Profit*	
Married	115	92	207
Unmarried	29	07	36
Total	144	99	243

$$E_{11} = \frac{144 \times 207}{243} = 122.67$$

$$E_{12} = \frac{99 \times 207}{243} = 84.33$$

$$E_{21} = \frac{144 \times 36}{243} = 21.33$$

$$E_{22} = \frac{99 \times 36}{243} = 14.67$$

$$X^2 = \frac{(115-122.67)^2}{122.67} + \frac{(92-84.33)^2}{84.33} + \frac{(29-21.33)^2}{21.33} + \frac{(7-14.67)^2}{14.67}$$

$=$

$=0.48 + 0.7 + 2.76 + 4.01$

$=7.95$

Thus, calculated value (7.95) > Tabulated value (3.841).

It can be seen from Table 15.5 that married entrepreneurs perform better than their unmarried counterparts as is indicated by a quite higher calculated value (7.95) than the tabulated value (3.841) at 1 d.f. at 5%.

Thus, our hypothesis that the married entrepreneurs are more successful than their unmarried counterparts is held true. This is because (i) Since marriage takes place relatively at an older age which implies more maturity on the part of the entrepreneurs. Maturity enables entrepreneurs to cope better with business problems and, in turn, perform better. (ii) Marital (married) status especially with children involves more obligations and responsibilities to be discharged which obviously raises one's need for more income or higher performance.

Though we could not classify entrepreneurial performance in relation to marital status by sex, yet our observation suggests that like elsewhere in India (Gibb 1992:1-15), married female entrepreneurs are more successful than their male counterparts. The reasons attributable to this are: (i) Female entrepreneurs especially with grown up children experience reduced duties associated with their reproductive roles (child bearing and rearing, household tasks and care of the elderly) which enables them to focus more on their business and, in turn, perform better. The most successful female entrepreneurs like Shanaz Hussain and Kiran Mazumdar–Shaw and many well performing ones lend support to our above observation-cum-finding. In fact, marital status and age run parallel for female entrepreneurs. (ii) The civic status also plays an important role for women in the Indian society. Once a woman marries, she is seen to be more secure and well protected. As a result, she enjoys more liberty to take up a new venture that originates from her 'real home' which is her husband's or her in–law's home. The husband, more often than not, becomes a source of strength to run her venture. (iii) Moreover, more facilities and incentives are available for female entrepreneurs.

Locus of Control

A person when thinks to embark on an enterprise formation,

one major concern haunts him/ her whether he /she will be able to sustain the enterprising spirit or drive and energy required to overcome the *inertia* in establishing an enterprise and also manage and make it grow. The answer to it lies in one's locus of drive toward enterprise. As per the behavioural sciences, one who thinks that he/ she has control over the success or failure of his/her venture is termed as a person with *'internal locus of control'*. On the contrary, one who thinks that the success or failure of his/her venture is beyond his/ her control is termed as a person with *'external locus of control'*. Research is so far inconclusive about the definite role of *'locus of control'* in entrepreneurship (Rotter 1966). Nonetheless, most of the studies report that more successful entrepreneurs are decidedly with internal locus of control, and the entrepreneurs overall are more internal than the general populace (Brockhaus 1980: 368-72 and Brockhaus and Nord 1979 : 364-68).

As regards the role of locus of control in the performance of our sample entrepreneurs, it is found that the larger number of successful entrepreneurs is with internal locus of control whether indicated by the number of internals earned profit out of total entrepreneurs earned profit (60.4% or 87 out of 144 entrepreneurs) or the number of entrepreneurs earned profit out of total entrepreneurs with internal locus of control (73.7% or 87 out of 118 entrepreneurs).

Table 15.6: Entrepreneurial Performance in Relation to Locus of Control

Marital Status	*Performance*		*Total*
	Profit	*No Profit*	
Internal	87(73.7)	31(26.3)	118
External	57(45.6)	68(54.4)	125
Total	144	99	243

Note: Figures within parentheses denote percentage to total.

The entrepreneurial history is replete with evidences that one's self-efficacy and strong determination, to a great extent, overcome external barriers and pitfalls on the way of one's entrepreneurial journey.

The internal locus of control of Shahnaz Hussain, one of the most successful women entrepreneurs in the world, supports it: **"I do not believe in destiny- the word 'fail' does not exist in my dictionary. I never fail, because I tried things with sheer grit and determination and succeeded and only succeeded."** Similar was the internal locus of control displayed by Abraham Lincon: **"Always remember in your mind that your own resolution to succeed is more important than any one thing".**

Family Background

The research findings on the relationship between one's business family background and the success in business have so far been inconclusive. For example, there are research studies reporting that the entrepreneurs belonging to business background perform better than those with non-business background. (Khanka 1990:107 -108, Kazmi 1999:70). The main reason ascribed to such finding was the family business background serves as a cushion for entrepreneurial activity. Contrary to it, a study on the characteristics of entrepreneurs conducted in Kerala (Nair & Pandey 2006: 57) indicated that the spirit of entrepreneurship and the degree of entrepreneurial success were not directly related to the family business background of the entrepreneurs.

Evidence of our 243 sample entrepreneurs given in Table 15.7, does not lend much support to the view that the entrepreneurs' family business background matters in success in business (as being the calculated value 0.0086 is quite lower than the tabulated value 3.841). A close look at the total number of entrepreneurs belonging to business background and out of those earned profit is suggestive of the fact that one's business background may be helpful in entering the business but not necessarily to become successful in it. The success stories of some of our exemplary entrepreneurs like (Late) Dhiru Bhai Ambani, N. R. Narayana Murthy, Kiran Mazumdar-Shaw, and Sunil Bharati Mittal who came from non- business background, lend support to our finding.

Table 15.7: Entrepreneurial Performance in Relation to Family Background

Family Background	*Performance*		*Total*
	Profit	*No Profit*	
Business background	127	87	214
Non Business background	17	12	29
Total	144	99	243

$$E_{11} = \frac{144 \times 29}{243} = 16.71$$

$$E_{12} = \frac{99 \times 29}{243} = 11.81$$

$$E_{21} = \frac{144 \times 214}{243} = 126.81$$

$$E_{22} = \frac{99 \times 214}{243} = 87.19$$

$$X^2 = \frac{(127-126.81)^2}{126.81} + \frac{(87-87.19)^2}{87.19} + \frac{(17-16.71)^2}{16.71} + \frac{(12-11.81)^2}{11.81}$$

$$= 0.0002 + 0.0004 + 0.005 + 0.003$$

$$=0.0086$$

Two reasons can be attributed to our findings. *One,* one's non-business background is, to a large extent, compensated by the various incentives, concessions, and facilities. offered by the government to attract people to become entrepreneurs. This has helped the people without business background become entrepreneurs. That is the reason how entrepreneurship in India, of late, has become broad-based. *Second,* the ever increasing emphasis on entrepreneurship development through education and training interventions has helped shape and mould the attitude and orientation of the people suitable for business.

Added to these is the erstwhile rule of thumb practice in running business is no longer effective in today's highly competitive business environment. In today's era of the *'survival of the fittest'*, one requires specialized knowledge, skills, and techniques to run business effectively and successfully.

Entrepreneurship Development Programmes (EDPs)

In India, EDPs have been conducted since 1971 with an objective to develop entrepreneurship and, in turn, small-scale enterprises in the country. Today, India operates the oldest and largest programmes for entrepreneurship development in any developing country. The Indian model of entrepreneurship development is being adopted by some of the developing countries of Asia and Africa. In view of this, any attempt on studying entrepreneurship development will remain incomplete without examining the impact of EDPs on entrepreneurship development of a region. It is against this backdrop, we have also tried to examine the impact of EDPs on the performance of our sample entrepreneurs mainly with regard to two aspects: (i) Awareness of promotional activities and facilities, and (ii) Attending the EDPs.

That the awareness of promotional activities and facilities helps the entrepreneurs perform better is well evidenced by 72.8% or 134 out of 184 entrepreneurs with awareness of promotional activities and facilities earned profit as against merely 16.9% or 10 out of 59 entrepreneurs without awareness of promotional activities and facilities (see Table 15.8). This is also duly substantiated by an exceedingly higher calculated value (57.76) than the tabulated value (3.841). The reason is not difficult to seek. The awareness of promotional activities and facilities enables the entrepreneurs to complete the procedural formalities more smoothly involved in availing of facilities offered for running an enterprise. This, in turn, helps the entrepreneurs run their enterprises more effectively and successfully.

Table 15.8: Entrepreneurial Performance in Relation to Their Awareness of Promotional Facilities

Awareness	*Performance*		*Total*
	Profit	*No Profit*	
Aware	134 (72.8)	50 (27.2)	184
Unaware	10 (16.9)	49 (83.1)	59
Total	144	99	243

N.B. : Figures in parentheses denote percentage total.

$$E_{11} = \frac{144 \times 184}{243} = 109.04$$

$$E_{12} = \frac{99 \times 184}{243} = 74.96$$

$$E_{21} = \frac{144 \times 59}{243} = 34.96$$

$$E_{22} = \frac{99 \times 59}{243} = 24.04$$

$$X^2 = \frac{(134-109.04)^2}{109.04} + \frac{(50-74.96)^2}{74.96} + \frac{(10-34.96)^2}{34.96} + \frac{(49-24.04)^2}{24.04}$$

$$= 05.71 + 08.31 + 17.82 + 25.92$$

$$= 57.76$$

Like other studies (Awasthi & Sebastian 1996 and Dutta 2000), the evidence given in Table 15.9 lends support to the view that attending EDPs has been quite effective in entrepreneurial performance. Going merely by the absolute number, 93 % or 40 out of 43 entrepreneurs who attended EDPs, earned profit as against 52% or 104 out of 200 entrepreneurs who did not attend. Further, a quite higher calculated value (24.67) than tabulated value (3.841) also confirms the significance of EDPs in improving entrepreneurial performance. The reason being the participants during the EDP are being exposed to almost all aspects of an enterprise starting from the identification and selection of a business idea to actual running of an enterprise.

Table 15.9: Entrepreneurial Performance in Relation to EDPs Attended

EDPs	*Performance*		*Total*
	Profit	*No Profit*	
Attended	40	03	43
Not –Attended	104	96	200
Total	144	99	243

N.B. : Figures in parentheses denote percentage total.

$$E_{11} = \frac{144 \times 43}{243} = 25.48$$

$$E_{12} = \frac{99 \times 43}{243} = 17.52$$

$$E_{21} = \frac{144 \times 200}{243} = 118.52$$

$$E_{22} = \frac{99 \times 200}{243} = 81.48$$

$$X^2 = \frac{(40-25.48)^2}{25.48} + \frac{(03-17.52)^2}{17.52} + \frac{(104-118.52)^2}{118.52} + \frac{(96-81.48)^2}{81.48}$$

$$= 08.27 + 12.03 + 01.78 + 02.59$$

$$= 24.67$$

Such an exposure obviously facilitates the entrepreneurs perform their roles more effectively and, in turn, run their enterprises smoothly and successfully. There is research evidence to support our above inference that the entrepreneurial success and direct supervision with managerial ability are positively associated (Panda 2000: 210). Reverse is also confirmed by research studies reporting that around two-thirds of industrial units fell sick due to poor management, or say, mismanagement of one type or other (Mehta 1988:186 and Srivastava and Yadav 1986.)

Concluding Remarks

As regards the entrepreneurial performance, it relates to both performance (economic) and reward (psychic) incomes. Research studies report that psychic income matters more than economic performance to sustain the entrepreneurial pursuit. We have assessed the performance of our sample entrepreneurs based on sole criterion of profitability. An analysis of the entrepreneurial performance in relation to various variables like the locational origin of entrepreneurs, location of enterprise, gender, education, marital status, locus of control, family background, awareness about entrepreneurship development programmes (EDPs), and participation in EDPs affect the entrepreneurial (economic) performance. While some variables like local, male, married, and with internal locus of control affect the entrepreneurial performance positively, others like formal education and business background affect adversely. The training interventions in terms of EDPs are found helpful in improving entrepreneurial performance.

16

The Entrepreneurial Problems and Prospects

Introduction

The concerted efforts in the field of entrepreneurship development in India formally started by the Gujarat Industrial and Investment Corporation (GIIC) in 1970. Since then there is no looking back in this direction. It's a cliché to mention that Assam has been among the pioneers in developing entrepreneurship development with a noble intervention named 'Entrepreneurial Motivation Training Centres (EMTCs')' in India, yet there has not been any expected and perceptible dent in the entrepreneurial and industrial front in Assam and North-East India. But unfortunately that is the case. It, then, implies that there are still some problems or lacunae or weaknesses in our endeavour of entrepreneurship and/or enterprise development. Efforts have already made by the researchers to find out the same. (Awasthi and Sebastian 1996, Dutta 2000, Ahluwalia 2001).

There are reasons and evidences to believe that the problems and prospects for any type of development are context specific and, therefore, are likely to vary from context (region) to context (region). Keeping this in view, it seems quite logical and pertinent to try to probe into the specific problems of entrepreneurship development in the North East India, in general, and in Assam, in particular.

The Entrepreneurial Problems

For the convenience of analysis, we have classified the entrepreneurial problems into two broad categories: I. Problems Based on the Primary Data, and II. Problems Based on the Secondary Sources. These are discussed one by one.

Based on Primary Data

Based on previous researches, evidences, and observations, we inserted specific problems of entrepreneurship development in our Questionnaire. While processing the data, we noticed that, like factors of motivation in Chapter 14, some entrepreneurs reported only one major problem while others counted more problems than one as major problems in entrepreneurship or enterprise development. We found it difficult to categorize them into degrees and types. Therefore, in order to regard all the respondents at par, only the most crucial problem was taken into consideration in all cases. This signifies the fact that one specific problem might have been regarded by all the entrepreneur-respondents as the most crucial one faced by them in developing their enterprises. The distribution of such entrepreneurs on the basis of their most crucial problem faced in entrepreneurship or enterprise development is presented in Table 16.1.

Table 16.1: Problems of Entrepreneurship Development

Problems	*Male*	*Female*	*Total*
• Raw Material	12 (6.38)	01 (3.12)	13 (5.99)
• Capital	23 (12.33)	11 (34.37)	34 (15.67)
• Market	34 (18.08)	06 (18.75)	40 (18,43)
• Infrastructural Facilities	38 (20.21)	05 (15.63)	43 (19.81)
• Manpower	11 (5.85)	02 (6.24)	13 (5.99)
• Law and Order	39 (20.74)	03 (9.36)	42 (19.35)
• Procedural Formalities	28 (16,41)	04 (12.53)	32 (14.76)
Total	185 (100.00)	32 (100.00)	217 (100.00)

It is seen from Table 16.1 that the major problems of entrepreneurship development in the study region are the problems relating to infrastructural facilities (19.81%), law and order (19.35%), market (18.43%), and procedural complexities (14.76%) in that order. Yes, as is reported in other studies as well (Nair & Pandey 2006), there is significant variation in the intensity of these problems between male and female entrepreneurs which is understandable in the sense of gender distinctiveness with regard to entrepreneurial career. For example, while the problems of law and order and infrastructural facilities are the two most serious problems faced by the male entrepreneurs, the problem of capital and market turn out as the most serious problems for the female entrepreneurs for which the reasons are not difficult to seek. Females in general lack in both own fund and also the possibility for obtaining fund from institutional sources because of lack of collaterals on their names to pledge against the loans. As regards the market problem, it can be attributed to two reasons: *one,* lack of knowledge about the market, and *two,* lack of required resources like skill and capital for advertising and sales promotion of one's product or service among the prospective customers. The problems of market and infrastructural facilities rank the third serious most problems for male and female entrepreneurs respectively. However, the problem of procedural complexities turns out the fourth major problem in entrepreneurship development for both male and female entrepreneurs. It is believed that both the governmental efforts to simplify the procedural formalities like *'Single Window System'* and increasing awareness about formalities to be completed by the entrepreneurs have eased the procedural complexities, to a large extent. This belief is supported by the validity of our hypothesis, in Chapter 15, that both the awareness and participation in entrepreneurship development programmes by the people help them perform better. The problems of raw material and manpower rank the lowest in order because most of the enterprises established in the region are based on local resources and skill.

Let us discuss some of these serious problems in more detail.

Problems of Infrastructural Facilities: There is research evidence to believe that a minimum level of prior built-up infrastructural development is required to undertake any economic activity including industrial activity (Papola & Tiwari 1981). Thus, there is a positive relationship between infrastructural development and industrial development. But, that the level of infrastructural development is at a quite low level in the North East Region (NER) as compared to the country as a whole is indicated by various indicators of infrastructural facilities shown in Table 11.1. For instance, the credit-deposit ratio, the common indicator of fund availability for industrial purposes in the NER is as low as just the half (28.31%) of the national average (57.20%). Similarly, the development of transport facility, i.e. roads has been at a very low level in the NER is well indicated by the 54.80% kms. Length of roads per 100 sq. kms area as against 74.90 kms per 100 sq. kms area in the country as a whole. The result is the lack of minimum level of required infrastructural facilities holds the region back in making use of advantages and resources the NER holds within its fold for enterprise and economic development of the region. As such, problem relating to infrastructural facilities has turned out as the most serious problem for the entrepreneurs of the study (19.81%).

Unstable and Uncertain Law and Order Situation: The highly unstable and uncertain law and order situation hovering the North-East India for quite long time has been reported by our sample entrepreneurs as the second most serious problem (19.35%) in entrepreneurship or enterprise development in the region. Evidences available from both within and outside India confirm that the unstable law and order situation makes the environment as non-conducive for enterprise development. The problem of terrorism prevalent in the Indian Punjab in the past confirms this. The consequence is while the number of well-established entrepreneurs both local and migrant entrepreneurs have been either closing or shifting their enterprises to outside the NER is continuously on increase, on the one hand, the new entrepreneurs are hesitant rather scared to establish industries in the disturbed NER, on the other. According to a study conducted by the Indian Institute of Entrepreneurship (IIE), Guwahati, about 24 per cent of industrial units have been closed in the entire NER in 1998 and 85 per cent of sick small-scale industries are non-viable, i.e. these are on the verge of their closure. The plight of industries in the region is by all indicators dismal and prognostic.

Problem of Market: As per our sample entrepreneurs, market has turned out as yet another major problem (18.43%) in entrepreneurship or enterprise development. The various problems relating to marketing include the lack of knowledge in marketing; lack of marketing facilities like transportation, cold storage, fare price, etc; sales promotion; and competition with products manufactured by medium and large-scale enterprises. The problem of marketing is more serious for women entrepreneurs (18.75%) as compared to male entrepreneurs (18.08%) mainly due to the gender reasons.

Promotional Formalities: An entrepreneur has to follow a prescribed procedure in establishing his /her enterprise. The entrepreneur has to approach to the officials of different Departments which are often located at different places. The money, time and energy of the entrepreneur to be spent in the process lower his enthusiasm to establish an industry. So much so, the entrepreneur being so much fed up or puzzled with the complex and cumbersome process gives up idea of establishing any industry. Besides, the time-consuming procedure leads to cost overrun. The result is the enterprise falls prey to the inadequacy of funds, or say, suffers from malnutrition since birth. M/S Saraswati Woollen Mills (P) Ltd., Ranikhet (Uttaranchal) represents the classical example of cost-overrun and time-overrun on account of procedural delays (Khanka 1990). This mill was registered in 1973 and it got an industrial license two years later, it took about 9 years for it to build the factory shed, install the machinery and go into production. The evil effects of the procedural delays were seen in the cost escalation of the project from Rs. 32 lakhs in 1973 to Rs. 56 lakhs in 1981.

Problem of Capital: Earlier the lack of required capital used to be one of the major problems faced by the entrepreneurs in establishing and running their enterprises. However, the availability of capital/funds on soft terms from the banks and financial institutions, on the one hand, and requirement for relatively less capital for establishing small-scale enterprises, on the other, have eased the problem of capital for enterprise development. Nonetheless, that capital has still been a problem faced by the entrepreneurs is indicated by the fact that one out of every six entrepreneurs still faces the problem of capital in establishing and developing his / her enterprise. Further, that the problem of capital is graver for women entrepreneurs is revealed from the fact that one out of every three women entrepreneurs has reported the problem of capital. The reason for this is not difficult to seek. Women in India still do not have properties in their names and, as a result, they fail in providing the collaterals to the funding agencies against the loan asked by them. Added to this is their overall weak economic condition that makes even the friends and relatives hesitant to extend financial help to the women entrepreneurs.

Based on Secondary Data

In this section, we present the problems in entrepreneurship development based on excursion into the previous researches, reports, and programmes to substantiate our findings on the problems of entrepreneurship/enterprise development as discussed earlier under section *Based on Primary Data.* For the convenience of presentation, we have classified the evidences from secondary sources into two broad categories, namely:

I. Entrepreneurial Interventions

II. Entrepreneurial Schemes

These are discussed in seriatim.

I. Entrepreneurial Interventions: Realizing that the development of required human resources, rechristened as 'entrepreneurs' is a pre-condition for establishing and successful running of enterprises, the Government of India embarked on conducting entrepreneurial interventions popularly known as EDPs since 1970. Since then, there is no looking back in this direction. By now, EDP in India has emerged as a national movement. However, the success in this endeavour is not satisfactory as only around 26% of the EDP trainees actually establish enterprises (Awasthi & Sebastian 1996 and Dutta 2000). Obviously, a question arises is why the success or effectiveness of the EDPs is so low. The answer to this question, as reported in some research studies, is a host of factors are responsible for such low effectiveness of EDPs. The major ones among them are the wrong selection of EDP trainees, inadequate infrastructural facilities, lack of skilled and trained instructors, the antithetic attitude on the part of concerned officers towards EDPs, and absence or inappropriate method devised to measure the effectiveness of EDPs.

II. Entrepreneurial Schemes: With a view to compliment the entrepreneurial interventions, the entrepreneurial schemes and policies are devised and offered to the entrepreneurs to make their enterprises successful. There are reasons and evidences to believe that these schemes for one reason or other have, however, not been proved effective as expected. Of the major reasons are discussed hereunder:

(i) Procedural Complexities: That the procedure involved in availing of facilities like concessions, subsidies, tax exemptions, etc. is complex and cumbersome is a common feature of our promotional schemes. Research findings (Papola and Tiwari 1981) report that even after completing the cumbersome procedural formalities, the entrepreneurs get only meager help which they do not find worth in terms of time, energy, and money spent by them to avail of it. In simple words, the benefits received are less than the costs incurred by the entrepreneurs. Hence, the most of the entrepreneurs give up the idea to apply for availing of the benefits offered under different schemes. Then, this serves as an unhappy example for the prospective entrepreneurs as well. Thus, the procedural complexities adversely affect the both-the present entrepreneurs and prospective entrepreneurs.

(ii) Lack of Complimentary Facilities: Evidences are available to confirm that enterprise establishment and development is a function of different factors and/or efforts that are often complimentary to each other. So to say, one's absence or ineffectiveness renders the other/s too as infructuous. From this point of view, the availability of concessions, subsidies, and incentives is not found to adequately compensate for the lack of basic infrastructural facilities (Papola and Tiwari 1981 and Khanka 1994). This has resulted in the Governmental facilities as non-attraction for people to establish industries to avail of the facilities, on the one hand, and the emergence of pseudo entrepreneurs to avail of various promotional facilities offered by the Government, on the other. One of the evil effects of the lack of infrastructural facilities for enterprise development also leads to the misuse of the facilities towards non-enterprise purposes. These are *inter alia* the reasons why sickness in small-scale enterprises has been continuously on increase in spite of the Governmental support and facilities extended to the entrepreneurs.

Lack of Required Human Resources

The problem of unemployment and uncertain law and order situation hovering the Region has propelled mainly the males to migrate to outside the NER in search of education and job. The increasing outflow of males from the NER has been continuously on increase for quite some years. If this trend is not curbed, it is going to create serious implications from more than entrepreneurial angle. The immediate consequence of the absence of many young men from the region results in increase in the proportion of other groups, namely, women, children, or the old in the population. A higher sex-ratio in the NER (for example, 978 in Manipur and 975 in Meghalaya) is well indicative of it (see Table 11.1) . In nutshell, out–migration of males results in denudation of population with such qualities as skills, education, entrepreneurship and beacon of new orders (Oberai and Singh 1983 and Khanka 1984). Such a population structure has its own implications for economic activities like entrepreneurial and industrial activities.

The Prospects

The remote and undulating topography of the NER not only poses problems for economic and entrepreneurship development, but also possesses good prospects within its fold for its development (Anonymous 2002). The trite saying of "poverty amidst plenty" squarely holds true of the NER. There are few regions in the world that can boast of the treasure house of variety of resources that North-East India possesses. Here is an overview of the same:

- The region has about 8 percent of the country's total land space with 4 percent of the country's population. Thus, NE enjoys a distinct demographic edge over the rest of the country.
- It is an emergency market of 400 million people.
- It has potential to be India's future powerhouse by having 38 percent of hydropower potential of the country because of the presence of the country's largest perennial water system, natural gas reserves of 190 billion cubic meters, coal reserves of 909 million tones, hydroelectric potential estimated at 49,000 MW, oil reserves of 513 million tones.
- Large mineral resources including limestone reserves of 4,933 million tones and a forest cover which is 25 percent of the country's total forest area.
- Enjoys phenomenal bio-diversity be it the forest wealth, agro-base, fruit and vegetables, herbs, aromatic, plants, exotic flowers, other flora and fauna.
- Almost 98 percent of its boarders form India's international boundaries- a veritable gateway to the South-East and, in turn, to the world. China to the North, Bangladesh in the South-West, Myanmar in the East and Bhutan in the North-West share borders with the North East Region (NER) of India. Thus, the NER possesses strong potential to be a future international trading *hot spot* and a strategic base for foreign and domestic investors to tap the vast contiguous markets of Mynmar, China, Malaysia, Thailand, Singapore, Philippines, Indonesia and other East and South East Asian Countries. It is this vast potential that the Government of India is giving increasing

emphasis to its *"Look East Policy through North East"*

- It has also proximity to SAARC countries like Bangladesh, Nepal and Bhutan offering enormous possibilities for trade and investment.
- It's a region with very high literacy rate of over 68 percent. It has more people who are fluent in English than any other region in the country. Thus, it has a strong potential for growth of information technology enabled services.
- It's also a region of virtually tax-free fiscal package.
- The NER is also blessed with breath taking beauty, and has within its fold, some of the most scenic spots in the country, prompting many comparisons like the "Scotland of the East" and "Switzerland of India". Be it wild life sanctuaries, adventure tourism, eco-tourism, hill stations, lakes, cultural and historical heritage- the NER has it all in full and plenty. Recognizing the vast potential for tourism development, the Government of India has notified the NER as *"Hot spot in Tourism " like "Hot Spot in Biodiversity"*.

Thus, it is evident that the NER is a region in India waiting to things happen because vast opportunities are yet unexplored and unexploited which , in turn, means ample possibilities for entrepreneurship development and, in turn, industrial and economic development of the region.

Concluding Remarks

Like elsewhere in the country, the NER also suffers from the common nature of problems of entrepreneurship development. However, this region is plagued with certain distinct but grave problems of entrepreneurship such as the problems of insurgency and law and order hovering the land for quite some years. In fact, these two problems bear far reaching effects on all aspects of the economy including entrepreneurial aspects. Other problems, to a large extent, can be overcome by the strategic choices of the entrepreneurs, but not these two. These two problems have rendered all the developmental measures and efforts of the Government as infructuous.

Nonetheless, the NER holds good prospects for the entrepreneurial and industrial development within its fold. It is a treasure trove of several natural resources. It possesses minerals, oil reserves, water resources, places of scenic beauty, rich bio-diversity, world famous parks, and wild life centauries, in full and plenty within its fold. In fact, the problem is not of lack of resources for entrepreneurship development, but it is of non-exploitation and non-utilizations of resources available in full and plenty.

17

Summary of Findings

The focus of the present study was primarily on the delineation of the profile of entrepreneurship development so far taken place in the North-East India, with special reference to Assam. The structure of research was designed accordingly by dividing it into two major aspects. Considering that perspective affects and also gets affected by any type of development including entrepreneurship / enterprise development, the study, therefore, began with delineating the (entrepreneurial) perspective in existence in the NER as the research scaffolding. A major portion of the present research was devoted to the exploration of entrepreneurial dynamics consisting of who the entrepreneurs are and what they do. Now that the study is complete, we can profitably recapitulate the major finding flowing from it.

Major Findings

These are presented chapter-wise as follows:

Research Paradigm on Entrepreneurship

Entrepreneurship being a discipline of behavioural science, on the one hand, and its *primum mobile* role in industrial and economic development of an economy, on the other, has produced volume of prodigious research on it over the period. By now, entrepreneurship has emerged as a hyperactive area of research. Almost all researches in entrepreneurship are carried out either based on 'population ecology model', also called 'environmental determinism perspective' or strategic choice model, also called 'entrepreneurial determinism perspective.' Researchers have provided empirical evidences to explain their entrepreneurial model or perspective. Nonetheless, more studies focus on entrepreneurial perspective than the environmental perspective as an element of entrepreneurship development. As is evident from survey of research in entrepreneurship, see Table 2.2, a paradigm shift in entrepreneurship research has already taken place in the West from environment to entrepreneur. In nutshell, the paradigm shift in entrepreneurship research has taken place in exploring "what the entrepreneurs do" rather "who the entrepreneurs are?"

The Environmental Context or Perspective

Just like the development of any type is context specific, entrepreneurship development so is also. The context, in a way, means environment. Evidences are available to believe that environment determines the nature and extent of entrepreneurship development. The favourable environment, some call it '*task environment*", promotes entrepreneurship development and unfavourable one deters it. The factors like availability of materials, manpower, capital, market, suppliers, favourable government policies, accessibility to transportation, respective population, availability of supporting services, etc. constitute favourable or task or conducive environment for entrepreneurship development. In fact, favourable environment and entrepreneurship sustain each other in a virtuous cycle: favourable environment produces entrepreneurial opportunities and entrepreneurial initiatives strengthen and promote environment. The cases of Mahashrastra, Gujarat, and Punjab support to this virtuous relationship between the two.

Considering the various components, or say, indicators of environment (see Table 11.1), the entrepreneurial environment of the NER cannot be considered as favourable but unfavourable one. The factors like lack of infrastructural facilities, problems of insurgency and law and order hovering the NER for quite some years make the entrepreneurial environment as unfavourable or non-conducive. The unfavourable environment and entrepreneurship harm each other in a vicious cycle. That is, unfavourable environment reduces entrepreneurial opportunities and entrepreneurial initiatives do not strengthen but weaken the environment. This goes on and on. In fact, the NER is very much reeling under this vicious cycle of the two.

The Entrepreneurial Profile

Almost all research studies in entrepreneurship report that the entrepreneurs form a distinct class in the society in many respects. The entrepreneurs of our study also squarely confirm it. Our entrepreneurs consist of any persons with educational, occupational background, age, with or without work experience, etc. They are both male and female, belong to different races, and religions. Thus, the entrepreneurs of our study have come from the highly heterogeneous backgrounds. Thus, we had no hesitation in accepting our first hypothesis:

(i) **"The entrepreneurs are drawn from varied socio-economic backgrounds particularly when specific incentives and facilities are provided to establish industries."**

The majority of entrepreneurs (48.56 %) are local ones mainly due to *"Homeland Factor"* or *"the Son of the Soil"* psychology. The majority of entrepreneurs (60.49%) coming from business background indicates that business background still serves as a cushion for entry into entrepreneurial career. Profession as family occupation facilitating entry into entrepreneurship comes second in order. Similarly, exceedingly higher dominance of males (85.19%) in business reveals the outstanding fact that, like in other parts of the country, the enterprise/business is still male-dominated activity in the region. While relating an overwhelming majority (85.10%) of married entrepreneurs and a higher average age with more than two-thirds (65%) holding University degrees or technical diplomas and nearly 30% as student unemployed clearly shows that the entrepreneurs especially from non-business background had to rely on academic effulgence and prior work experience. Thus, we uphold the hypothesis:

(ii) **" The entry into entrepreneurship especially from non-business background is characterized by the academic effulgence and prior experiential learning."**

The Entrepreneurial Motivation

Almost all human behaviour is motivated. So is true of entrepreneurial behaviour also. Given the highly heterogeneous background of entrepreneurs, it would be of research interest to probe into whether the entrepreneurs are motivated by a common factor or different factors. If the motivational factors change along with change in the entrepreneurial background or the motivation of the same entrepreneur undergoes changes in pursuant to entrepreneurial experience. In order to find out answers to these questions, we inserted 15 motivational statements, based on entrepreneurial literature, in our questionnaire to be rated on the Likert type 5-point scale. The rationale behind this rating scale was that different entrepreneurs may be motivated by a single factor in varying degrees. Of the 15 statements to be rated, on an average, an entrepreneur checked 11 of them. This implies that the entrepreneurial motivation is multi-dimensional. This is not unlikely. Because, except in extreme cases of deprivation, human beings seek simultaneous satisfaction of their different desires. We, therefore, have no hesitation to accept the hypothesis:

(iii) **"There is more than a reason or motive for an individual's plunge into entrepreneurship."**

The major factor of entrepreneurial motivation has been self-actualization or self-fulfillment in terms of economic, self-expression, doing something new and path-breaking followed by nature of work, power, status and affiliation motives in that order. Thus, it can be concluded that the major motivational factors to start their own enterprises are survival, financial independence and security, personal growth, and recognition.

Apart from the diversified pattern of entrepreneurial motivation, we also endeavoured to explore into if the motivation of an entrepreneur changes in pursuant to his/her entrepreneurial experience. Taking cues from Abraham Maslow's need hierarchy theory of motivation, it is likely that the motivation to start an enterprise and to remain there could be different. Though our findings in this regard did not indicate a complete transformation in entrepreneurial motivation, yet some changes in entrepreneurial motivation in the wake of entrepreneurial experience were quite evident. The two motives, namely, self-actualization and affiliation have not changed, i.e. remained the same what at the time of start were. The ascent of the economic motive in the motivational list of the entrepreneurs is understandable and can be explained on a number of counts. Given the serious threats posed by the business environment, small-scale enterprises need to earn certain revenue to survive in the competitive market. Likewise, moving up of status and deontic motives two steps each seems perfectly in order because having fulfilled the economic requirements, the entrepreneur may perceive the need for status and recognition in the society. This is just like Maslow's need-order from security to social need. The entrepreneur may also have a feeling to contribute to the well-being of those with whom he is affiliated like family members. Yes, a complete metamorphosis in autonomy and power moving down from third rank at the start to the last rank six in the wake of entrepreneurial experience over the period is worth noticing. This is also not unlikely. As the business develops and expends, the entrepreneur finds himself unable to look after all the business matters especially in the today's highly competitive business world. Then, what he does is delegates the authority and decentralizes the decision making process. This enables him/her to multiply his / her business ability and capability. Now, his role changes from as an owner to as a manager. As such, desire for authority and power are likely to get lower rungs to run the business effectively. Based on these evidences, we uphold the hypothesis:

(iv) **"Entrepreneurial motivation changes in pursuant to entrepreneurial experience."**

The Entrepreneurial Performance

The entrepreneurial performance can be assessed in terms of both economic performance and psychic reward. Given the complexities involved in assessing the psychic reward of entrepreneurs, we have assessed the entrepreneurial performance based on a sole criterion of profitability. The justification is that the psychic reward ultimately boils down to economic performance, i.e. profitability. Different variables affect the entrepreneurial performance differently.

The local entrepreneurs have performed better than the migrant ones because of the *"son of the soil factor."* The local or native element of entrepreneur bestows on him/her certain edges like awareness about the place, people, policies, organizations which help one get one's things done more effectively. We have, therefore, rejected our hypothesis:

(v) "The migrant entrepreneurs are more successful than the local ones."

As regards entrepreneurial performance by sex, it is found insignificant. Thus, the evidence provided by the study indicates that sex does not matter in entrepreneurial performance.

Business history is replete with evidences that some of the illiterate and/or high school drop- out entrepreneurs like Andrew Carnegie, Henry Ford, Thomas Edison Alwa, William Durant, and Dhirajlal Hirachand Ambani made remarkable success as entrepreneurs. These cases suggest that it is not the entrepreneur's education, but his / her entrepreneurial acumen that matters and makes all the difference in the entrepreneurial performance. Then, our finding that education does not lend much support to entrepreneurial performance seems perfectly in order. Therefore, we do not hesitate to reject our hypothesis:

(vi) The formal education positively influences the entrepreneurial performance.

Advancement in age enriches one in many respects like improved rationality, maturity, awareness, perseverance, etc. The average age at which our entrepreneurs started their entrepreneurial career is relatively at an old age. Most of them entered into entrepreneurial career after marriage. While male joined entrepreneurship after having some work experience, females joined after the children completed their school level education. Thus, work experience, maturity, and more time to devote in entrepreneurial activities helped them perform better than young and unmarried ones.

Our study is focused on the 'strategic choice model', or say, 'individualistic model of entrepreneurship' The finding of the study seems well in conformity with the model. That the entrepreneurs with strong determination and self-efficacy have performed better than those with external locus of control is indicated by an exceedingly higher percentage of former than the latter. Thus, we accept the hypothesis:

(vii) "Entrepreneurs with internal locus of control perform better than those with external locus of control."

The entrepreneurship intervention programmes commonly known as EDPs expose the participants to all activities involved in establishing and running an enterprise. The behavioural inputs designed thoughtfully shape and mould the participants' attitude towards entrepreneurial career. Such an exposure of matters relating to enterprise breaks the inertia of participants toward entrepreneurial career. In line with the findings of research studies that EDP is found helpful to make the participants ready establish their enterprises and run these effectively; our study also finds that EDP participants perform better in their entrepreneurial pursuits. Thus, we have no hesitation to accept our hypothesis:

(viii) Participation in EDPs helps perform better in entrepreneurial activities.

The Entrepreneurial Problems and Prospects

The low level of entrepreneurship and industrial development in the NER is indicative of problems in entrepreneurship development in the region. While there are some common problems faced in entrepreneurship development every where in the country, yet there are some region-specific, or say, context specific. The problems of insurgency, disturbed law and order situation, and lack of infrastuctural facilities are the specific problems of entrepreneurship development in the NER. These problems frustrate the developmental efforts, on the one hand, and discourage the prospective entrepreneurs to assume the entrepreneurial career, on the other. As such, while hardly any new industry, in real term, is established in the private sector in the NER in the recent years, a good number of existing ones have been closed and several are in the process of closure.

However, the NER also holds good promises within its fold for entrepreneurship and enterprise development. It is treasure trove of natural resources that any other regions can hardly boast of. It is 'hot spot' of bio-diversity and 'paradise unexplored' for tourism development.

Scope for Further Research

Research is a continuous academic exercise either of the same problem from different perspectives or the different problems from the same perspective or the same problem from the same perspective in different times. Just digging deeper and deeper gives soil with different colours, researching a particular problem also provides different insights about the same problem. That is precisely the reason why a problem, for example, entrepreneurship development, is being researched again and again by different researchers or by the same researcher from time to time (see Table 2.2). In our country, research on entrepreneurship has customarily been carried out focusing on "who the entrepreneurs are", whereas the focus of entrepreneurship research in the West has been exploring "what the entrepreneurs do". Considering the dynamics of entrepreneurship phenomenon, the desirability of extending the entrepreneurship research in these dimensions in our case may also be examined and explored.

Having studied the dynamics of entrepreneurial development in the NER, the present study gives insights about certain other relevant areas as further research topics / problems on entrepreneurship development of the region. We have classified these into two broad categories:

1. Environment-Related Research Areas
2. Entrepreneur-Related Research Areas

Environment-Related Research Areas

1. Tourism Entrepreneurship
2. Rural Entrepreneurship
3. Micro Entrepreneurship
4. Community-Based Entrepreneurship
5. Agripreneurship
6. Local-Resource Based Entrepreneurship

Entrepreneur-Related Research Areas

1. Caste-Based Entrepreneurship
2. Family-Business Based Entrepreneurship
3. Gender-Based Entrepreneurship
4. Copreneurship
5. Intrapreneurship

Research in entrepreneurship is so far conducted, more often than not, following the reactive approach. We believe that, in order to understand the dynamics of entrepreneurship in a better sense, research studies in entrepreneurship also need to be initiated and encouraged following the proactive approach. An example of proactive approach in entrepreneurship research can be tracing out the prior status of entrepreneurs with their attitudinal and behavioural characteristics. In other words, what happened before the enterprise actually came into existence could also be a fertile subject of research interest. A research study on intentions to become entrepreneurs among the students across the disciplines, for example, can bring out some significant cues about entrepreneurial phenomenon.

The above mentioned list of topics for further research in entrepreneurship is not a comprehensive one. This is an illustrative one only indicating some of the broad areas for future researches in entrepreneurship subject. There can be set of sub-topics of research under each broad area.

Bibliography

Ahluwalia, Bharat (2001): "Indian Small Business: Languishing at Death's Door," *Business Today,* April 21.

Alexander, A.P. (1964): *Greek Industrialists,* Athens: Centre for Planning and Economic Growth.

Anonymous (2000): "25 Events That Shaped Business," *Business World,* January 3.

Anonymous (2006), "B.P. Reflections," *A Monthly Newsletter of Oil India Limited,* Dliajan (Assam), December 1 (4).

Aris, S. (1970): *The Jews in Business,* London: Jonathan Cape.

Awasthi, D.N. (1997): *Dynamics of Industrial Clusters in India,* Ahmedabad: Entrepreneurship Development Institute of India.

Awasthi, D.N. and Jose Sebastian (1996): *Evaluation of Entrepreneurship Development Programmes,* New Delhi: Sage Publications.

Bagchi, A.K. (1970): European and Indian Entrepreneurship in India 1900-1930, In: E. Leach & S. N. Mukherjee (Eds.): *Elites in South Asia,* Cambridge: Cambridge University Press.

Baldwin, G.B. (1959): *Industrial Growth in South India: Case Studies in Economic Development,* Glencoe, Illinois: The Free Press.

Behari, Bipin (1976): *Rural Industrialization in India,* New Delhi: Vikas Publishing House Pvt. Ltd.

Bennis, Warren and Burt Nanus (1985): *Leaders: The Strategies for Taking Charge,* New York: Harper & Row.

Berna, James J. (1960): *Industrial Entrepreneurship in Madras State,* Bombay: Asia Publishing House.

Bezbaruah, M.P. (2001): *Frontiers of New Tourism,* New Delhi: Gyan Publishing House.

Bhargava, Shivganesh (2007): "Entrepreneurship Development in the 21st Century," In: Shivganesh Bhargava (Ed.): *Developmental Aspects of Entrepreneurship,* New Delhi, Response Books.

Bhat, Ganesh (1999): "Rural Entrepreneurship and NGOs," *Kurukshetra,* November.

Bhatt, Ela (1989): Toward Empowerment, *World Development,* Volume 17, Number 7.

Bird, B. J. (1989): *Entrepreneurial Behaviour,* Glenview, IL: Scott, Foresman & Co.

Birley, S. (1989): "Female Entrepreneurs: Are They Really Different," *Journal of Small Business Management,* XXVII-I.

Boserup, Ester (1970): *Women's Role in Economic Development,* New York: St. Martin's.

Boyle, E. (1994): The Rise of Reluctant Entrepreneurs, *International Small Business Journal,* Vol. 2, No. 2, January-March.

Brimmer, A. F. (1955): The Setting of Entrepreneurship in India, *Quarterly Journal of Economics,* L 20 (4), November.

Brockhaus, Robert H. (1980): Psychological and Environmental Factors Which Distinguish the Successful from the Unsuccessful Entrepreneurs, *Proceedings of the 40th Annual Meeting of the Academy of Management,* August.

Brockhaus, Robert H. and W. R. Nord (1979): An Exploration of Factors Affecting Entrepreneurial Decisions: Personal Characteristics versus Environmental Conditions, *Proceedings of the 39th Annual Meeting of the Academy of Management,* August.

Bruno, Albert V. and Tyebjee (1982): "The Environment for Entrepreneurship," In: Valvin A. Kent, Donald D. Sexton, and Carl H. Vesper (Eds.): *Encyclopedia of Entrepreneurship,* Englewood Cliffs NJ: Printice-Hall, Inc.

Burns, James M. (1978): *Leadership,* New York: Harper & Row.

Cantillon, Richard (1971): In Peter Kilby (Ed.): *Entrepreneurship and Economic Development*, New York: The Free Press.

Danhof, Clarence (1949): "Observation in Agriculture," In: A. Cole (Ed.): *Change and the Entrepreneur*, Cambridge: Harvard University Press.

David, N. (1992): "Development of Micro-Enterprises by Women," In: S. Beaumont, K. Singh, & K. Ramachandran (Eds.): *Development of Micro-Enterprises by Women*, New Delhi: British Council and Indian Institute of Management, Ahmedabad.

Dees, J. Gregory (1998): "Enterprising Non-profits: What Do You Do When Traditional Sources of Funding Fall Short?" *Harvard Business Review*, January/February.

Cantillon, Richard (1755): *Essai Sur La nature du Commerce en general*, London: (quoted in Kilby, Peter (1971).

Cardulla, M. W. (1999): *Technological Entrepreneurism*, Baldock: Research Studies Press.

Carroll, J. J. (1965): *The Filipino Manufacturing Entrepreneur: Agent and Product of Change*, Ithaca: Cornell University Press.

Chandra, P. (1985): Reliance: The Man Behind the Legend, "*Business India*," 17-30 June.

Chandrakandan, K. (2001): Agribusiness Management: Basic Issues, *International Extension Forum Newsletter*, 7 (3-4).

Chary, S. N. (2002): *Business Gurus Speak*, New Delhi: Macmillan India Ltd.

Chell, E. and J. M. Haworth (1988): Entrepreneurship and Entrepreneurial Management: The Need for a Paradigm, *Graduate Management Research*, Winter.

Chernovskaya, Valentina (2005): *Indian Entrepreneurship: Its Past and Present*, Delhi: Shipra Publications.

Cochran, T. C. (1949): "Approaches to Entrepreneurial Personality," In: *Change and the Entrepreneur*, Prepared by the Research Centre in Entrepreneurial History, Cambridge, MA: Harvard University Press.

Cole, A. H. (1949): "Entrepreneurship and Entrepreneurial Histroy," In: *Change and the Entrepreneur*, Prepared by the Research Centre in Entrepreneurial History, Cambridge, MA: Harvard University Press.

Collins, O. F. and D. G. Moore (1964): *The Enterprising Man*, East Lansing, MI: Michigan State University.

Cooper, A. C. (1973): "Technical Entrepreneurship: What Do We Know?," *R & D Management*, Volume 3, pp. 59-64.

Dana, Leo Paul (1992): "A Look at Small Business in Austria," *Journal of Small Business Management*, Volume. 30, Number. 4.

Das, Mallika (1999): "Women Entrepreneurs from South India: An Exploratory Study," *The Journal of Entrepreneurship*, Volume 8, Number 2, July-December.

Dasgupta, A. (1969): *Indian Business and Management*, New Delhi: University of Delhi, Department of Business Management and Industrial Administration.

Davis, K. (1975): *The Challenge of Business*, New York: McGraw-Hill.

Davis, Keith (1977): *Human Behaviour at Work*, New Delhi: Tata McGraw-Hill Publishing Company.

Dees, J. G. (2001): *The Meaning of Social Entrepreneurship Revisited*, Working Paper, Stanford University Graduate School of Business.

Desai, Vasant (1992): *Dynamics of Entrepreneurial Development and Management*, Bombay: Himalaya Publishing House.

Deshpande, M. U. (1984): *Entrepreneurship of Small-Scale Industries*, New Delhi: Deep & Deep Publications.

Drucker, Peter F. (1968): *The Practice of Management*, Bombay: Allied Publishers.

Drucker, Peter F. (1985): *Innovations and Entrepreneurship*, London: William Heinemann Ltd.

Dutt, Ruddar and K. P. M. Sundharam (2005): *Indian Economy*, New Delhi: S. Chand & Company Ltd.

Dutta, Gautam (2000): "Developing Entrepreneurship in the North East Through Training Interventions," In: D. D. Mali (ED.): *Entrepreneurship Development in North East*, Guwahati: Indian Institute of entrepreneurship.

Emerson, Jed and Fay Twerksy (Eds.) (1996): *New Social Entrepreneurs: The Success, Challenge and Lessons of Non-profit Enterprise Creation*, San Francisco: The Roberts Foundation, Homeless Economic Development Fund.

Friedman, Milton (1962): *Capitalism and Freedom*, Chicago: University of Chicago Press.

Gadgil, D.R. (1959): *Origins of the Modern Indian Business Class: An Interim Report*, New York: Institute of Pacific Relations.

Gaikwad, V.R., H. Gor and U. Pareek, T. V. Rao, H. C. Shah, B.G. Shah and M.C. Shetty (1974): *Entrepreneurship Development Programmes: An Evaluation (Research Report)*, Ahmedabad: Indian Institute of Management.

Gaikwad, V. R. and R. N. Tripathi (1970): *Socio-Psychological Factors Influencing Industrial Entrepreneurship in Rural Areas*, Hyderabad: National Institute of Community (now Rural) Development.

Ghosh, Ratna, Meenakshi Gupta and S. Nina Dhar (1998): Women and Entrepreneurship in India, In: Rabindra N. Kanungo (Ed.): *Entrepreneurship & Innovation*, New Delhi: Sage Publications.

Gibb, A. A. (1992): "Assisting New Female Entrepreneurs – Is Support Geared to Reality?" In: S. Beaumont, K. Singh and K. Ramachandran (Eds.): *Development of Micro enterprises by Women*, New Delhi: British Council and Ahmedabad: Indian Institute of Management.

Glade, W. (1967): "Approaches to a Theory of Entrepreneurial Formation," *Explorations in Entrepreneurial History*, Volume 3.

Gnyawali, D.R. and D.S. Fogal (1994): "Environments for Entrepreneurship Development: Key Dimensions and Research Implications," *Entrepreneurship Theory and Practice*, Vol. 18, No. 4, Summer.

Goldstein, Kurt (1939): *The Organism*, New York: The American Book.

Gopakumar (1995): Entrepreneurship in Economic Thought: A Thematical Review, *Journal of Entrepreneurship*, Vol. 4, No. 1.

Government of Kerala (1984): *Women's Industries Department*, Trivandrum.

Greshenkron, A. (1968): The Entrepreneur, *American Economic Review*, Volume 58, No.

Guha, Amlendu (1970): Parsi Seths and Entrepreneurs: 1750-1890, *Economic and Political Weekly*, Vol. 5, No. 35, August.

Gulati, M. (1997): *Restructuring and Modernisation of Small and Mediuym Enterprise Clusters in India*, UNIDO.

Gupta, C.B. and N. P. Srinivasan (1992): *Entrepreneurial Development*, New Delhi: Sultan Chand & Sons.

Gupta, C.B. and S. S. Khanka (1996): *Entrepreneurship and Small Business Management*, New Delhi: Sultan Chand & Sons.

Gupta, M.C. (1987): *Entrepreneurship in Small-Scale Industries*, New Delhi: Anmol Publications.

Hagen, E.E. (1962): *On the Theory of Social Change: How Economic Growth Begins?* London: Tavistock Publications.

Haan, H.H. (1980): *Rural Industrialization in India*, Rotterdam: Discussion Paper No. 53, Erasmus University for Development Planning.

Hannan, M.T. and J.H. Freeman (1977): "The Population Ecology of Organisations," *American Journal of Sociology*, Vol. 82, No. 5, pp. 929-964.

Hansra, B.S and K. Vijayaragavan (Eds.) (2003): *Agri-business and Extension Management*, New Delhi: Concept Publishing Company.

Haq, M. (1992): The Development of Micro Enterprises by Women: BRAC's Experiences, In: S. Baumont, K. Singh and K. Ramachandran (Eds.): *Development of Micro Enterprises by*

Women, New Delhi: British Council and Indian Institute of Management, Ahmedabad.

Harbison, Frederick (1956): Entrepreneurial organization as a Factor in Economic Development, *Quarterly Journal of Economics*, August.

Herzberg, F., B. Mausner, and B. Snyderman (1959): *The Motivation to Work*, New York: John Wiley.

Hisrich, R. D. (1990): *Entrepreneurship / Intrapreneurship*, American Psychologist, Volume 45, No. 2.

Hisrich, R. D. and M. P. Peters (1995): *Entrepreneurship-Starting, Developing, and Managing a New Enterprise*, Boston: Irwin.

Hisrich, R. D. and M. P. Peters (2002): *Entrepreneurship*, New Delhi: Tata McGraw-Hill Publishing Company Limited.

Hooks, B. (1984): *Feminist Theory from Margin to Center*, Boston, MA: South End Press.

Hoselitz, B. F. (1960): *Sociological Aspects of Economic Growth*, Bombay: Vakil Feffer and Simmons.

Jain, Pankaj S. (1994): Managing for Success: Lessons from Asian Development Programmes, *World Development*, Volume 22, Number 9.

Jayachandran, G. B. Vijayalakshmi and D. Hemachalam (1998): "Entrepreneurial Profile in Industrial Estates," *SEDME*, Vol. 25, No. 3, September.

Jha, Alok (2009), Role of Dairy and Food Processing Industries for Promoting Agri-Business and Entrepreneurship, Paper resented in the *National Conference on Entrepreneurial Opportunities in Agri-Business: Challenges and Prospects*, organised by the Faculty of Management Studies, Banaras Hindu University, Varanasi, November 23, 2009.

Joshi, Arun (1975): *Lala Shri Ram: A Study in Entrepreneurship and Industrial Management*, New Delhi: Orient Longman.

Kamalanabham, T. J. (2001): "Personality Inventory for Selection of Potential Entrepreneurs: An Evaluation," *Management & Change*, Vol. 5, No. 1, January-June.

Kanitkar, Ajit and Nalinee Contractor (1994): *In Search of Identity: The Women Entrepreneurs of India*, Ahmedabad: Entrepreneurship Development Institute of India.

Kanungo, Rabindra N. (Ed.) (1998): *Entrepreneurship & Innovation (Models for Development)*, New Delhi: Sage Publications.

Kanungo, Rabindra N. & J. A. Conger (1995): "Model Orientation in Leadership Research and Their Implications for Developing Countries," In: R. N. Kanungo (Ed.): *New Approaches to Employee Management, Vol. 3: Employee Management in Developing Countries*, Greenwich, Conn: JAI Press.

Khandwalla, P. N. (1985): *The P I Motive: A Base for Development*, Working Paper No. 558, Ahmedabad: Indian Institute of Management.

Kazmi, Azhar (1999): "What Entrepreneurs and Do? A Study of Second-Generation Entrepreneurs," *The Journal of Entrepreneurship*, 8 (1), January - June.

Kennedy, Robert E. Jr. (1962): The Protestant Ethic and Parsis, *The American Journal of Sociology*, L 18 (I), July.

Khandwalla, Pradip N. (1977): *Design of Organizations*, New York: Harcourt Brace Jovanovich.

Khanka, S.S. (1984): Migration from Kumaun Region- Some Findings Based on the Sample Study of Pithoragarh District, *The Indian Journal of Labour Economics*, Volume 26, Number 4, January.

Khanka, S. S. (1990): "Entrepreneurship development in a Notified Backward Economy," *Decision*, Volume 17, Number 2, April-June.

Khanka, S.S. (1990): *Entrepreneurship in Small-Scale Industries*, New Delhi: Himalaya Publishing House.

Khanka, S.S. (1992): "Industrial Sickness in India," *Indian Management*, Volume 31, Number 5, October.

Khanka, S. S. and Anjan Bhuyan (2004): *Potential for Rural Tourism in Assam* (Mimeograph), Tezpur: Department of Business Administration, Tezpur University.

Kilby, Peter (1971): Hunting the Heffalump, In: Peter Kilby (Ed.): *Entrepreneurship and Economic Development*, New York: The Free Press.

Kirzner, I.M. (1979): *Perception, Opportunity and Profit: Studies in the Theory of Entrepreneurship*, Chicago: The University of Chicago press.

Knight, E.H. (1965): *Risk, Uncertainty and Profit*, New York: Harper & Row.

Krebs, D. (1982): "Altruism: A Rational Approach," In: H. Eizenberg (Ed.): *The Development of Pro-social Behaviour*, New York: Academic Press.

Kristiansen, Stein (2001): "Promoting African Pioneers in Business: What Makes a Context Conducive to .Small-Scale Entrepreneurship?," *The Journal of Entrepreneurship*, Volume 10, Number 1, January-June.

Kuchhal, S.C. (1963): *The Industrial Economy of India*, Allahabad: Chaitanya Publishing House.

Kunkel, J.A. (1970): *Society and Economic Growth: A Behavioural Perspective of Social Change*, New York: Oxford University Press.

Leavitt, H. (1986): *Corporate Pathfinders*, Homewood: Irwin.

Leibenstein, H. (1968): Entrepreneurship and Development, *American Economic Review*, Volume 58, No. 2.

Levenstein, M. (199 McClelland, David C. 5): "African-American Entrepreneurship: The View from the 1910 Census," *Business and Economic History*, Vol. 24, No. 1, Fall.

Lovell, Catherine H. (1992): *Breaking the Cycle of Poverty: The BRAC Strategy*, West Hartford, CT: Kumarian Press.

MacMillan, I.C. and J. Block (1985): Milestones for Successful Venture Planning, *Harvard Business Review*, Volume 63, Number 5.

Mali, D.D. and R. Bandopadhyay (1993): *Small-Industry Development in North- East India – Status and Strategy*, New Delhi: Omsons Publications.

Malenbaum, W. (1962): *Prospects for Indian Development*, Glancoe: The Free Press.

Manimala, Mathew J. (1986): Founder-Culture in Organisations: Its Impact on Organisational Growth, Dynamics and Innovativeness, *Abhigyan*, Autumn.

Manimala, Mathew J. and Alan W. Pearson (1995): *Growth Venture Policies and Founder Characteristics: Evidence from British High-Growth and Low-Growth Ventures*, Paper presented at the EFER 6th Conference held at Gent, Belgium, November 16-18.

Manimala, Mathew J. and Alan W. Pearson (1998): Entrepreneurial Motivation revisited, In: Rabindra N. Kanungo (Ed.): *Entrepreneurship & Innovation* (Models for Development), New Delhi: Sage Publications.

Marshall, Alfred (1936): *Principles of Economics*, London: Macmillan.

Martin, Roger L. and Sally Osberg (2007): Social Entrepreneurship: The Case for Definition, *Stanford Social Innovation Review*, Spring.

Maslow, Abraham H. (1954): *Motivation and Personality*, New York: Harper & Row.

Matthai, Raul J. (1978): "Rural Entrepreneurship: A Framework," In: U. Pareek and M. Nandkarni (Eds.): *Developing Entrepreneurship*, New Delhi: Learning Systems.

McClelland, David C. (1961): *The Achieving Society*, New York: The Free Press.

McClelland, David C. (1965): "N-achievement and Entrepreneurship: A Longitudinal Study," *Journal of Personality and Social Psychology*, Volume I.

McClelland, David C. and D. Burnhom (1976): "Power is the Great Motivator," *Harvard Business Review*, Vol. 54, No. 2, pp. 110-110.

McClelland, David C. and D. G. Winter (1969): *Motivating Economic Achievement*, New York: The Free Press.

McClelland, David C. (1971): "The Achieving Motive in Economic

Growth," In: Peter Kilby (Ed.): *Entrepreneurship and Economic Development*, New York: The Free Press.

McGregor, Douglas (1960): *The Human Side of Enterprise*, New York: McGraw-Hill.

Medhora, Phiroze B. (1965): "Entrepreneurship in India," *Political Science Quarterly*, L 30.

Mehta, S.S. (1988): "Sick Industry Syndrome in India," *Decision*, Vol. 15, Nos. 3 & 4, July – October.

Mendonca, manuel and Rabindra N. Kanungo (1998): "Ethical Entrepreneurship: Challenges and Rewards," In:abindra N. Kanungo (Ed.): *Entrepreneurship & Innovation* (Models for Development), New Delhi: Sage Publications.

Ministry of Industry (1997): *Report of the Expert Committee on Small Enterprises* (Chairman: Abid Hussain), New Delhi: Ministry of Industry, Government of India.

Moharana, S. (2006): "Entrepreneurial Opportunities in the Agri-business Sector: Some Emerging Issues," In: S. Moharana (Ed.): *Entrepreneurship and Agri-business Enterprise*, Bhubaneshwar: Department of Commerce, Utkal University.

Murray, H.A. (1938): *Explorations of Personality*, New York: McGraw-Hill.

Nafziger, E.W. (1979): The Relationship between Education and Entrepreneurship, *The Journal of Developing Areas*, Volume 4, Number 3.

Nagayya, D. (2000), "Entrepreneurship Development in North Eastern Region: Retrospect and Prospect," In: Mali, D.D. (Ed.): *Entrepreneurship Development in North East*, Guwahati: Indian Institute of Entrepreneurship.

Nair, K.R.G. and Anu Pandey (2006): *Characteristics of Entrepreneurs: An Empirical Analysis*, The Journal of Entrepreneurship, Volume 15, Number 1.

Narayana Murthy, N.R. (2001): "Blissful Knowledge: Six Pillars of Corporate Wisdom," *Times of India*, Friday, August 10.

Nath, V. (2000): "Entrepreneurship by Regions and Castes: A Survey," *Economic and Political Weekly*, Volume 35.

National Knowledge Commission (2008): *Entrepreneurship in India*, New Delhi: National Knowledge Commission.

Nirodbaran(1990): *Sri Aurobindo for All Ages*, Pondicherry: Sri Aurobindo Ashram.

Oberai, A. S. and H. K. M. Singh (1983): *Causes and Consequences of Internal Migration: A Study in the Indian Punjab*, New Delhi: Oxford University Press.

Panda, G. (1984): "Growth of Entrepreneurship," *Financial Express*, 13 February.

Panda, N. M. (2000): "What Brings Entrepreneurial Success in a Developing Region?" *The Journal of Entrepreneurship*, Vol. 9, No. 2.

Papanek, G.F. (1962): "A Century of Gestation: Relevance of Non-Economic Factors in Development Studies," *Economic Weekly*, Vol. XIV, No. 38, 22 September.

Papola, T. S. (1982): *Rural Industrialization (Approaches and Potential)*, New Delhi: Himalaya Publishing House.

Papola, T.S. and R.T. Tiwari (1981): *Impact of Concessional Finance on Industrial Development of Backward Areas* (*A Study in Uttar Pradesh*), Mimeo, Lucknow: Giri Institute of Development Studies.

Papola, T.S. (1985): *Rural Industrialisation* (*Approaches and Potential*), New Delhi: Himalaya Publishing House.

Pavlov, V. T. (1964): *The Indian Capitalist Class: A Historical Study*, New Delhi: People's Publishing House.

Planning Commission (1997-2002): *Ninth Five-Year Plan* (*Approach Paper*), New Delhi: Government of India.

Planning Commission (2002): *Tourism in Assam: Status and Prospects*, New Delhi: Government of India.

Poon, A. (1993): *Tourism, Technology and Competitive Strategies*. Oxford: CAB Wallingford.

Prag, C. Mirjam Van and Hans an Ophem (1995): "Determinants and Willingness and Opportunity to Start as an Entrepreneur," *Kyklos*, Volume 48.

Prasad, Lallan (1983): *Industrialization–Concepts and Issues,* New Delhi: S. Chand & Company Limited.

Raghupati, T. (1995): *Decision Making Process and Information Requirements of Entrepreneurs for Location of Medium and Small-Scale Industries,* New Delhi: Indian Council of Social Science Research (ICSSR).

Raj, Rituparna (2001): *A Study in Business Ethics,* New Delhi: Himalaya Publishing House.

Rao, R.V. (1969): *Indian Handidicarfts,* Hyderabad: Bookhomes Private Limited.

Ronstadt, R.C. (1983): "Initial Venture Goals, Age and Decision to Start an Entrepreneurial Career," *Proceedings of the 43rd Annual Meeting of the US Academy of Management,* August.

Rose, Kalima (1992): *Where Women are Leaders: The SEWA Movement in India,* London: Zed Books Ltd.

Rotter, J. (1966): *Generalized Expectancies for Internal vs. External Control of Reinforcement,* Psychological Monograph, General and Applied (Number 80).

Sinclair, M.T. and M. Stabler (1997): *The Economics of Tourism,* London: Rutledge.

Sangita, S.N. (1990): Self-Employment Programmes for Rural Youth: The Role of NGOs, *IIBM Management Review,* Vol. 5, No. 2.

Saxena, Anand (2005): *Entrepreneurship: Motivation, Performance, Rewards,* New Delhi: Deep & Deep Publications Pvt. Ltd.

Say, Jean-Baptiste (1827): *A Treatise on Political Economy: Or, the Production, Distribution and Consumption of Wealth,* New York: A.M. Kelley.

Say, Jean Baptiste (1827): *Production, Distribution and Consumption of Wealth,* Philadelphia: John Grigg No. 9.

Sayigh, Y.A. (1962): *Entrepreneurs of Lebanon,* M.A.: Harvard University Press.

Schumpeter, Joseph A. (1934): *The Theory of Economic Development,* Cambridge, Massachusetts: Harvard University Press.

Schumpeter, Joseph A. (1939): *Business Cycles*, New York: McGraw-Hill Book Co.

Schwartz, H.S. (1983): "A Theory of Deontic Work Motivation," *Journal of Applied Behavioural Science*, Volume 19, Number 2.

Sethi, Jyotsna (1999): *Development of Women Entrepreneurs in India*, Unpublished Ph. D. Thesis, Delhi: University of Delhi.

Shapero, A. (1975): Who Starts news Businesses? The Displaced Uncomfortable Entrepreneur, *Psychology Today*, 9, November.

Shapero, A. and L. Sokol (1982): The Social Dimension of Entrepreneurship, In: C. A. Kent, D. L. Sexton and K. H. Vesper (Eds.): *Encyclopedia of Entrepreneurship*, New Jersy: Printice-Hall.

Sharma, K. L. (1975): *Entrepreneurial Performance in Role Perspective*, New Delhi: Abhinav Publications.

Sharma, K.L. (1976): *Entrepreneurial Growth and Industrial Development Programmes in Punjab and Uttar Pradesh: A Comparative Study of Small Entrepreneurs* (Mimeo), Ludhiana: Department of Economics and Sociology, Punjab agricultural University.

Sharma, R.A. (1980): *Entrepreneurial Change in Indian Industry*, New Delhi: Sterling Publishers.

Sharma, S.V. S. (1979): *Small Industry Development in Select Asian Countries*, New Delhi: Light Publishers.

Sharma, S.V. S. and M. M. P. Akhouri (1978): *Small Entrepreneurial Development – Indian Experiences in the North Eastern Region*, Hyderabad: SIET Institute.

Shaw, Gareth and Allan M. Williams: (2002) *Critical Issues in Tourism*, Oxford: Blackwell.

Sherrif, M. (1958): Super-Ordinate Goals in the Reduction of Inter-Group Conflict, *American Journal of Sociology*, Volume 63, Number 4.

Shridharan, L. and Mathew J. Manimala (1999): Promoting Industrial Clusters: Review of Experiences in Europe, East

Asia and India, *The Journal of Entrepreneurship,* Volume 8, Number 2, July-December.

Sigurdson, Jon (1977): *Rural Industrialization in China,* London: Harvard University Press.

SIET Institute (1974): *Evaluation of Entrepreneurial Motivation Training Programmes in Assam,* Hyderabad: Small Industries Extension and Training Institute.

SIET (1974): *Socio-Psychological Factors Influencing the Adoption of the Innovations of Starting a Small Industry Unit,* Hyderabad: Small Industries Extension Training Institute.

Singh, N.P. (1992): "NGOs Fireplay towards Developing Entrepreneurship in Asia," *Asian Entrepreneur,* Autumn, Vol. 2, No. 2.

Singh, Pritam (1966): "The Role of Entrepreneurship in Economic Development," In: D. H. Butani & Pritam Singh (Eds.): *Economic Development: Issues and Policies,* Bombay" Vora & Co. Publishers Pvt. Ltd.

Sinha, Atul (2002): *Tourism Development of India,* http:www.pib.com/feature/

Smith, Adam (1776): *The Wealth of Nations,* New York: Random House.

Soundarapandian, M. (1999): Development of Rural Industries: Issues and Strategies, *Kurukshetra,* November.

Spodek, Howard (1965): The Manchestrisation of Ahmedabad, *The Economic Weekly,* 17 (11), March 13.

Sreenivasan, Jyotsna (2000): *Ela Bhatt: Uniting Women in India,* New York: Feminist Presso f the City, University of New York.

Srivastava, S. S. and R. A. Yadav (1986): *Management and Monitoring of Industrial Sickness,* New Delhi: Concept Publishing Company.

Shrivastava, Arun and Singh Thakur, Guman (2002), *Rural Tourism in the Seraj Valley.*

Himachal Pradesh, http:www.mtnforum.org— —(2003), Tourism, http:www.pib.com.govt.of India/factsheet/.

Stanworth, M. J. K. and J. Curran (1973): *Management Motivation in the Small Business*, Essex: Gower Press.

Stevenson, H. H. and J. C. Jarillo (1990): "A Paradigm of Entrepreneurship: Entrepreneurial Management," *Strategic Management Journal*, Volume 11.

Stevenson, L. A. (1986): "Against All Odds: The Entrepreneurship of Women," *Journal of Small Business Management*, Volume XXIV, Number 4.

Storey, D. J. (Ed.) (2000): *Small Business: Critical Perspectives on Business and Management*, London: Routledge.

Surya Kumar, P. V. S. (1999): "Export Oriented Agriculture – The Powerhouse of Agribusiness in India," *SBI Monthly Review*, June.

Thompson, J. D. (1967): *Organisations in Action*, New York: McGraw Hill. Timberg, T. A. (1978): *The Marwaris: From Traders to Industrialists*, New Delhi: Vikas Publishing House Pvt. Ltd.

Tripathi, Dwijendra (1971): "Indian Entrepreneurship in Historical Perspective: A Reinterpretation," *Economic and Political Weekly*, 6 (2), May 29.

Tripathi, Dwijendra (1981): "Occupational Mobility and Industrial Entrepreneurship in India: A Historical Analysis," *The Developing Economies*, Vol. XIX, No. 1, March, pp. 52-68.

Tripathi, Dwijendra (2004): *The Oxford History of Indian Business*, New Delhi: Oxford University Press.

Tripathi, Dwijendra and Makrand Mehta (1990): *Business Houses in Western India: A Study in Entrepreneurship Response (1850-1956)*, New Delhi: Manohar Publications.

United Nations (1955): *Process and Problems of Industrialization in Underdeveloped Countries*, New York: United Nations.

Upadhaya, Carol and Mario Rutten (1997): "In Search of a Comparative Framework: Small-Scale Entrepreneurs in Asia and Europe," In: Rutten, Mario and Carol Upadaya (Eds.):

Small Business Entrepreneurs in Asia and Europe, New Delhi: Sage Publications India Pvt. Ltd.

Venkataraman, S. (2000): The Promise of Entrepreneurship as a Field of Research, *Academy of Management Journal*, Volume 25.

Vijaya, V. and T.J. Kamalanabhan (1998): A Scale to Access Entrepreneurial Motivation, *The Journal of Entrepreneurship*, Volume VII, Number 2.

Weber, Alfred (1910): *Theory of Location of Industry*, Chicago: The University of Chicago Press.

Weber, Max (1930): *The Protestant Ethic and the Spirit of Capitalism* (trans. By Talcott Persons), New York: Charles Scribner's Sons.

Weber, M. (1930): *The Prostestant Ethic and the Spirit of Capitalism*, New York: Talcott Parsons.

Worchem, S., J. Cooper and G. Goethals (1988): *Understanding Social Psychology*, Chicago: Dorsey.

Young, F.W. (1971): "A Micro-Sociological Interpretation of Entrepreneurship," In: Peter Kilby (Ed.): *Entrepreneurship and Economic Development*, New York: The Free Press.

Yunus, Muhammad (1995): *Banker to the Poor: Micro Lending and the Battle against World Poverty*, New York: Public Affairs.

Yunus, Muhammad (1997): "The Grameen Bank Story: Rural Credit in Bangladesh," In: Anirudh Krishna, Norman Uphoff and Milton J. Esman (Eds.): *Reasons for Hope: Instructive Experiences in Rural Development*, West Hartford, CT: Kumarian Press.

Index

***